# A clear and present word

Titles in this series:

NEW STUDIES IN BIBLICAL THEOLOGY 21

*Series editor: D. A. Carson*

# A clear and present word

## THE CLARITY OF SCRIPTURE

*Mark D. Thompson*

APOLLOS

INTERVARSITY PRESS
DOWNERS GROVE, ILLINOIS 60515

APOLLOS (an imprint of Inter-Varsity Press)
*Norton Street, Nottingham NG7 3HR, England*
*Website: www.ivpbooks.com*
*Email: ivp@ivp-editorial.co.uk*

INTERVARSITY PRESS
*PO Box 1400, Downers Grove, Illinois 60515, USA*
*Website: www.ivpress.com*
*Email: mail@ivpress.com*

*First published 2006*

**British Library Cataloguing in Publication Data**
A catalogue record for this book is available from the British Library.

UK ISBN–13: 978–1–84474–140–3
UK ISBN–10: 1–84474–140–0

**Library of Congress Cataloging-in-Publication Data**
These data have been requested.

US ISBN–13: 978–0–8308–2622–3
US ISBN–10: 0–8308–2622–X

Set in Monotype Times New Roman
Typeset in Great Britain by Servis Filmsetting Ltd, Manchester

With thanks to God for three wise theological guides: *Alan D. Catchpoole*, Principal, Capernwray Bible College, Australia (1970–1982); *D. Broughton Knox*, Principal, Moore Theological College (1959–1985); *Peter F. Jensen*, Principal, Moore Theological College (1985–2001), Archbishop of Sydney (2001–).

# Contents

# Series preface

*New Studies in Biblical Theology* is a series of monographs that address key issues in the discipline of biblical theology. Contributions to the series focus on one or more of three areas: 1. the nature and status of biblical theology, including its relations with other disciplines (e.g. historical theology, exegesis, systematic theology, historical criticism, narrative theology); 2. the articulation and exposition of the structure of thought of a particular biblical writer or corpus; and 3. the delineation of a biblical theme across all or part of the biblical corpora.

Above all, these monographs are creative attempts to help thinking Christians understand their Bibles better. The series aims simultaneously to instruct and to edify, to interact with the current literature, and to point the way ahead. In God's universe, mind and heart should not be divorced: in this series we will try not to separate what God has joined together. While the notes interact with the best of scholarly literature, the text is uncluttered with untransliterated Greek and Hebrew, and tries to avoid too much technical jargon. The volumes are written within the framework of confessional evangelicalism, but there is always an attempt at thoughtful engagement with the sweep of the relevant literature.

It is a pleasure to include in the Series this volume by Dr Mark Thompson. I suppose one might initially question why his work has been included in a series devoted to biblical theology. His earlier work on Luther was essentially an historical study; the present work, it might be argued, belongs at least as obviously to the domain of systematic theology as to biblical theology. But that is just the point. NSBT is interested in how biblical theology contributes to related disciplines, and while this present work addresses historical and dogmatic questions, on several fronts its fulcrum is responsible biblical theology.

Certainly there are few topics more pertinent in the first decade of the twenty-first century. A strange combination of collective

theological amnesia and an uncritical acquiescence in the least discip-
lined forms of postmodernism have made many Christians highly
suspicious of hearing any sure or clear Word from Scripture. The
'perspicuity of Scripture' (often designated *claritas Scripturae*) has
fallen on hard times. Dr Thompson's clearly written and robust articulation of the clarity of Scripture will help many people think
about these matters knowledgably, crisply, faithfully, pointedly. The
purpose of such an exercise, of course, can never be an end in itself:
the purpose is to handle Scripture itself with greater wisdom and confidence. That is why this book deserves the widest circulation.

*D. A. Carson*
*Trinity Evangelical Divinity School*

# Author's preface

The five chapters of this book were originally the Annual Moore College Lectures, delivered in August 2005. It was an enormous privilege to be invited by the Principal, Dr John Woodhouse, to deliver those lectures. His encouragement during the study leave granted for the purposes of preparation kept the project on track when a myriad of other demands threatened to derail it. I join with many others in thanking God for his gifted and godly leadership of the Moore College community and I am grateful for this opportunity to record my own extensive debt to his faithful ministry of the word of God.

Like many before me, I have found that one of the great benefits of working in a theological college is the opportunity to wrestle in fellowship with faithful and insightful colleagues and highly motivated and gifted students about questions such as the clarity of Scripture. I have greatly benefited from conversations on this topic with Drs Peter Jensen, Robert Doyle, Peter Bolt, Andrew Shead, Mike Ovey and Peter O'Brien. A number of former students at Moore College have also investigated these questions and shared the results of their work. While there are undoubtedly others, I owe a particular debt to Stephen Anderson, Hefin Jones and Orlando Saer. Outside this environment I am glad to acknowledge the philosophical insights of Mr Shane Waugh.

In researching this subject, as previously, I have been much more than adequately equipped by the resources of the Moore College Library. I found that almost everything I needed to explore these questions was already held by the library and in those rare cases where something was not, Mr Kim Robinson ensured that it was ordered or borrowed with unusual speed. I am very grateful to him and the rest of the library staff.

Professor John Webster of the University of Aberdeen has been extraordinarily generous, allowing me to read his own treatment of this topic prior to its publication in his book *Confessing God*. The book appeared as these lectures were being delivered and the extent of my debt to his stimulating treatment of the topic will be obvious.

I hope he will understand where I have continued to walk a somewhat different path.

I have valued the encouragement I have received over many years now from Professor Don Carson. We first spoke about this topic back in 1996 in a little restaurant in Oxford. Years later he was one of those who convinced me to make this the topic of the lectures when he first heard that I had been invited to deliver them. His own model of wide and generous reading, his humble and constant submission to the word of the living God, and his determination to honour God by speaking his truth and confronting error or sheer sloppy academic work have encouraged me and many others. His graciousness and generosity to me personally, not least in accepting this book as a volume in the New Studies in Biblical Theology series, is something for which I continue to give great thanks to our God.

The book is dedicated to three theologians who have all left their mark on my own thinking and that of countless others. Alan Catchpoole was the first to show me how to think theologically. His passion for explaining the teaching of Scripture in a systematic way opened up a new world. Broughton Knox was nearing the end of his long tenure as Principal of Moore College when I began studying there in 1983. His capacity to excite students is now almost legendary in Sydney and elsewhere. He modelled a kind of theological reflection that refuses to be distracted from the words of Scripture, allowing every system and every thought to be challenged by what God has said to us in the Bible. Peter Jensen, who succeeded Broughton Knox in 1985, has been an outstanding mentor both theologically and personally. Though called to a different role amongst God's people in 2001, he has continued to encourage me to think hard, read widely and speak with clarity and boldness.

Yet the one person without whom not a single word that follows could have been produced is my wife Kathryn. She makes life and ministry a joy and is the ever-present reminder of God's wonderful goodness to me. Eternity alongside her is a marvellous prospect.

In the remarkable kindness of God he has equipped his people for life in a fallen world by giving them his Spirit and his word written. If what follows encourages men and women to read the Scriptures with confidence in God's goodness, expecting to be addressed by him in the words he has caused to be written for us, then it will have served its purpose.

*Mark D. Thompson*
*August AD 2005*

# Abbreviations

| | |
|---|---|
| *ANF* | *The Ante-Nicene Fathers: Translations of the Writings of the Fathers Down to A.D. 325*, ed. A. Roberts and J. Donaldson, 10 vols., Grand Rapids: Eerdmans, repr. 1985 |
| ANTC | Abingdon New Testament Commentaries |
| AV | Authorized Version (of the Bible) |
| BST | The Bible Speaks Today |
| *CCSL* | *Corpus christianorum series latina*, 176 vols., Turnholt: Brepols, 1954– |
| *CD* | K. Barth, *Church Dogmatics*, ed. T. F. Torrance and G. W. Bromiley, trans. G. Thomson, H. Knight et al., 4 vols., Edinburgh: T. & T. Clark, 1956–74 |
| *ChrCent* | *Christian Century* |
| *CTJ* | *Calvin Theological Journal* |
| ESV | English Standard Version (of the Bible) |
| FS | Festschrift |
| *HTR* | *Harvard Theological Review* |
| *IJST* | *International Journal of Systematic Theology* |
| *JETS* | *Journal of the Evangelical Theological Society* |
| JSNTSup | Journal for the Study of the New Testament Supplement Series |
| *KD* | K. Barth, *Die Kirchliche Dogmatik*, 4 vols., Zollikon: Evangelischer, 1932–67 |
| LCC | Library of Christian Classics |
| *LW* | *Luther's Works*, ed. J. Pelikan and H. T. Lehmann, 55 vols., St. Louis: Concordia; Philadelphia: Fortress, 1955–86 |
| NICOT | New International Commentary on the Old Testament |
| NIGTC | New International Greek Testament Commentary |
| *NPNF,* 1st Series | *A Select Library of the Nicene and Post-Nicene Fathers of the Christian Church*, 1st Series, ed. P. Schaff, 14 vols., Grand Rapids: Eerdmans, repr. 1979 |

| | |
|---|---|
| *NPNF,* 2nd Series | *A Select Library of the Nicene and Post-Nicene Fathers of the Christian Church,* 2nd series, ed. P. Schaff and H. Wace, 14 vols., Grand Rapids: Eerdmans, repr. 1982 |
| NSBT | New Studies in Biblical Theology |
| OTL | Old Testament Library |
| *PG* | *Patrologiae, cursus completus, patres ecclesiae, series graeca,* ed. J.-P. Migne, 162 vols., Paris: Migne, 1857–66 |
| *PL* | *Patrologiae, cursus completus, patres ecclesiae, series latina,* ed. J.-P. Migne, 221 vols., Paris: Migne, 1844–64 |
| *RTR* | *Reformed Theological Review* |
| *SBET* | *Scottish Bulletin of Evangelical Theology* |
| *SJT* | *Scottish Journal of Theology* |
| SP | Sacra pagina |
| *ThTo* | *Theology Today* |
| *TJ* | *Trinity Journal* |
| *WA* | *D. Martin Luthers Werke: Kritische Gesamtausgabe, Schriften,* ed. J. K. F. Knaake, G. Kawerau et al., 66 vols., Weimar: Böhlaus Nachfolger, 1883– |
| *VE* | *Vox evangelica* |
| WBC | Word Biblical Commentary |
| *WTJ* | *Westminster Theological Journal* |
| WUNT | Wissenschaftliche Untersuchungen zum Neuen Testament |
| *ZTK* | *Zeitschrift für Theologie und Kirche* |

Open my eyes, that I may behold wondrous things out of your law.

(Ps. 119:18)

But this is the one to whom I will look: he who is humble and contrite in spirit and trembles at my word.

(Isa. 66:2b)

If God spare my life ere many years I wyl cause a boye that dryveth the plough shall know more of the scripture than thou dost.

(Tyndale 1521)

Christ has not so enlightened us as deliberately to leave some part of his word obscure while commanding us to give heed to it, for he commands us in vain to give heed if it does not give light.

(Luther 1525: 95)

In the fog of this intellectual life of ours the word of God, which is clear in itself, always becomes obscure.

(Barth 1938: 716 [*KD* I/2, 803 = *CD* I/2, 716])

No confession concerning Scripture is more disturbing to the church than the confession of its perspicuity.

(Berkouwer 1966–7: 288)

Behind the argument about the clarity of Scripture is an argument about whom Scripture belongs to and whether it is a means of control.

(Goldingay 1994: 345)

We can cloak our own darkness by calling it the obscurity of the text; we can evade the judgement which Scripture announces by endless hermeneutical deferral; we can treat Scripture not as the clear Word of judgement and hope but as a further opportunity for the imagination to be puzzled, stimulated and set to work . . . That is why the promise of *claritas scripturae* is inseparable from the prayer: 'Open my eyes, that I may behold wondrous things out of thy law' (Ps. 119:18).

(Webster 2005: 67)

Chapter One

# Oh sweet obscurity: The absurdity of claiming clarity today

'Did God really say . . . ?'

By almost any measure a bold and confident use of the Bible is a hallmark of evangelical Christianity. Whether it be the sophisticated sociohistorical analysis of David Bebbington, who ranks 'biblicism' as the third of his four characteristics of evangelical religion,[1] or the simple and direct statement of evangelical leader John Stott, 'It is the contention of evangelicals that they are plain Bible Christians,'[2] explorations of evangelical identity routinely acknowledge the decisive role of the Bible in shaping thought and practice. Billy Graham's insistent appeal to 'the Bible says' is emblematic for many. Convinced that what the Bible says, God says, classic evangelicalism appeals to the Scriptures for an understanding of God and his purposes as well as for the shape of an appropriate response to the words he has spoken.

Underlying such an appeal are a number of assumptions about the origin, nature and form of that collection of ancient narrative, poetry, proverb, law, vision and epistle that is the Christian Bible. What authority (if 'authority' is the right word) can such an anthology legitimately exercise over the thinking and behaviour of men and women two millennia after its completion? What gives these texts a priority over the plethora of other religious texts in the world, even just the ancient world? How does their undoubted variety in genre and historical perspective serve the interests of their message, if, indeed, we can be permitted to speak about 'message' in the singular at all? These are all legitimate questions that have occupied many,

[1] Bebbington 1989: 2–4, 12–14. Bebbington acknowledges that others such as J. C. Ryle, John R. W. Stott and J. I. Packer all mention the authority of Scripture as the leading principle of evangelical faith (Ryle 1871: 10; Stott 1977: 5–14; Packer 1978: 20).
[2] Stott 1970: 32.

especially in the last fifty years or so.[3] Yet even if there are very good grounds (and there are) for accepting the Christian Scriptures as the authoritative word of the living God, complete with a coherent story or meganarrative that appropriates rather than sublimates the genuine diversity to be found in these texts,[4] there is still another question that nags away at many: Can we really be certain about what it says or what it means?

In many ways this would appear to be the question of the hour. A lack of confidence that we do or even that we can know for sure what the Bible says is apparent in Western Christianity. Theologians, it seems, are more comfortable asking questions than giving answers or seeking to justify them. Ancient apophatic traditions with their appeal to mystery, to God's incomprehensible nature and his inscrutable will, are gaining a new prominence in mainstream denominations.[5] Silence is proposed as a more appropriate response to the reality of God's presence than bold proclamation.[6] Those who persist in an appeal to the clear teaching of Scripture face charges of hermeneutical naivety, entrapment in modernist assumptions, a lack of epistemic humility, or, worst of all, an act of 'communicative violence'.[7] You can't be sure that's what it means; and if you say you are, it is merely a ploy to coerce me to accept your point of view.

Despite a number of sophisticated explorations of the clarity or perspicuity of Scripture in recent decades,[8] this doctrine is either ignored or derided by many. It seems scarcely credible and even absurd given two thousand years of Christian biblical interpretation, let alone contemporary literary theory. What is more, it just doesn't

---

[3] The literature discussing the doctrine of Scripture more generally is immense. Amongst the most helpful and scholarly treatments of this doctrine and related issues in English are Berkouwer 1966–7, though note it has been extensively abridged by Jack B. Rogers; Vanhoozer 1994b; Gunton 1995; Wolterstorff 1995; Jensen 2002: 145–256; Horton 2002: 123–219; Ward 2002; and Webster 2003a. At a more popular level, the recent volume from N. T. Wright (Wright 2005) raises important questions, even if its argument is open to significant criticism at a number of points.

[4] For the distinction between *meganarratives* and *metanarratives* (the latter the target of Jean-François Lyotard's famous definition of the postmodern condition, Lyotard 1979: 7) see Westphal 2003. For a little more detail of what is involved see Westphal 2001: xi–xvi.

[5] Williams 1991: 5–6. Note John Webster's stinging retort: 'Apophasis does not secure freedom from idolatry, and, indeed, may be itself a form of idolatrous resistance to the human vocation to positive speech and action' (Webster 2003b: 121).

[6] Williams 1994a, 1994b; Muers 2004.

[7] Muers 2004: 215.

[8] E.g. Berkouwer 1966–7: 267–298; Sandin 1983; Callahan 2001; Webster 2005: 33–67.

seem to resonate with the experience of many Christians who struggle to make sense of what is being said at point after point. Should this doctrine and the rhetoric associated with it ('the plain meaning of the text') be quietly retired from Christian use? Is it not simply an uncomfortable reminder of those long-gone days when we took words at their face value, oblivious to the leaps of logic we made whenever we read the biblical texts? Berkouwer's forty-year-old observation appears vindicated in the current climate: 'No confession concerning Scripture is more disturbing to the church than the confession of its perspicuity.'[9]

There is undoubtedly a contemporary flavour to these objections to the doctrine of Scripture's clarity. The phenomenon known mostly as 'postmodernism' has reshaped old questions and generated new ones. Nevertheless, the debate itself is not new. Considerable ink has been spilt over the centuries in attempts to challenge or defend the idea that Scripture, both in form and in substance, is clear. It is one of the many examples of our arrogance mixed with ignorance that we at the beginning of the third millennium consider responsible hermeneutics a relatively recent acquisition. Christian teachers have been exegeting the Scriptures since the Day of Pentecost, if not before, and questions of interpretation, indeed of the relative clarity or obscurity of the ancient texts and their own, were recognized and addressed from the earliest days.[10] So before we explore a little more fully the particular shape objections to this doctrine have taken in more recent years, it is worth identifying the reasons why some in earlier times found it difficult to accept that Scripture is clear.

## Traditional objections to the doctrine of the clarity of Scripture

Objections to any suggestion that Scripture is clear and that, as a consequence, a direct appeal to the words of Scripture is enough to settle controversy, came from various directions. Nevertheless, it may be helpful to identify five basic protests and deal with more specific issues under those headings. As those who sought to defend this doctrine in the past made plain, none of these objections is unanswerable. However, no attempt will be made to rehearse those answers or

---

[9] Berkouwer 1966–7: 288.
[10] The most obvious example of such a concern in the New Testament is 2 Pet. 3:14–16.

to construct our own at this point. The objections themselves need to be taken seriously and the weight of the arguments borne in full. As the history of Christian theology more generally makes plain, far too much theologizing has in fact been a response to a caricature rather than engagement with an issue.

1. *The doctrine fails to take account of the transcendent mystery that is the subject of Scripture.* This was one of the chief objections raised against the idea of Scripture's clarity by the great early-modern humanist, Desiderius Erasmus (1466–1536). In his exchange with Martin Luther over the status of the human will, Erasmus objected that Luther's confident appeal to the Scriptures ran the risk of blasphemy, or at least of lacking the restraint necessary when speaking about God and his purposes on this side of the Lord's return. While not every passage of Scripture is opaque, it ought not to surprise us if many are, since God and his purposes are greater than the human mind. Does not Scripture itself say so? Erasmus' appeal at this point was to Romans 11:33 and Isaiah 40:13:

> Oh, the depth of the riches and wisdom and knowledge of God! How unsearchable are his judgments and how inscrutable his ways!
>
> (Rom. 11:33)

> Who has measured the Spirit of the LORD, or what man shows him his counsel?
>
> (Isa. 40:13)[11]

Paul and Isaiah, Erasmus suggested, tread a 'wiser and more reverent course' than the one to which Luther had committed himself. In fact, Luther's confidence was actually presumption. He had dared to reduce God to a series of doctrinal assertions without realizing that at significant points God's person and will go far beyond our linguistic capacity. Erasmus was protesting that all human language, including the language of Scripture, is stretched to breaking point when it comes to expressing the reality of God and his purposes.[12] From this perspective, insistence upon the clarity of Scripture represents a

[11] As translator Gordon Rupp points out, Erasmus (or his printer) misquotes Isaiah, replacing *adiuvit* with *audivit,* resulting in 'Who has heard the Spirit of the Lord . . .' (Erasmus 1524a: 38 fn. 11).

[12] This is part of what Rowan Williams describes as 'the sheer difficulty of talking about God' (Williams 2003).

failure at an elementary level: recasting God in the dimensions of his creatures. As Karl Barth would put it, 'The revelation attested in the Bible is the revelation of the God who by nature cannot be unveiled to men.'[13]

2. *The doctrine fails to acknowledge the God-given role of the church as the interpreter of Scripture.* This objection lay close to the heart of the dispute about Scripture's clarity at the time of the Reformation. Luther and those who stood with him reacted to what they saw as a radical inflation of the role of the church as guardian and interpreter of the Scriptures. Indeed, Luther considered that the papal claim to be the authoritative interpreter of Scripture was the second of three walls built to preserve the power of Rome and to stymie all attempts at reformation.[14] However, the idea that the church had an important role in guarding the integrity of the Scriptures and attesting genuine interpretations had a much more benign origin. Irenaeus, the second-century bishop of Lyons, sought to counter the appeal to Scripture by the heretics of his day by insisting that the church, led by bishops as successors of the apostles, is the guarantor of true interpretation:

> True knowledge is the teaching of the Apostles, the ancient con-stitution of the Church for the whole world, and the mark of Christ's body according to the successions of bishops, to whom they committed that Church, which is in every single place. [The Church] carefully and continuously comes to us without pre-tence, [providing] a very full handling of the Scriptures, and a legitimate exposition according to the Scriptures, careful, accepting neither addition nor subtraction, reading without falsification, without danger, and without blasphemy.[15]

It should be evident that Irenaeus considered the Scriptures to be inviolate and that the authority of the church does not extend to adding or subtracting from the biblical text. Yet the reality of hetero-dox appeals to the Old Testament or the writings of the apostles led him to insist upon an interpretative responsibility peculiar to the

---

[13] Barth 1932: 320 (*KD* I/1, 338 = *CD* I/1, 320). Note, as usual, that this is not all Barth has to say. In the pages that follow he will speak of God's 'permanent freedom to unveil Himself or to veil Himself' (342 = 324).

[14] Luther 1520a: 133–136 (*WA* VI, 411.8 – 412.38 = *LW* XLIV, 133–136).

[15] Irenaeus 189: 508 (*Adversus haereses* IV.xxxiii.8 [*PG* VII, 1077 = *ANF* I, 508]). The passage is notoriously difficult, being preserved partly in Greek and partly in Latin. The translation is my own. Cf. Irenaeus 189: 548 (*Adversus haereses* V.xx.2 [*PG* VII, 1177–1178 = *ANF* I, 548]).

orthodox churches.[16] Only by heeding the interpretative guidance of the true church could the danger of blasphemy be avoided.

This concern is even more obvious in one of the most famous statements about the church's role as guardian and interpreter of the Scriptures, from the *Commonitorium* of Vincent of Lérins written around AD 434:

> Here someone may possibly ask: Since the canon of the Scriptures is complete, and is abundantly sufficient for every purpose, what need is there to add to it the authority of the church's interpretation? The reason is, of course, that by its very depth the Holy Scripture is not received by all in one and the same sense, but its declarations are subject to interpretation, now in one way, now in another, so that, it would appear, we can find almost as many interpretations as there are men. Novatian expounds it one way, Sabellius another, Donatus another, Arius, Eunomius, Macedonius, another, Photinus, Apollinaris, Priscillian, all another, Iovinian, Pelagius, Celestius, still another, and finally, Nestorius another. For this reason it is very necessary that, on account of so great intricacies of such varied error, the line used in the exposition of the prophets and apostles be made straight in accordance with the standard of ecclesiastical and catholic interpretation. Likewise in the catholic church itself especial care must be taken that we hold to that which has been believed everywhere, always, and by everyone.[17]

The last line points us in the direction of the famous 'Vincentian Canon', three cardinal virtues that enable an interpreter to identify the church's authorized interpretation: ecumenicity (everywhere), antiquity (always) and consensus (by everyone).[18] But once again the concern is to *preserve* the meaning of Scripture rather than to *constitute* it. The church's role is to be a responsible guardian of this treasure entrusted to her, contending against diverse and idiosyncratic interpretations.

---

[16] See the complaints of Irenaeus about the interpretative practices of the heretics: Irenaeus 189: 320, 326 (*Adversus haereses* I.iii.6, I.viii.1 [*PG*, VII, 477, 521 = *ANF* I, 320, 326]). Cf. Tertullian 207: 377 (*Adversus Marcionem* IV.xix.6 [*CCSL* I, 592 = *ANF* III, 377]).

[17] Vincent 434: 132 (*Commonitorium* II.5 (*PL*, L, 640. My translation departs very little from that of C. A. Huertley in *NPNF*, 2nd Series, XI, 132).

[18] Vincent 434: 152 (*Commonitorium* XXVII.70 [*PL*, L, 674; *NPNF*, 2nd Series, XI, 152]).

However, in the centuries that followed, a shift took place that gave the church's interpretative function greater significance. In the wake of the Reformation, the Council of Trent declared in 1546 that the function of 'Holy Mother Church' is to 'pass judgment on the true meaning and interpretation of the Sacred Scriptures'.[19] The teaching of this council has been repeatedly affirmed in the centuries since. In its dogmatic constitution on divine revelation, *Dei verbum*, promulgated in 1965, Vatican II drew attention to God's continuing presence and activity in the church: 'God, who spoke of old, uninterruptedly converses with the bride of His beloved Son.'[20] It then continued:

> But the task of authentically interpreting the word of God, whether written or handed on, has been entrusted exclusively to the living teaching office of the Church, whose authority is exercised in the name of Jesus Christ. This teaching office is not above the word of God, but serves it, teaching only what has been handed on, listening to it devoutly, guarding it scrupulously and explaining it faithfully in accord with a divine commission and with the help of the Holy Spirit, it draws from this one deposit of faith everything which it presents for belief as divinely revealed.
>
> It is clear, therefore, that sacred tradition, Sacred Scripture and the teaching authority of the Church, in accord with God's most wise design, are so linked and joined together that one cannot stand without the others, and that all together and each in its own way under the action of the one Holy Spirit contribute effectively to the salvation of souls.[21]

Until recently it may have been possible to characterize this line of argument as a peculiar conviction of the Roman Catholic Church. However, increasingly Protestant writers have also been willing to admit a much more corporate dimension to Christian interpretative responsibility, one that calls into question traditional appeals to the clarity of Scripture. To be sure, this has somewhat different contours

---

[19] 'Decretum de editione et usu sacrorum librorum', Council of Trent, Session IV, 8 April 1546.

[20] Vatican II, *Dei verbum*, II.8 available online at http://www.vatican.va/archive/hist_councils/ii_vatican_council/documents/vat-ii_const_19651118_dei_verbum_en.html.

[21] Vatican II, *Dei verbum*, II.10.

23

from the classic statements of Catholic doctrine, but lines of convergence are apparent. So Robert Jenson writes:

> The primary hermeneutical principle for the church's reading
> of Scripture is – I want to insist – simply the church's own life
> ... What God uses to guide our reading of the Bible is first and
> foremost the church's liturgy and devotion and catechesis and
> homiletics, as Scripture has its particular place in them.[22]

Elsewhere he declares, 'The slogan *sola scriptura*, if by that is meant "apart from creed, teaching office, or authoritative liturgy", is an oxymoron.'[23]

Once again those who put forward such an argument against the clarity of Scripture have often appealed to the Scriptures themselves.[24] Do they not teach that the same Spirit who moved the prophets to speak and to write (2 Pet. 1:21) has been given to the church to guide her 'into all truth' (John 16:12–15)? Did not the apostle Peter expound with decisive authority the prophecies of Joel on the Day of Pentecost (Acts 2:14)? Did not the Jerusalem church decide, in Acts 15, that Paul's gospel was a right and proper understanding of the Scriptures in the light of Jesus' life, death and resurrection? Does God not manifest his glory 'in the church' (Eph. 3:21)? God's involvement with his people did not cease with the production of the biblical texts. The Bible does not stand alone and the Christian person's experience of the Bible occurs in a context. Indeed, a case can be mounted for a certain priority of the church, at least from a historical perspective, since the community predates the texts addressed to it. Nevertheless, the most important part of the objectors' argument is their insistence that God continues to be present amongst his people by his Spirit, guiding and teaching through the authorized teachers of the church.

3. *The doctrine fails to take seriously the nature of the words of Scripture.* Whatever else we might say about the Bible, we cannot deny that these pages are full of words, human words, arranged according to the conventions of human language. Furthermore, these

---

[22] Jenson 1995: 90.

[23] Jenson 1997: 28. See also Franke 2004: 192–193.

[24] E.g. 'To remove the Bible from its organic churchly setting and to attempt to "exegete" it outside its ecclesial context is itself "uncritical" and "unscientific," since such a method of reading and interpreting the Scriptures is contrary to the testimony of the writings themselves, as well as the testimony of the church that produced them' (Hopko 1995: 116).

words are each used from within a particular historical and social context. The recognition of these simple truths about Scripture lie behind the third classic objection to declarations of Scripture's clarity, which insists that such declarations regularly fail to take this genuine humanity of the biblical text seriously. Not only does the humanity of the text stand in stark contrast to the transcendence of God himself (objection 1 above), human language, especially in its written form, is a notoriously frail and fallible means of communication. We habitually mishear and misread each other, we choose the wrong words and convey our meaning obliquely. Those with malicious intent use words to cloak their intentions rather than make them known. Of course, communication is still possible; most of the time we do succeed in making ourselves, our thoughts, desires and plans known to each other through human words. Yet it *is* difficult. Human language is neither pristine nor ideal. In short, declarations of Scripture's clarity, especially those of a more absolute type, expect more of these words than they are able to deliver.

Some would suggest that such claims for clarity in fact arise from the belief that we need to affirm certain perfections of the biblical text in order to secure its authority in theology and the Christian life more generally. At times when the authority of the Bible seemed threatened, new and inflated claims were made by conservative forces. The usual suspects are the Lutheran and Reformed theologians of the seventeenth century and the 'heirs' of Hodge and Warfield in the twentieth. Karl Barth and others have argued that the rationale for this move is entirely mistaken and insist instead upon 'the vulnerability of the Bible' as a necessary corollary of its genuine humanity.[25] Barth himself warns that 'we must not compromise either directly or indirectly the humanity of its form and the possibility of the offence which can be taken at it':[26]

[25] Barth 1938: 509 (*KD* I/2, 565 = *CD* I/2, 509). Rachel Muers speaks of God making his word 'vulnerable to mishearing' (Muers 2004: 116, 119).

[26] Barth 1938: 528 (*KD* I/2, 587 = *CD* I/2, 528). This is one feature of Barth's 'distinction yet relatedness' of witness and word, of the Bible and revelation: 'In the Bible we meet with human words written in human speech, and in these words, and therefore by means of them, we hear of the lordship of the triune God . . . If we want to think of the Bible as a real witness of divine revelation, then clearly we have to keep two things constantly before us and give them their due weight: the limitation and the positive element, its distinctiveness from revelation, in so far as it is only a human word about it, and its unity with it, in so far as revelation is the basis, object and content of this word. To avoid this, there is no point in ignoring the writtenness of Holy Writ for the sake of its holiness, its humanity for the sake of its divinity' (Barth 1938: 463 [*KD* I/2, 512 = *CD* I/2, 463]).

> This offence is therefore grounded like the overcoming of it in
> the mercy of God. For that reason it must not be denied and
> for that reason, too, it must not be evaded. For that reason
> every time we turn the Word of God into an infallible biblical
> word of man or the biblical word of man into an infallible
> Word of God we resist that which we ought never to resist, i.e.
> the truth of the miracle that here fallible men speak the Word
> of God in fallible human words – and we therefore resist the
> sovereignty of grace, in which God Himself became man in
> Christ, to glorify Himself in His humanity.[27]

Barth's direct target in this paragraph is any insistence upon the infal-
libility or inerrancy of the biblical text. Yet a little further along in
the same volume of the *Church Dogmatics* he makes clear that for
very similar reasons claims for the clarity of Scripture need careful
qualification:

> In order to be proclaimed and heard again and again both in
> the Church and the world, Holy Scripture requires to be
> explained. As the Word of God it needs no explanation, of
> course, since as such it is clear in itself. The Holy Ghost knows
> very well what He has said to the prophets and apostles and
> what through them He wills also to say to us. This clarity
> which Scripture has in itself as God's Word, this objective *per-
> spicuitas* which it possesses, is subject to no human respon-
> sibility or care . . . But this Word in Scripture assumes the form
> of a human word. Human words need interpretation because
> as such they are ambiguous, not usually, of course, in the
> intention of those who speak, but always for those who hear.[28]

It is this line of thinking that leads Gerrit Berkouwer to suggest
that at least some appeals to the clarity of Scripture 'lack respect for
the words of Scripture'.[29] They arbitrarily impose a special linguistic
property upon the text that is not possessed by other human
writing.[30] Indeed, some suggest that their unintended result is a kind

---

[27] Barth 1938: 529 (*KD* I/2, 588 = *CD* I/2, 529).

[28] Barth 1938: 712 (*KD* I/2, 798–799 = *CD* I/2, 712).

[29] Berkouwer 1966–7: 279. Berkouwer's targets here are 'spiritualism' and the insistence of a simple clarity that renders unnecessary continual detailed exegesis of
Scripture.

[30] Anderson 1967: 67, 70.

of docetism, where the humanity of the biblical text proves to be unimportant or, more seriously, merely apparent.[31] To take the humanity of the text seriously means grappling with the imprecision of human language: there is rarely a mathematical exactness to human words. It also means grappling with the historical location of the biblical texts and the distance that creates between it and all but the original readers.

The genuine humanity of Scripture, including its historical location, is highlighted by the fact that most of its readers down through the ages have encountered it as a translated text. Without the activity of translators, transposing the original words into the vernacular of a myriad of people groups around the globe, the Scriptures would be accessible only to those trained in ancient Hebrew and Greek. Yet this very phenomenon of translation introduces its own problems.[32] At one level, there is the loss, to a greater or lesser extent, of the form of the original text. The most obvious example is Hebrew poetry, particularly the acrostic psalms. 'Translation is always a treason' the Italian proverb insists, and a Chinese author once likened its best products to 'the reverse side of a brocade – all the threads are there, but not the subtlety of colour or design'.[33] However, at another level, given that all translation involves interpretative choices and that alternative translations are often available (especially in languages such as English), an element of uncertainty can easily enter the process of reading the Bible. Even translations at the literal end of the spectrum can tend to close off interpretative options. Which form of the text, then, are we to consider clear? If most of us approach the text only as far as a translation will allow, does it make any sense to talk about the clarity of Scripture?

More than two centuries of historical criticism has raised additional questions about any robust affirmation of Scripture's clarity.[34] Taking the words of Scripture seriously, its practitioners suggest, means acknowledging that very little about this text is simple or straightforward. Opponents of the doctrine at the time of the

[31] France 1982: 236.
[32] Silva 1987: 79.
[33] Okakura 1906: 19.
[34] De Senarclens spoke of how historical criticism sought 'to rediscover the humanity of the Bible' and to free the Word of God from a 'novel and illegitimate incarnation' in order to 'restore to Jesus Christ his living authority' (de Senarclens 1959: 287). Others speak of how historical criticism was, at its heart, a revolt against the Augustinian worldview, with its supernaturalist perspective and its priority of divine initiative over human action (Harrisville & Sundberg 2002: 5, 26–29).

Reformation had pointed to difficulties in the text such as apparent contradictions, ambiguities, broken syntax and even verses out of place in a narrative.[35] Yet the critical biblical scholarship that emerged in the wake of the Enlightenment went much further. It insisted that we cannot always move directly from the biblical narratives to the historical events to which they refer. Imagination, symbolism and different historiographical conventions make the move more complex than we might first suppose. There is a palpable diversity between – and in some cases within – the texts that complicates the picture further. Appeals to the clarity of Scripture may too easily be attempts to avoid messy historical realities and retreat behind traditional interpretations in defiance of the tremendous advances in specialist knowledge over the past two hundred years. Does a careful, scholarly examination of the text we actually have really lead to the doctrine of Scripture's clarity, or is it something brought to, indeed imposed upon, the Bible by those who refuse to look too closely?

4. *The doctrine fails in practice given the reality of diverse interpretations.* This ancient objection points to the most glaring empirical counter-evidence against the clarity of Scripture. If Scripture is clear, its true and normative meaning accessible and intelligible to all, then why are there so many different and even conflicting interpretations? We have already seen that this reality demanded explanation during the time of Irenaeus and Vincent of Lérins. It was even more of an embarrassment during the time of the Reformation, when the differences were not merely between Catholics and Protestants but between the Protestants themselves. Luther's protracted dispute with Zwingli and others over the words of Jesus at the Last Supper was merely the most notorious example.[36] Some scholars detect a retreat on the part of the Reformers themselves: a movement away from their early hermeneutical optimism forced upon them by the reality of such undeniable differences between equally learned and godly men.[37] It was one thing to write boldly about the clarity of Scripture in 1525; it was quite another to rehearse those same sentiments in 1530. A supposedly clear and compelling word had failed to bring unanimity of opinion.

The Catholic opponents of the Reformers did not hesitate to capitalize on this 'inconsistency'. Roberto Bellarmino used the old

---

[35] See Whitaker's careful account of this objection by Bellarmino and his point-by-point response (Whitaker 1588: 377–379).

[36] Thompson 1998a.

[37] McGrath 1999: 161. For a different view see Steinmetz 1984: 96–97. For a more detailed treatment of the idea in Luther's thought see Thompson 2004: 198–209.

figure of Scripture as a wax nose (*cereus nasus*), a text malleable in a variety of directions as heretics attempt to cloak their perfidy. In the absence of a judge to decide between them, people would simply concoct their own interpretation as a way of justifying their personal convictions. The so-called 'right of private judgment' (a much later term) was undeniably the path to theological anarchy.[38]

The same arguments have been repeated many times since the sixteenth century. Today a preponderance of biblical commentaries is cited as further evidence that the question of Scripture's meaning remains an open one.[39] Furthermore, some long-held understandings have been shown to be untenable given a better knowledge of the languages of Scripture and careful attention to the context and to biblical theology. Few today would insist with Luther and his contemporaries that the 'man of lawlessness' in 2 Thessalonians 2 or the 'antichrist' of 1 John 2 is the pope.[40] In some cases differences of opinion, such as that between Luther and Zwingli over the words 'this is my body', have hardened into firm theological positions with little prospect of reconciliation. Hard cases make bad law, it is true, but what are we to do with continuing differences over who is the 'I' in Romans 7, or what it means to be baptized for the dead in 1 Corinthians 15, or when and how Jesus preached to the spirits in prison in 1 Peter 3? An honest look at the history of exegesis or simply at the current state of Old Testament or New Testament study, we are told, exposes the folly of any talk about the clarity of Scripture.

  5. *The doctrine fails by its own criterion, since Scripture confesses its own obscurity*. This final objection opens up the possibility not only that we could claim more for Scripture than it does for itself, but that we might be claiming what Scripture explicitly denies. Once again the classic presentation of this argument comes from Bellarmino in the sixteenth century who well understood its psychological impact. If his opponents claimed to be obedient to the Scriptures, if their basic stance on authority for Christian thinking and living was truly represented by the principle *sola scriptura*, then to demonstrate that Scripture did not claim what they were claiming for it and in fact acknowledged its own obscurity would be a powerful blow to the entire

---

[38] Abraham sees other serious theological problems generated by the Reformers' advocacy of the clarity of Scripture and its inevitable compromise by the disputes between them (Abraham 1998: 151–152).

[39] Carnley 2004: 105.

[40] Luther 1535–45: II, 383 (*WA* XLII, 536–537 = *LW* II, 383); Luther 1535: 335 (*WA* XL, 516 = *LW* XXVI, 335); Luther 1527: 252 (*WA* XX, 667–669 = *LW* XXX, 252).

Protestant system. This potential of Bellarmino's argument was recognized by those who sought to reply to him, such as William Whitaker in the sixteenth century and François Turretin in the seventeenth.[41]

We will return to Bellarmino's arguments in more detail in the final chapter. For our present purposes we need only note his appeal to David's prayer for understanding in Psalm 119, the interpretative assistance given to the disciples on the Emmaus road and also to the eunuch on the road to Gaza, and the promise of the Spirit to guide the disciples into all truth. None of these would be necessary, he argued, if the meaning of Scripture was clear, accessible and intelligible to all. Furthermore, this same pattern of conscious dependence upon the interpretative assistance of the church could be discerned in the writings of the early church Fathers as they sought to explain Scripture. Those who had proposed and defended the doctrine of the clarity of Scripture had presented the world with an unbiblical theological novelty.

It is evident just from this brief sketch that many of the questions surrounding this doctrine have been raised repeatedly (and answered repeatedly) over the last two thousand years. Although the debate was most prominent in the early church and again in the sixteenth and seventeenth centuries, an argument can be mounted that even the medieval conversations about the priority of the literal or historical sense and the legitimacy of allegorical interpretation were largely variations on this same theme.[42] However, significant new dimensions have been added to the discussion since the 1970s. These present new challenges to those who would affirm the clarity of Scripture in the third millennium.

## The contemporary context of this discussion

Since the 1970s we have witnessed a massive shift in intellectual commitments, not least in the fields of philosophy, literary theory and theology. The challenge of postmodernism, both a protest at and the progeny of modernism in all its forms, has dramatically changed the landscape and any affirmation of the clarity of Scripture (inseparable as it is from questions of the Bible's truth and authority) must take it into account. Postmodernism cannot be ignored, even if there are

[41] Whittaker 1588: 367–370; Turretin 1679–85: 145–146.
[42] Callahan 2001: 105–126. For more detail on relevant developments in this period see Smalley 1941; Evans 1984, 1985.

already signs that the ground is beginning to shift again.[43] We will keep returning to an engagement with postmodern perspectives in the chapters that follow. However, in order to help us appreciate the world into which any restatement of the doctrine of Scripture's clarity must venture, we turn now to look briefly at the three academic fields I have mentioned as they bear upon the question.

## Postmodern philosophy: Radically questioning epistemological certainty

There is a strongly reactive element to postmodernism, especially in its philosophical mode.[44] It is a repudiation of the central features of what is often called 'the Enlightenment project'. Chief amongst these is what might be termed 'modernist epistemology', a set of convictions about the capacity of human beings to know or apprehend reality and so to speak about truth. Epistemological questions have interested philosophers since at least the time of the protosceptic Xenophanes of Colophon (c. 570–475 BC). He recognized that the process of gaining and validating knowledge was not as straightforward as many thought. The same issues kept resurfacing in different forms through the centuries, with important contributions by Zeno of Citium, Plato, Aristotle, Augustine and Aquinas. However, it was René Descartes (1596–1650) who famously raised the profile of epistemology with his search for an indubitable foundation upon which to reconstruct human knowledge in the face of a resurgent scepticism. He finally located that foundation, he believed, in the human ego, the 'I' of his famous 'I think therefore I am'. Here was a reliable starting point: the simple and undeniable fact that when I doubt everything, it is 'I' who doubts. From this foundation, through the application of a rigorous method, we can know the truth about things.[45] Whether through

---

[43] Parker 2004. For a strong challenge to postmodernism, especially as it has influenced evangelical theology, see the other essays in that volume: Moreland and De Weese 2004; Smith 2004; Caneday 2004; and Wellum 2004.

[44] Cf. David Tracy's assessment, Tracy 1994:16. Paul Lakeland suggests that 'the postmodern elements in our contemporary world are all manifestations in one way or another of a breakdown of what have previously been taken to be "givens", fundamental coordinates of experience' (Lakeland 1997: 2). As we have already noted, Jean-François Lyotard famously summed up the postmodern condition as 'an incredulity toward metanarratives' (Lyotard 1979: 7). Helpful and accessible discussions of postmodernism from the perspective of evangelical Christianity include Carson 1996: 57–137 (simplified and updated in Carson 2005: 87–124); Hicks 1998; and Groothuis 2000.

[45] Strictly speaking, the ego is only one of Descartes's indubitable foundations. Another is the conviction that, because he is perfect, God is no deceiver (Descartes 1641: 37–38).

careful logical argument or scientific measurement, observation and testing, we can proceed from the knowing subject to the truth of reality.

Mathematical precision became the ideal to which all the endeavours of human reason aspired. The ancient concern of philosophy for questions of metaphysics (loosely, the nature of reality) was swamped by the new priority given to questions of how and what we know.[46] This shift of emphasis in philosophy was reinforced by the repudiation of supernatural explanations, given intellectual credibility by the geological studies of James Hutton (1785) and Charles Lyle (1830–3), and Charles Darwin's work on biological evolution (1859, 1871). The result was a remarkable optimism about the accessibility of objective, universally applicable truth. This optimism seemed to be vindicated by the extraordinary achievements in the natural sciences and the development of technology through the application of critical methods of observation and testing.

Of course over the next three and half centuries there were protests. Not everyone was as persuaded as Descartes and his successors that some kind of purchase on objective truth was possible. David Hume embraced a profound scepticism, which prompted Immanuel Kant to explore the valid exercise of human reason as well as its limits. The so-called 'masters of suspicion' raised the possibility that our perception of reality, our convictions about what is true, might be shaped by our own vested interests: economics (Marx), psychosexuality (Freud) or the exercise of personal or corporate power (Nietzsche). There were also sophisticated attempts to correct the preoccupation with objectivity and to insist that there is a critical personal element to all our knowledge (Polanyi).[47] Some abandoned epistemology for linguistic analysis (Wittgenstein) or existentialism (Kierkegaard, Heidegger). More recently, others have pursued an alternative in the internalist epistemology associated with Laurence Bonjour and Roderick Chisholm.[48] Nevertheless, the dominant note

[46] 'The reign of epistemology has ended in European philosophy and theology' (Tracy 1994: 133). Carl Raschke credits Hegel with a critical climactic move here with his 'absorption of the Being into thought' (Raschke 2004: 40–41).

[47] Polanyi's 1951–2 Gifford Lectures explained, 'We must now recognise belief once more as the source of all knowledge. Tacit assent and intellectual passions, the sharing of an idiom and of a cultural heritage, affiliation to a like minded community: such are the impulses which shape our vision of the nature of things on which we rely for our mastery of things. No intelligence, however critical or original, can operate outside such a fiduciary framework' (Polanyi 1962: 266).

[48] Here a claim to knowledge is justified by conditions appropriately internal to the knower's perspective rather than some external foundation (Greco 2000: 181). See also Sosa & Bonjour 2003.

was one of optimism about the human capacity to grasp reality and identify objective truths about it.

Postmodernism has amplified the protests of the past and generated a series of fresh challenges to the confident epistemology of modernism. In a world where cultural and religious pluralism are non-negotiable realities, the claim that we are capable of gaining access to universally valid truths, indeed the notion of absolute truth itself, is highly problematic. It smacks of imperialism and bigotry. It would compel you to use the words 'no' and 'wrong' in a world where some argue that these words are themselves violations of the rights of others. Nietzsche's suspicion that all claims to know what is true are in reality covert attempts to manipulate people has been developed in the detailed studies of Michel Foucault.[49] There is always a reason why you want to say this or that is true. The binary thinking of 'true and false' is not only archaic; it is self-interested (and self-interest may be personal or corporate).

Furthermore, our perceptions of reality and declarations of truth are more dependent upon our context than we often realize or admit. Pure objectivity is mythological. Hans-Georg Gadamer, amongst others, argued persuasively that we cannot detach ourselves or our situation from our history. It is important to unmask modernism's 'prejudice against prejudice' and recognize that our foremeanings and presuppositions help to shape the 'event' of understanding.[50]

> Reason exists for us only in concrete, historical terms – i.e., it is not its own master but remains constantly dependent on the given circumstances in which it operates . . . Long before we understand ourselves through the process of self-examination, we understand ourselves in a self-evident way in the family, society, and state in which we live. The focus of subjectivity is a distorting mirror. The self-awareness of the individual is only

[49] 'The important thing here, I believe, is that truth isn't outside power, or lacking in power: contrary to a myth whose history and functions would repay further study, truth isn't the reward of free spirits, the child of protracted solitude, nor the privilege of those who have succeeded in liberating themselves. Truth is a thing of this world: it is produced only by virtue of multiple forms of constraint. And it induces regular effects of power. Each society had its regime of truth, its "general politics" of truth: that is, the types of discourse which it accepts and makes function as true; the mechanisms and instances which enable one to distinguish true and false statements, the means by which each is sanctioned; the techniques and procedures accorded value in the acquisition of truth; the status of those charged with saying what counts as true' (Foucault 1977: 72–73).
[50] Gadamer 1984: 271.

a flickering in the closed circuits of historical life. *That is why the prejudices of the individual, far more than his judgments, constitute the historical reality of his being.*[51]

Modernist epistemology, according to such thinking, is based on a series of illusions. We cannot, nor should we, escape the contingency of our truth claims. Of course we can still live with a degree of confidence. We can still make sense to each other within our particular 'language game' (Wittgenstein's overused and often misunderstood expression). Yet to make a claim for truth that extends beyond our own sociolinguistic community, beyond the particular story in which we locate ourselves, is either naive or manipulative (and perhaps both). Simply put, 'when people defend their worldview or some system of thought, they are simply defending their own fragile self-identity'.[52]

It is not difficult to see how these developments impact upon any attempt to speak about the clarity of Scripture. This doctrine is suspected of operating totally within the epistemological framework of modernism. It is far too committed to the project of achieving certainty. In particular, it is sometimes argued that a particular form of modernist epistemology, the Common Sense Realism associated with the eighteenth-century Scottish philosopher Thomas Reid, is the real driving force behind the doctrine as it was classically defined.[53] This can be seen in the introduction to one contemporary textbook on hermeneutics:

> In the last century, however, the application of Scottish Common Sense Realism to Scripture has led many to assume that everyone can understand the Bible for themselves, that the surface of the text is sufficient to produce meaning in and of itself. Therefore, the need for hermeneutical principles to bridge the cultural gap was ignored, and individualistic interpretations abounded. For some reason, no one seemed to notice that this led to multiple meanings. The principle of perspicuity was extended to the hermeneutical process as well,

[51] Gadamer 1984: 276–277.
[52] Carson 1996: 31.
[53] Reid's own words help identify the heart of this approach: 'All knowledge, and all science, must be built upon principles that are self-evident; and of such principles, every man who has common sense is a competent judge, when he conceives them distinctly' (Reid 1785: 268).

leading to misunderstanding in popular interpretation of Scripture and a very difficult situation today. Hermeneutics as a discipline demands a complex interpretive process in order to uncover the original clarity of Scripture.[54]

By binding itself so tightly to modernist epistemology, it is argued, twentieth-century doctrines of Scripture, and perhaps especially the doctrine of the clarity of Scripture, doomed itself to the same fate. There are no unshakeable foundations upon which to build a certain knowledge of reality. Likewise, interpretation is a complex process and the clarity of Scripture is something that needs to be uncovered. A clear and universally accessible Scripture in fact functions for evangelical theology in much the same way as Descartes's indubitable foundation operates in modernist epistemology more generally.[55] Many have seen the implication: we are as removed from the meaning of Scripture as we are from a grasp on reality itself and absolute truths about it.[56]

[54] Osborne 1991: 9–10. Common Sense Realism is regularly demonized and association with it taken to discredit the way Charles Hodge and Benjamin Warfield expounded the doctrine of Scripture (Ahlstrom 1955; Rogers & McKim 1979: 323–351; Vander Stelt 1978: 166–184; Marsden 1980: 110–115; Noll 1994: 84–99; McGrath 1996: 168–170; Raschke 2004: 120–131). More nuanced than most criticisms is that of Harriet Harris: 'The Scottish Common Sense philosophy has influenced fundamentalist thought, but its influence is neither specific nor comprehensive. It is not specific because fundamentalist theologians have not engaged with the arguments of Common Sense philosophers and the philosophy does not lead obviously in a fundamentalist direction. It is not comprehensive because many fundamentalist characteristics – even those which have parallels in Common Sense philosophy – derive from aspects of the Christian tradition which predate that philosophy . . . Common Sense philosophy provided a framework within which to produce a conservative biblical apologetic in a scientific age' (Harris 1998: 13–14). However, outside theological circles, especially those interacting with classical evangelicalism, there is a growing appreciation of Reid's philosophical contribution (Cuneo & Woudenberg 2004). The shallowness of the argument that dismisses Princetonian doctrines of Scripture by simple appeal to its association with Scottish Common Sense Realism has repeatedly been exposed in recent years; e.g. Carson 1996: 153–154; Helseth 2004.

[55] Greer 2003: 37–38.

[56] So James K. A. Smith: 'everything is a matter of interpretation, including those interpretations described as core orthodoxy. We never have the crisp, unadorned voice of God because it is always heard and read through the lens of our finitude and situationality. Even when someone purports to deliver to us the unadorned voice of God, or "what God meant", we always receive only someone's interpretation, which is wearing the badge of divinity' (Smith 2000: 44). For a critique of what he labels Smith's 'hermeneutical Pelagianism' see Webster 2003a: 100.

## Postmodern literary theory: From author to text to reader to interpretative community

There is, as one might expect, considerable overlap between developments in the field of philosophy and those in the field of literary theory and hermeneutics.[57] Similar concerns about the confident claims of modernism to be certain, this time about *the* meaning of a given text, have echoed throughout the massive output of literary critics since the 1960s or 1970s. Schleiermacher's definition of the technical side of interpretation has been a particular target: 'The point of the task is to understand the particular part of a coherent utterance as belonging in the specific sequence of thoughts of the writer.'[58]

The impact of postmodern literary theory on contemporary biblical hermeneutics is so significant that it will be a particular focus of our attention in later chapters. However, it may be worth providing a very brief orientation at this point.[59] With the broadest possible strokes we might say that literary theory has moved away from classical notions that the meaning of texts is determined, either entirely or in large measure, by the author's intention, through a fascination with structural features of the text as the carriers of meaning, to a greater appreciation of the contribution the reader brings to the task of understanding, and finally to an emphasis upon the role played by the interpretative community in shaping the reader's expectations of and stance towards the text. This should not be misunderstood as a lineal development with each perspective neatly building upon and eventually taking over from the one that preceded it. Indeed, many have continued to affirm the importance of traditional elements in the approach to texts, albeit in a modified way, while at the same time registering genuine appreciation of the important insights of other approaches. For our current purposes, though, we might simply highlight four general features of the discussions in this field that impact the work of biblical scholars.

---

[57] See Richard Rorty's perceptive, though dated, chapter entitled 'From Epistemology to Hermeneutics' (Rorty 1979: 315–356).

[58] Note that Schleiermacher was concerned that this be understood as a linguistic task: the thought-content he had in mind is 'known grammatically via the language' (Schleiermacher 1809–10: 254). See the discussion of how Schleiermacher has been misunderstood in Wolterstorff 2001: 73–75.

[59] Perhaps the best detailed treatment of these developments remains Vanhoozer 1998: 37–195. Note also the brief but stimulating treatment in Wolterstorff 2001: 73–82.

1. *The author does not have all the answers.* Roland Barthes once famously complained that 'The image of literature to be found in contemporary culture is tyrannically centered around the author, his person, his history, his tastes, his passions . . .'[60] Building upon the work of the French poet Stephané Mallarmé, Barthes insisted that the notion of an author was an unnecessary limitation on textual meaning with palpable theological dimensions. If we insist upon an author and focus our interpretative efforts on seeking to establish the author's intention or message we are in effect closing off all other options.[61] Once we feel we have established the author's intention we have *the* authoritative interpretation. The need of the moment, he argued, was the 'anti-theological activity' of refusing to fix meaning in this way. 'To refuse to fix meaning is', he argued, 'in the end to refuse God and his hypostases – reason, science, law.'[62]

Barthes, with his suggestion that 'the birth of the reader must be at the cost of the death of the author' is one of the most aggressive pro-testors at the traditional preoccupation with the author as the one who designates 'the' meaning of the text.[63] Michel Foucault is another, who describes the author as 'the ideological figure by which one marks the manner in which we fear the proliferation of meaning'.[64] However, they are part of a larger disquiet (not only amongst postmodern writers it should be said) over the role attrib-uted to the author in establishing the meaning of his or her text. Two problems seem to loom large. First, how are we to establish the inten-tion of the author, especially if it is not explicitly expressed? Second, how are we to overcome the possibility that the text may have turned out quite differently from the way the author intended?[65] Yet there is in fact a third and perhaps most critical danger: does not the very attempt itself reduce the shape of the interpretation either to biog-raphy or to psychological analysis? Is every text really only about its author in the end?

---

[60] Barthes 1968: 126. A similar protest had been voiced earlier by advocates of the so-called New Criticism, notably in a previously mentioned article on 'the intentional fallacy' by William Wimsatt and Monroe Beardsley (Wimsatt & Beardsley 1946).

[61] 'To give a text an author is to impose a limit on that text, to furnish it with a final signified, to close the writing' (Barthes 1968: 129).

[62] Barthes 1968: 129.

[63] Barthes 1968: 130.

[64] Foucault 1979: 119.

[65] Wolterstorff 2001: 75–76. In the background of many of these discussions is the famous article by Wimsatt and Beardsley on 'the intentional fallacy' (Wimsatt & Beardsley 1946).

Paul Ricœur also spoke of what he called 'the semantic autonomy of the text'. It is important for him that a distinction be made between speaking and writing as modes of communication. Writing is not just a more permanent form of communication than speaking. When speech is transformed into writing very significant changes occur at a number of different levels. In speech the speaker and hearer are in the same 'dialogical situation'. There is the possibility of referring back to the speaker for clarification or explanation. Yet in writing and reading the relation is nowhere near as immediate; in his words, 'the dialogical situation has been exploded'.[66] The critical effect of this is that 'the author's intention and the meaning of the text cease to coincide'. [67]

We will return to Ricœur in a moment. In the meantime it is worth considering the impact of so detaching the text's meaning from the author's communicative intention. Claims to an authoritative interpretation are now much more dubious. The door is opened to diverse interpretative possibilities, even conflicting or contradictory readings. There is a new unpredictability to the task of interpretation. This is compounded by the other end of the communicative chain, where a written text is potentially addressed to anyone who knows how to read. As Ricœur put it, 'It is part of the meaning of a text to be open to an indefinite number of readers and, therefore, of interpretations. This opportunity for multiple readings is the dialectical counterpart of the semantic autonomy of the text.'[68]

In such a context is it not simply naive to speak about the 'clarity' of a particular text and to suggest a particular reading commands the assent of all? This leads us to consider a second feature of contemporary literary theory.

2. *Reading is as socially located as writing.* David Tracy has identified a shift in the language of hermeneutics from a concern for 'historical context' to a recognition of 'social location'.[69] The significance

---

[66] Ricœur 1976: 29.

[67] 'This dissociation of the verbal meaning of the text and the mental intention of the author gives to the concept of inscription its decisive significance, beyond the mere fixation of previous oral discourse. Inscription becomes synonymous with the semantic autonomy of the text, which results from the disconnection of the mental intention of the author from the verbal meaning of the text, of what the author meant and what the text means. The text's career escapes the finite horizon lived by its author. What the text means now matters more than what the author meant when he wrote it. This concept of semantic autonomy is of tremendous importance for hermeneutics' (Ricœur 1976: 29–30).

[68] Ricœur 1976: 31–32.

[69] Tracy 1994: 135.

of each writer's linguistic community in shaping the texts he or she produces has long been recognized. In biblical studies this has meant extensive debate about the nature and impact of the Johannine community or the Graeco-Roman context of Paul's mission. However, Gadamer and, two decades later, Stanley Fish have emphasized the social location of all reading as well as all writing.

Gadamer's contribution is part of the larger theory of understanding we have already touched upon and was developed in his highly influential *Wahrheit und Methode*. In this book he built upon the work of his teacher Martin Heidegger, arguing that 'understanding is, essentially, a historically effected event' and that we who are trying to understand are 'always situated within traditions'.[70] We do not come to a text with a blank sheet, as if the text did all the work conveying its meaning. We come as those who have a 'horizon', a 'range of vision that includes everything that can be seen from a particular vantage point'.[71] The text has its own horizon as well and a significant part of the process of understanding is acknowledging both the distance between them and the need to bring them into relationship of some kind. In his words, 'understanding is always the fusion of these horizons supposedly existing by themselves'.[72]

Stanley Fish developed this notion of the social location of the interpreter in a new direction. Instead of speaking about horizons and traditions, he popularized the notion of 'interpretative communities'.[73]

> What I have been arguing is that meanings come already calculated, not because of norms embedded in the language but because language is always perceived, from the very first, within a structure of norms. That structure, however, is not abstract and independent but social . . .[74]

---

[70] Gadamer 1984: 300, 282. See Heidegger: 'Whenever something is interpreted as something, the interpretation will be founded essentially upon fore-having, fore-sight and fore-conception. An interpretation is never a presuppositionless apprehending of something presented to us' (1927: 191–192). For an account of the intriguing debate between Gadamer and Jürgen Habermas on the relation of prejudice (that which we bring to the text) and critical reflection, see Ferretter 2003: 109–118.

[71] Gadamer 1984: 302. Gadamer attributes this notion of 'horizon' to Edmund Husserl, though the latter may have been influenced by William James's idea of 'fringes' (245).

[72] Gadamer 1984: 306.

[73] His influential book *Is There a Text in This Class?* is subtitled *The Authority of Interpretive Communities* (Fish 1980).

[74] Fish 1980: 318.

Each reader approaches a text with a set of prejudices, interests and values, as well as a set of expectations about this particular text, which are all to various extents shaped by the cultural community in which he or she operates. There may indeed be aspects of a person's approach to the text that are idiosyncratic, yet the most basic parameters of expectation and method are determined by the community. As Fish himself put it:

> What I finally came to see was that the identification of what was real and normative occurred within interpretive communities and what was normative for the members of one community would be seen as strange (if it could be seen at all) by the members of another. In other words, there is no single way of reading that is correct or natural, only 'ways of reading' that are extensions of community perspectives.[75]

Meaning is, by and large, conventional. Its contours are shaped by the group to which we belong (there are fairly obvious echoes here of Wittgenstein).[76] Such a perspective on understanding texts has very serious implications for the doctrine of the clarity of Scripture. If meaning is largely or even entirely determined by the reader who resides within an interpretative community, then how can we possibly decide between suggested meanings? Even if we were to propose criteria for such a discussion, these would themselves be open to the charge that they are merely conventional, the product of a particular interpretative community's perspective on the nature of texts in general or of this text in particular. What seems clear to one group may not be so clear to another. Indeed, this is what we should expect: 'there is no single way of reading that is correct or natural'.

3. *The world that matters is the world of the text.* We have already seen how one constraint on interpretation, the communicative intention of the author, has been removed by writers such as Barthes and Ricœur. Yet traditionally language has been understood as a way of signifying something, or referring to reality.[77] This too has been seen by some contemporary theorists as an unnecessary, even arbitrary,

---

[75] Fish 1980: 15–16.

[76] There is undoubtedly much more to Fish's argument than this brief summary can convey. For the best recent engagements from a Christian perspective see Vanhoozer 1998: 168–174; Ward 2002: 182–185; Ferretter 2003: 130–138.

[77] The basic building blocks of the Western view of signification are to be found in Augustine's *De doctrina christiana*, completed about AD 426. See below, p. 116.

restriction on the possibilities of textual meaning. Early in the twentieth century Ferdinand de Saussure, one of the important sources of the 'structuralist' approach to linguistics and textual analysis, challenged any necessary connection between words and what is signified by words. In an important sense, the meaning of words is arbitrary, determined more by the place of the word in the total language system to which it belongs.[78] The structural relationship of words within a text became the important focus of attention for those who followed de Saussure. However, his challenge to the centrality of textual reference has been radicalized in more recent work.

Jacques Derrida and his program of 'deconstruction' is most often cited in this regard. Derrida's own language is famously tortuous. He is in fact suspicious of simplicity, once famously insisting that 'those who wish to simplify at all costs and who raise a hue and cry about obscurity because they do not recognize the unclarity of their good old *Aufklärung* are in my eyes dangerous dogmatists and tedious obscurantists'.[79] It is possible, even for powerfully influential thinkers, to confuse obscurity with profundity and simplicity with superficiality. Derrida calls into question the lingering sense of reference. He speaks of the 'transcendental signified', by which he means any proposed external reference of a text, either in terms of its author and his psychology or the nature of reality itself. If we are to take texts seriously, he argues, we need to recognize 'the absence of the transcendental signified'.[80] So devastating is his critique that, as one commentator notes, when Derrida is finished 'neither language nor human self-awareness conceals any thread of reference to things as they are'.[81] What we are left with is 'the infinite play of signification':

---

[78] De Saussure 1916: 8–11.

[79] Derrida 1988: 119. One writer critiquing Derrida's literary model was castigated in a review for his 'unproblematic prose and the clarity of his presentation, which are the conceptual tools of . . . conservatism' (Zavarzadeh 1982: 333).

[80] 'Henceforth, it was necessary to begin thinking that there was no center, that the center could not be thought in the form of a present-being, that the center had no natural site, that it was not a fixed locus but a function, a sort of nonlocus in which an infinite number of sign-substitutions came into play. This was the moment when language invaded the universal problematic, the moment when, in the absence of a center or origin, everything became discourse – provided we can agree on this word – that is to say, a system in which the central signified, the original or transcendental signified is never absolutely present outside a system of differences. The absence of the transcendental signified extends the domain and the play of signification infinitely' (Derrida 1967b: 351, 353–354).

[81] Raschke 1982: 4. Raschke uses these words to describe how 'the movement of deconstruction has set about to show that the cathedral of modern intellect is but a mirage in cloud-cuckoo land'.

one sign simply referring to another and that to another and so on.[82] Once we recognized this 'absence of the transcendental signified', writing, and indeed meaning itself, takes on a different appearance: 'From the moment that there is meaning there are nothing but signs. We think only in signs.'[83]

Derrida's talk of 'the infinite play of signification' has led some to suggest that a commitment to the essential indeterminacy of meaning is a critical element of his deconstructionist program. The play never ends and we cannot prematurely decide upon *the* meaning of a text. Certainly, when signs refer only to each other and 'acquire what sense they have from their contrast with other signs', meaning itself retains very little stability.[84] There is always another sign. In such a climate all talk of the clarity of this text, the Bible, sounds like a nostalgic if not frantic search for certainty and security. Such an interpretative utopia just doesn't exist. It is time to let go.

Once again Paul Ricœur has something to say at this point. Unlike Derrida, he wishes to retain a place for both sense (what is said) and reference (that about which it is said). Descriptive texts in particular do more than just endlessly move from sign to sign. Yet his idea of reference is not just a return to the classical model. Texts such as the Bible present their readers with a possible world, perhaps a number of such worlds, which they are invited to inhabit. There is still a world that matters and to which the text refers, but it is a world generated by the text itself.[85]

4. *We can no longer talk about 'the plain meaning' of a text.* This is the conclusion of much contemporary literary criticism. Against the temptation to be unequivocal and our constitutional tendency towards closure,[86] we are faced with the reality of interpretative difficulty and a variety of possible readings of any text, let alone the Bible. Not many take the extreme position of Derrida and suggest an inescapable and infinite play. Umberto Eco, for example, has insisted that the interpretative possibilities are not in fact limitless. We can in fact identify those interpretations that are contextually illegitimate.[87] Yet he too rejects any suggestion that there is a single plain meaning:

[82] Derrida 1967a: 49.
[83] Derrida 1967a: 50.
[84] Vanhoozer 1998: 62.
[85] Ricœur 1976: 36.
[86] Kermode 1979: 65. See the brief discussion in Callahan 2001: 259–262.
[87] '[M]any modern theories are unable to recognize that symbols are paradigmatically open to infinite meanings but syntagmatically, that is, textually, open only to the indefinite, but by no means infinite, interpretations allowed by the context' (Eco 1990: 21).

> To recognize this principle [the principle of contextual limitation] does not mean to support the 'repressive' idea that a text has a unique meaning, guaranteed by some interpretive authority. It means, on the contrary, that any act of interpretation is a dialectic between openness and form, initiative on the part of the interpreter and contextual pressure.[88]

The process of understanding a text as it has been unfolded since the 1960s or 1970s is indeed a complex one. To speak of the clarity of the Scripture in a context informed by that discussion sounds a little quaint or perhaps reactionary. It raises too many questions and ignores too much scholarship. Whose plain reading are you talking about? Aren't you prematurely closing down the conversation? What is left to justify your privileging of this particular perspective?

## Theology in the postmodern setting: A struggle for identity

Theology at the beginning of the twenty-first century has not escaped either the pressures of pluralism or the challenges to certainty and confidence that have made such a mark on contemporary philosophy and literary theory. Ecumenism and interfaith dialogue have become vital concerns of denominational bodies and are more insistent in their demands for a review of both the style and content of traditional theological work. From the other direction it appears as if the theological academy has rediscovered its ecclesial responsibilities, with a renewed emphasis on the community of faith as the proper context for theological reflection.[89] There is also a new tentativeness discernible in some contemporary theological writing, matched with (and perhaps arising from) a determination to avoid comparison with fundamentalism, a term that lost whatever residual value it might have had on 11 September 2001. Dogmatism is pounced upon wherever it appears.

A feature of theology in both its Protestant and Catholic modes since the 1970s has been a surge of interest in the doctrine of God, and more particularly the doctrine of the Trinity. When writing the preface for the second edition of his *The Promise of Trinitarian Theology* in 1997, Colin Gunton was led to remark, 'suddenly we are

---

[88] Eco 1990: 21.
[89] E.g. the collection of essays in honour of Thomas Gillespie entitled *Theology in the Service of the Church* (Aston 2000).

all trinitarians, or so it would seem'.[90] God is at the centre of theological reflection again, even those forms of it that accent the category of mystery and reappropriate the resources of the apophatic tradition. Of course in certain significant traditions God had never left centre stage, and certain forms of contemporary trinitarian reflection, it must be said, are overly concerned about the utility of the doctrine in a way that betrays a lingering inclination towards anthropocentric thinking. Nevertheless, this fresh appreciation of the fact that the way we think about God shapes the way we think about everything else has energized Christian theology at the turn of the millennium.

Some contemporary theologies have embraced postmodernism, arguing that it provides the tools with which to combat the aggressively secular and sometimes explicitly anti-Christian elements of modernism on the one hand and the rationalism of conservative elements within the Christian community on the other.[91] In a postmodern world, theology and church life need a new face, witness the arrival of post-conservative,[92] post-evangelical[93] and post-liberal[94] theologies, and, to choose just one example, the emerging church movement.[95] In a postmodern world, Christian evangelism and apologetics need not be constrained by modernist notions of proof and evidence. In a postmodern world, reflection means so much more than thinking, and theology means so much more than arguments about biblical texts and their implications. Postmodernism retains its flavour of protest even in the theological sphere, challenging authoritative traditions of exegesis and doctrine, and calling on us not to choose comfort and closure over authentic Christian existence. At its most radical edge, postmodern thinking provides 'a hermeneutic for the death of God'.[96] At its best, as David Tracy observes,

> postmodern theology is an honest if sometimes desperate attempt to let God as God be heard again; disrupting modern historical consciousness, unmasking the pretensions of modern

---

[90] Gunton 1997: xv.

[91] Some of the more positive Christian responses to postmodernism include those from John R. Franke, Stanley Grenz, Carl Raschke and Merold Westphal (Grenz & Franke 2001; Raschke 2004; Westphal 2001).

[92] E.g. Grenz 2000; Grenz & Franke 2001.

[93] Tomlinson 1995.

[94] Lindbeck 1984; Liechty 1990; Lindbeck 2002.

[95] Long 2004; McLaren 2004. See the recent response to the emerging church movement in Carson 2005.

[96] Taylor 1984: 6.

rationality, demanding that attention be paid to all those others forgotten and marginalized by the modern project. *Theos* has returned to unsettle the dominance of modern *logos*.[97]

Nevertheless, the influence of postmodernism on Christian theology has not gone unchallenged. A number of serious critiques have been published in recent years. The timely challenge to modernist hubris is applauded while some postmodern analysis is disputed and many of its own positive proposals are revealed to be incoherent and destructive of biblical and creedal Christianity.[98] Nevertheless, movements in theology always seem to lag behind larger intellectual currents, so while postmodernism may be beginning to fade in the academy generally, its challenge to classical Christian theology may well be felt for some time yet.

Once again these developments have had a significant impact on contemporary attempts to explain the Christian doctrine of Scripture in general and the clarity of Scripture in particular. In addition to rehearsing the traditional objections we examined earlier, classical accounts of the doctrine are regularly described today as rationalistic or overstated, even charged with attributing to the biblical text a perfection that is God's alone.[99] Some contemporary writers cast further doubt upon the doctrine by suggesting its natural home is nineteenth- and twentieth-century fundamentalism, replete as that was with debts to its modernist context. The clarity of Scripture is thus caught up in the persistent and somewhat frantic assaults upon the doctrine of biblical inerrancy.[100] Others draw attention to the way the doctrine functions within a particular theological tradition, arising out of a polemical context and reinforcing conservative readings. Here is a powerful instrument to effect theological closure, generating a 'totalising intepretation that brooks no dissent'.[101] Faced with such charges, contemporary accounts to affirm Scripture's clarity sometimes seem tangled, pessimistic and defensive.[102]

---

[97] Tracy 1994: 37.
[98] There are many such critiques, but amongst the most helpful are Carson 1996 and the stimulating collection of essays edited by Erickson, Helseth and Taylor (2004).
[99] Webster 2005: 35, 43.
[100] Harris 1998: 288–289.
[101] Cowdell 2004: 123.
[102] Callahan 2001: 48.

## A reason to think again

Given these challenges to the doctrine, some very ancient and others the product of contemporary trends in thought and practice, any restatement of the clarity of Scripture might seem doomed to derision. Perhaps this explains the virtual disappearance of the doctrine from recent theological discussion. However, this is an historical anomaly. The doctrine of the clarity of Scripture has a long and honourable pedigree. It is demonstrably more than a construct of the sixteenth-century Reformation or a nineteenth-century alliance with modernist epistemological optimism.[103] Affirmations of Scripture's clarity have stubbornly persisted despite the best efforts of their detractors, and most recently sophisticated theological arguments have been presented for taking those affirmations with the utmost seriousness.[104] There are good reasons to think again about this neglected doctrine.

Perhaps chief amongst them is the impact that the neglect of this doctrine has upon the lives of the people of God. Neglect or dismissal of the clarity of Scripture almost inevitably undermines all talk of the authority of Scripture. How is a text supposed to function authoritatively if its meaning is considered to be inaccessible? The history of the European churches in the centuries just prior to the Reformation would seem to be eloquent testimony to the reality of such a consequence. As one contemporary writer puts it, 'yielding to the word is premised upon its clarity'.[105] The outworking of this principle in a negative direction can be seen in a number of current ethical debates. Few are willing to deny the authority of Scripture in principle, but there is a disturbing reluctance on the part of many to allow Scripture to have the final word, precisely because this conviction concerning its clarity has been lost.

All the objections and qualifications we have examined in this chapter are answerable and in fact have been answered in the long history of this doctrine. It is surprising how little is really new in the contemporary confusion. Classic Christian confidence that the

---

[103] See, amongst others, Whitaker 1588: 393–401; and Callahan 2001: 50–159. Note Callahan's conclusion that 'the subject of Scripture's clarity and obscurity neither begins nor ends with the Protestant Reformation', even if 'what Protestantism does with perspicuity is somewhat unique in that the subject becomes more prominent in its own right' (159).

[104] I think particularly of recent work by John Webster of the University of Aberdeen. Webster 2003a: 91–101; 2005: 33–67.

[105] Callahan 2001: 268. See also Carson 1997: 97.

ordinary man or woman (the ploughboy of Erasmus, Tyndale and Luther) can read and understand the Scriptures is well grounded. Yet today the doctrine needs a robust theological exposition rather than a purely historical or literary one. To such an exposition we now turn.

# Chapter Two

# The effective communicator: God as the guarantor of scriptural clarity

'So shall be the word that goes out from my mouth'

I begin with five observations about Christian theology. They are not meant to be comprehensive, nor will any of them be argued in full. This is, after all, not meant as a treatise on theological method.[1] Nevertheless, each of these preliminary observations will help us to orient appropriately our discussion of Scripture's clarity. They will help ensure that our construal of this doctrine is not open to the charge of being abstract, impersonal or mechanistic. I hope to show that when the clarity of Scripture is investigated with this basic framework in mind it takes on a new significance. There is much at stake in an affirmation or denial of the clarity of Scripture, something that has long been recognized by the most important classical treatments of the doctrine.

The first of these five observations is, perhaps, most critical for our purposes: *Christian theology, at its most basic, is talk about God.* This is more than just a simple etymological observation, that *theologia* is a compound of the Greek words *theos* (God) and *logia* (words).[2] Rather, it has to do with the very nature of theology itself. In all its variety and in whatever context, theology is concerned with God. There are, of course such things as theological anthropology and political theology and even a theology of nature. But in so far as these are *theological*, they speak of humanity or the organization of

---

[1] For a more thorough treatment of the issues from differing perspectives see Barth 1932: 3–87 (*KD* I/1, 1–89 = *CD* I/1, 3–87); 1938: 797–884 (*KD* I/2, 890–990 = *CD* I/2, 797–884); Torrance 1969; Wells 1991; Vanhoozer 1994a; Jensen 1997; Webster 1997; Thompson 2000; Webster 2003a: 123–135.
[2] For a discussion of the term 'theology' and alternatives see Barth 1932: 3–24 (*KD* I/1, 1–23 = *CD* I/1, 3–24); Pannenberg 1988: 1–26; and especially Gunton 1999.

societies or the world around us *as these are related to God*.[3] There have been times in the history of theology when theologians conceived of their task differently, as when Schleiermacher famously defined Christian doctrines as 'accounts of the Christian religious affections set forth in speech'.[4] Such an anthropological orientation to theology was rightly overturned by Karl Barth in 1921, even though it continues to linger on in some quarters and resonates with the pluralist and relativist agenda we briefly touched upon in chapter one.[5] It is worth remembering that there has always been a danger of distraction. For that reason, as much as any, Christian theologians must keep insisting, 'But God . . .'[6]

To insist that Christian theology at its heart is talk about God leads directly to our second observation about it: *Christian theology is essentially and unavoidably trinitarian.* Although once again it is Barth who famously insisted that 'the doctrine of the Trinity is what basically distinguishes the Christian doctrine of God as Christian', this conviction is something he held in common with the mainstream of the Christian tradition.[7] It arises from a recognition that Jesus and his history are not something extrinsic to God. He is the eternal Son who was incarnate to make the Father known and who 'through the eternal Spirit offered himself without blemish to God'.[8] Christian theology cannot conceive of God apart from Jesus Christ and so it can neither dispense with the doctrine of the Trinity nor treat it as an

[3] This is little more than a development of Calvin's starting point in the *Institutes*: 'Nearly all the wisdom we possess, that is to say, true and sound wisdom, consists of two parts: the knowledge of God and of ourselves' (Calvin 1559: 35 [*Inst*. I.i.1]). Calvin reflects upon the relation of these two parts and concludes, 'the order of right teaching requires that we discuss the former first, then proceed afterward to treat the latter' (Calvin 1559: 39 [*Inst*. I.i.3]). More recently Torrance has made the same point: 'Theological thinking is *theo*-logical, thinking not just from our own centres, but from a centre in God, from a divine ground' (Torrance 1969: 29). Michael Horton makes the same point using the language of Reformed orthodoxy: God is not only 'the *principium essendi* (foundation for existing) and the *principium cognoscendi* (foundation for knowing)' but also 'the *principium loquendi* (foundation of saying)' (Horton 2002: 186).
[4] Schleiermacher 1830: 76.
[5] Barth published the second edition of his Romans commentary in 1921 (Barth 1918). This is the edition that catapulted him to prominence and raised the ire of his liberal teachers. However, the turnaround in his own thought can be seen earlier, in his famous lecture from 1917, 'The Strange World of the Bible'. There he insisted that what matters most in theology is not 'the right human thoughts about God' but 'the right divine thoughts about men' (Barth 1917: 43).
[6] The classic biblical instance of this correction to anthropocentric thinking is Luke 12:20. Cf. Luke 16:15; Acts 2:24; and Eph. 2:4.
[7] Barth 1932: 301 (*KD* I/1, 318 = *CD* I/1, 301). Cf. Calvin 1559: 122 (*Inst*. I.xiii.2); Bavinck 1895: II, 260; Knox 1982: 49.
[8] John 1:18; Heb. 9:14.

appendix with no real connection to its other interests.[9] It is, of course, not the only Christian doctrine. Distortion and misappropriation are possible when the doctrine of the Trinity is isolated from God's redemptive purposes fulfilled in the death and resurrection of Jesus. Nevertheless, even the atonement must be viewed from a trinitarian perspective if it is not to fall prey to the kind of caricature represented in some popular literature.[10] The God of whom Christian theologians speak eternally exists as Father, Son and Holy Spirit. Our point of access to his purpose and character is the person of Jesus Christ, but we are only enabled to recognize Jesus for who he is by the work of the Spirit, in order that our life of faith might be to the glory of our heavenly Father.

Yet to speak about such a God is not self-evidently a possibility for human beings. How can our talk about God be seen as anything more than the product of imaginative ingenuity or whimsical projection? The Christian answer to this question is in fact our third observation about Christian theology: *Christian theology is talk about God made possible by God's prior decision to be known.* God, while self-sufficient, has not chosen to remain in splendid isolation from the world that he has made. It is God's desire to be known by his creatures, freely to enter into a relationship with them, to share with them the fellowship that is a feature of his own eternal nature, to invite them into his rest.[11] John Calvin summed up this determination on God's part as his 'benevolence (*benevolentia*) towards us'.[12] It is a free decision but not an arbitrary one. It arises from the character and nature of God as love and as such it is a purpose from which God will not be deterred. God will be known and nothing, not the primeval fall into sin, nor the persistent failure of the children of Israel, nor the murder

---

[9] '[T]he one true God is actually and intrinsically triune and cannot be truly conceived otherwise' (Torrance 1996: 15).

[10] I have in mind the long-standing objections to penal substitution raised by Peter Carnley, recently retired Archbishop of Perth, and recent books by Joel Green and Mark Baker in the US and Steve Chalke in the UK. See Carnley 2004: 128–150; Green & Baker 2000; and Chalke 2003.

[11] This emphasis on the initiative of God which makes all theology possible is an important feature of those theologies that are structured around the notion of God's covenant. See, most recently, Michael Horton's significant and yet incomplete project 'to integrate biblical theology and systematic theology on the basis of scripture's own intrasystematic categories of covenant and eschatology' (Horton 2002: 1; 2005). However, note the long tradition that goes back through Barth and Calvin to at least the epigram of Hilary of Poitiers: 'For He whom we can know only through his own utterances is a fitting witness concerning himself' (Hilary, *De Trinitate* I.xviii; *PL* X, 38 = *NPNF*, 2nd Series, IX, 45). See also Torrance 1996: 13–14.

[12] Calvin 1559: 551 (*Inst.* III.ii.7).

of the prophets and finally of his own Son, will prevent this purpose from being fulfilled. God is determined to have a people for himself who know him and rejoice in his purpose for the world.

Furthermore, God has acted upon this determination, making his character and purpose known in both words and deeds in the midst of human history. God has both acted and spoken. He has acted in such a way as to overcome the obstacles of our finitude and our sinfulness and he has given these actions their own authoritative explanation. The anchoring of all talk about God in his own exposition of his character and action leads to our fourth observation: *Christian theology can only claim truth and authority in so far as it conforms to God's self-revelation.* What God himself has done and said lies at the heart of our talk about him. This will inevitably draw us once again to the person and work of Jesus Christ but not in any way that bypasses the words God has spoken through him and about him.[13] As I will go on to argue later in this chapter, the Scriptures are to be located at this point. They are not so much a human report of or commentary on God's revelation as part of that revelation itself. They are, to use an older idiom, the word of God written. For this reason, in all their talk of God and his purposes, of humanity or our social constructs or the world around us as they are related to God, Christian theologians have a responsibility to expound the Scriptures.[14] Freshness and creative thinking are entirely appropriate but they must always remain in service to the critical reiterative function of theology. It is the 'faith once for all delivered to the saints' (Jude 3) – in all its richness and never-ending relevance – that Christian theologians seek to pass on undiminished and unaugmented by their endeavours. Precisely because the knowledge of God is given by God, theology must strive for faithfulness above novelty. In the end that faithfulness is most unambiguously demonstrated by direct appeal to the words of Scripture in their context.[15]

---

[13] As Kevin Vanhoozer puts it, 'one can begin with Christ only by attending to the apostolic (divinely authorized) testimony about him' (Vanhoozer 2002: 38 n. 55).

[14] Equally any such exposition of the Scriptures must be responsible. See Carson 1991.

[15] An endemic weakness of much contemporary theology is its reluctance to address the content of biblical teaching in biblical categories. This is not always the result of a fascination with novelty (though there is undoubtedly much of that). Nor is it always a reflection of a commitment to abstract and opaque language as the signs of true theological sophistication (though there is, alas, too much of that as well). I suspect that much of it is borne of genuine apologetic concerns: seeking to proclaim and defend the gospel in a way that communicates effectively with the wider culture.

The fifth and final observation to be made in this regard is this: *Christian theology is talk about God that takes place in the presence of God and in the eyes of the world.* The phenomenon of the word of God written is not an alternative to the active presence of God in the world and amongst his people. God accompanies his own word, bringing about the appropriate human response to that word. It is the present and active God who directs Joshua to meditate on the Book of the Law day and night while at the same time promising 'I will not leave you or forsake you' (Josh. 1:1–9). The apostles were sent to teach all that Jesus had commanded them to the disciples they would make 'of all nations' and in doing so were to remember his promise 'I am with you always, to the end of the age' (Matt. 28:18–20). Paul could call on God to bear witness to his words as well as his motivation in speaking them (1 Thess. 2:1–8). We do not speak of God in his absence or behind his back. The first audience of Christian theology is God himself, which is why the boundaries between declaration and doxology have been so regularly blurred, not only in the New Testament but throughout the history of theology. Paul moves effortlessly from an exposition of God's sovereignty exemplified in the history of Israel to praise and adoration (Rom. 11:33–36). Augustine's *Confessiones* are addressed to God. Needless to say, when this simple fact is taken seriously, bold confidence must go hand in hand with humility. In God's presence we cannot afford to claim we know more than is appropriate or less than he has revealed.[16]

Yet talk of God occurs in the world as well. It retains the character of proclamation. The principal beneficiaries of Christian theology may well be believing men and women, but its declaration of God and his purposes is both a challenge and an invitation to all who will hear. After all, the God of whom we speak is no tribal deity but the Creator of all. His purposes have a cosmic scope: the creation itself will be redeemed and every human being will stand before the judgment seat of Christ (Rom. 8:19–23; 2 Cor. 5:6–10). In such a context Christian theology cannot afford to be simply an in-house conversation, the intellectual self-indulgence of a privileged group. There is an urgent necessity about theology's engagement with the thinking and behaviour of the world in which we live. Such engagement is not of course without its dangers. One such danger is that of recasting the

---

[16] Note Moses' warning to the second generation of Israelites in Deut. 29:29. Barth spoke of the way dogmatics must always be undertaken as 'an act of penitence and obedience' (Barth 1932: 22 [*KD* I/1, 21 = *CD* I/1, 22]).

teaching of Scripture as simply a theological justification of contemporary values and commitments. There have always been attempts to domesticate the word of God and Christian theologians have been right to protest that God may just as likely be challenging entrenched attitudes and patterns of behaviour as endorsing them. Yet equally dangerous is the belief that the integrity of Christian doctrine can be preserved only by repeating verbatim its classic formularies without any attempt to understand the way in which our contemporaries think. Christian theology has a public face; it is not the private language of a secret wisdom.

All of this is vitally important when we come to consider the doctrine of Scripture or, more specifically, the doctrine of the clarity of Scripture. In contrast to claims made by some and a caricature drawn by others, this doctrine is not part of a prolegomenon to theology, a methodological introduction necessary before we turn our attention to the real thing. This doctrine says something about God. Scripture should not be considered in isolation, as if it exists somehow independently of God. What we say about the Bible has important implications for our understanding of God and his purposes, and these lines of connection run in both directions. Furthermore, the triune nature of God, and in particular the identity of Jesus as the Word incarnate, bears directly upon this doctrine as well. We are rightly warned about the incongruity of a doctrine of Scripture that consigns Jesus to the periphery.[17] The initiative of God and his determination to be known are also critical considerations. God's communicative activity is intentional and our knowledge of God is not a human achievement but a divine gift. It is also important to remember that what we say about the clarity of Scripture must be faithful to the actual teaching of Scripture. Claiming more for Scripture than it claims for itself is a counterproductive strategy, to say the least. Finally, the unique situation of God as author accompanying this text into the world will need to be taken into account.

As we begin a theological construal of the doctrine of Scripture's clarity, the obvious starting point is with God himself and in particular God as he has shown himself to be in the gospel of the Lord Jesus Christ. It is in the gospel preached by Jesus (Mark 1:14–15) and the apostles (1 Cor. 9:16) that we find the fullest exposition of God's character and intention. It is through this message that the Christian first encounters the living God, and this message provides the basic

---

[17] Watson 2002: 288.

contours of an entirely new worldview.[18] Whatever we might subsequently say about the Bible itself must make sense in this context.

# The God of the gospel

At the very beginning of his letter to the Christians at Rome, Paul speaks about 'the gospel of God (*euangelion theou*)' (Rom. 1:1). This message, which he has been set apart to proclaim amongst the nations, takes precedence over all other *euangelia* because its source is God himself.[19] It is a message for which there has been extensive preparation: God's promises throughout human history have been made with a particular series of events in mind, including this announcement to the world at large, an announcement that itself brings those promises to their fulfilment (Rom. 1:2). It is a powerful message that transforms the situation of those who embrace it, for in it 'the righteousness of God is revealed' (Rom. 1:16–17).[20] God is shown to be who he really is in the gospel. Yet at its heart it is a declaration about Jesus Christ: 'the gospel of God' is the gospel 'concerning his Son' (Rom. 1:3).[21] In an important sense, what follows in Paul's apostolic letter is an exposition of this gospel, one which makes clear that to understand the God of the gospel we must pay attention to Jesus Christ, who he is and what he has done.[22]

## *Jesus the exegete of God*

The gospel is the message about Jesus and what he has done to rescue human beings from the awful consequences of their rebellion against God. It identifies him as the Lord. God become one of us in order to die in the place of sinners and rise again on the third day (Phil. 2:5–11). It proclaims his triumph over death and the forgiveness of sins that he has secured for those who are joined to him by faith (Acts 13:38). The

---

[18] See Jensen 2002: 31–83; Watson 2002: 287–288.

[19] Köstenberger & O'Brien 2001: 271–274.

[20] For the scholarly debate about the important expression *dikaiosynē theou*, see Seifrid 2000.

[21] Paul is able to speak both of the 'gospel of Christ' (Rom. 15:19; 1 Cor. 9:12; 2 Cor. 2:12; 9:13; 10:14; Gal. 1:7; Phil. 1:27; 1 Thess. 3:2; 2 Thess. 1:8) and 'the gospel of God' (Rom. 15:16; 1 Thess. 2:2, 8, 9).

[22] Peter Jensen rightly stresses that the apostles 'preached a sentence, not a name' in the face of some contemporary suggestions that the gospel is 'Jesus Christ' *simpliciter* (Jensen 2002: 55). However, perhaps more needs to be said. The gospel is not just a statement about who Jesus is but also about what Jesus has done. The person and work of Christ are mutually explanatory. See Paul's summary of those things that are 'of first importance' in 1 Cor. 15:3–5.

right and proper judgment of God against our rebellion has not been overturned; it has been exhausted, embraced in full by the eternal Son of God himself (Rom. 3:21–26; Gal. 3:10–14). This gospel holds out the hope of an eternal future anchored in the promises of Jesus without ignoring its impact on the present. Paul can in effect summarize that impact with the words 'There is therefore *now* no condemnation for those who are in Christ Jesus' (Rom. 8:1; my emphasis).

At the heart of the gospel message, then, is the fulfilment of God's ancient intention through the extraordinary life, death and resurrection of Jesus Christ. It is a message of salvation won and offered freely to all who come to him in faith. It is a message addressed to the most fundamental need of human beings, a message that refuses to ignore the reality of our guilt before God and the inevitable judgment we face. Yet at the same time it is a message that has as its focus the one who brings forgiveness and freedom from condemnation. Those who hear are called to repentance and faith because of who *he* is and what *he* has done. To preach the gospel is to preach Christ.

There is a sense in which the whole of Christian theology – in particular, evangelical theology – is an exposition of the gospel and its implications. Two thousand years of reflection have not exhausted the wonder of it. The gospel enabled the apostles and those who came after them to think afresh about the character and purposes of God, because of their conviction that Jesus Christ is God 'become genuinely human'. In the words of the Johannine prologue, 'No one has ever seen God; the only God, who is at the Father's side, he has made him known' (John 1:18). As the early church soon realized, everything hangs on the personal identity of Jesus as God.[23] The Nicene formula 'of one being with the Father'[24] and the Chalcedonian Definition 'truly God and truly man . . . without confusion, without change, without division, without separation'[25] were in large measure defences of the gospel. Unless God really is as he has shown himself to be in Jesus Christ we have no certain knowledge of him, and the biblical doctrine of atonement begins to unravel.[26]

So it is the gospel of Jesus Christ that shapes the Christian understanding of God. That is not to deny a real knowledge of God and

---

[23] Torrance 1996: 14.

[24] *homoousion tō patri.*

[25] *theon alēthōs kai anthrōpon alēthōs [. . .] asynchytōs atreptōs adiairetōs achōristōs.*

[26] 'He is in himself not other than what he is towards us in his loving, revealing and saving presence in Christ' (Torrance 1996: 18).

his purposes in the Old Testament, prior to the coming of Christ. Rather, it is to recognize that such knowledge was not only partial (Paul makes clear that is true of the Christian's knowledge of God as well, 1 Cor. 13:12) but radically prospective. The Old Testament believer's knowledge of God had a future orientation, one that generates a certain restlessness in the narrative and the prophetic material alike. The apostle Peter speaks of the prophets who inquired about the things they announced, and were told they were serving others yet to come (1 Pet. 1:10–12). Paul spoke about the mystery hidden for ages but now at last made known (Rom. 16:25–27). Yet we must also say that on this side of the cross and resurrection of Jesus it is simply impossible to return to that Old Testament situation. Any attempt to speak truly of God in the last days cannot avoid Jesus who comes to us, in Calvin's phrase, 'clad in his promises'.[27] To attempt such a thing would be just another manifestation of our rebellion. What is it then that the gospel makes known about God?

## God revealed in the gospel

The gospel reveals that God is sovereign and his purposes will be fulfilled. What God proposes to do will be accomplished and there is nothing that can stand in the way of its fulfilment. Prior to his death and resurrection, Jesus insisted repeatedly that what was about to happen must take place that the Scriptures might be 'fulfilled' (e.g. Matt. 26:54; Luke 22:37). Afterwards he rebuked the disciples on the Emmaus road with the words 'Was it not necessary that the Christ should suffer these things and enter into his glory?' (Luke 24:26) God's declared purpose will not be overthrown or diverted. Even the acme of human self-assertion, the arrest, trial and execution of God's own Son, ends up being 'according to the definite plan and foreknowledge of God' (Acts 2:23). God is unfailingly effective in what he sets out to do.

This unfailing effectiveness is tied to the nature of all God's activity as free. God is not compelled or constrained by anything other than his own character. Creation is not a necessary extension of his being. Redemption is not something forced upon him by the victory of the serpent in the Garden of Eden. They are, of course, both perfectly consistent with his eternal character as love and in an important sense they arise out of it. Yet creation and redemption remain sovereign decisions of God. 'Let us make' is more than merely a

---

[27] Calvin 1559: 426 (*Inst*. II.ix.3).

poetic flourish in Genesis 1. It grounds the creation of all things in the will and purpose of God. The apostle Paul likewise grounds the redemption of men and women in God's choice made 'before the foundation of the world' (Eph. 1:3–14).[28]

Of particular significance is the freedom of the decision of the eternal Son to be incarnate, to take the form of a servant and to die bearing the sins of the world. These decisions are described in the New Testament in terms of obedience (Phil. 2:5–11; Heb. 5:7–10) but in each instance it is important that this obedience is freely given out of a determination he shares with the Father. The sense of necessity we noted earlier is never taken to mean that this is a path forced upon Jesus, one he did not freely choose for himself. The temptation scene at the beginning of his public ministry and the prayer in the Garden of Gethsemane just prior to his arrest make that point forcefully (Luke 4:1–13; 22:39–46). So too does the decision to 'set his face to go to Jerusalem' in full knowledge of what awaits him there (Luke 9:51; cf. 9:21–22, 43–45; 18:31–34). Rather than being compelled by circumstances or the actions, words or intentions of others, these decisions reflect the unity between the Father and the Son in their concern for the salvation of men and women (John 10:22–30).

The genuine humanity of Jesus is not a hindrance to the divine freedom. It is the means by which this freedom is exercised. He is genuinely human. He does tire and grow hungry. He eats and sleeps. He will bleed and die. All of these are possible only because he has taken on 'the likeness of sinful flesh' (Rom. 8:3). Yet none of them distorts the character or intention of God; rather, they give it a human expression. There is never any suggestion that the incarnation makes a genuine revelation of God's mind and character more difficult, that flesh and blood, human mobility or human means of communication are somehow obstacles to be overcome. The waves and wind obeyed when Jesus uttered the ordinary human words 'Peace! Be still!' (even if no-one is quite certain today whether he uttered them in Greek or Aramaic, Mark 4:39). Those who heard him teach using the language of the crowds were able in those words to recognize his authority (Matt. 7:29). Even his enemies understood that he was claiming the power to do what only God can do (Mark 2:7; cf. John 5:18). There is no hint of a lisp as God incarnate speaks to other human beings

---

[28] 'To say that election took place before creation indicates that God's choice was due to his own free decision and love, which were not dependent on temporal circumstances or human merit' (O'Brien 1999: 100). See also his discussion of the common rather than corporate nature of this election on the previous page.

about himself and his Father's purpose.[29] When some fail to understand or refuse to respond appropriately to the teaching of Jesus, it is explained in other ways (e.g. Luke 18:23).

The gospel is, above all else, a demonstration of God's love (Rom. 5:8; Eph. 2:4–5; 1 John 4:10). God's determination to save men and women arises out of his compassion, a key aspect of his character according to both the Old and New Testaments. He is committed to the welfare of his people. He is not mischievous or malevolent. The salvation he brings about through Jesus is no mirage: it is not something forever held tantalizingly out of reach. It is both real and effective. Jesus said, 'Come to me, all who labour and are heavy laden, and I will give you rest' (Matt. 11:28), and all those the Father draws do come and find life (John 6:43–47). The gospel is preached amongst the nations and 'as many as were appointed to eternal life believed' (Acts 13:48).

This astounding benevolence of God, his willingness to reach out to us while we were still sinners determined to resist him at all points (Rom. 5:8, 10), generates confidence and trust. In the light of the gospel, we know that God is good and will bring about what is best for us. Suffering is viewed in a new light, as a preparation for glory. The day of judgment is welcomed rather than dreaded, as God's good order will be affirmed throughout his creation. The commands of God are embraced as liberating and life-giving, not resented as restrictions on our personal freedom or right of self-determination. The language of suspicion, of the covert exercise of power, or manipulation or tyranny is entirely out of place when speaking about God's dealings with his people. The gospel demonstrates that God's sovereignty has a very different complexion: his irresistible rule is exercised in humble service. In the imagery of the book of Revelation, the lion of Judah *is* the lamb who was slain (Rev. 5).

The gospel is a message about salvation and life found only in Jesus Christ, who became one of us to die in our place and overcome the death and judgment we deserve. The God of the gospel is never thwarted in his purpose, and his purpose is to bring about the everlasting welfare of his people. He is both willing and able to do what is necessary to gather to himself a people who know him and trust him and rejoice in his purposes for the world.

[29] The allusion is to Calvin's famous expression 'God is wont in a measure to "lisp" in speaking to us' (Calvin 1559: 121 [*Inst.* I.xiii.1]). His target was those who took the anthropomorphisms of the Old Testament literally and thought of God as corporeal.

Yet how will such an understanding of God shape the way we talk about the Bible?

## The purposeful communicator

Our consideration so far has focused on the content of the gospel message and its implications. We have seen that the gospel reveals both the sovereign power and the determined love of God, both manifest in the person and work of Jesus Christ. In, not despite, Jesus' genuine humanity, God accomplishes his saving purpose. Yet in all of this we ought not to forget that the gospel is itself a *message*, an announcement. When proclaimed, it is a form of speech designed with a purpose and addressed to an audience.[30] As some contemporary philosophers of language would put it, the preaching of the gospel is a communicative act. This simple fact raises one of the most important issues surrounding the doctrine of Scripture and particularly any talk about its clarity. In what sense can we say that this is *God's* communicative act? Put another way, are we right to say that God is a speaking God? And what implications might such an observation have for how we talk about the Bible?

Quite a deal of sophisticated work has been done of late on the Christian claim that God speaks.[31] At the most basic level, it is not difficult to show that such a claim arises from the explicit teaching of the Bible. The writer to the Hebrews sums up God's dealings with humanity in just such terms: God, having spoken, spoke (Heb. 1:1–3). Indeed, the very first scene of the biblical meganarrative gains its momentum from the refrain 'And God said . . .' (Gen. 1:3, 6, 9, etc.), while the very last scene closes with words spoken by the glorified Christ, 'Surely I am coming soon' (Rev. 22:20). But there is no attempt to justify or explain the speech of God in either testament. God's capacity for speech is treated as self-evident and operates as one of the most basic and influential assumptions in Scripture. Even the tempter does not doubt that God has spoken, merely what God has said (Gen. 3:1).

Yet just what is involved in claiming that God speaks? Certainly, it is merely simplistic caricature to suggest it entails an anthropomorphic view of God with lips and a larynx.[32] Yet are we to take this

---

[30] The biblical writers rarely consider the gospel in isolation from its proclamation (Molland 1934: 48; Cranfield 1975: 54 n. 2; Köstenberger & O'Brien 2001: 173–174).

[31] Vanhoozer 1994b; Wolterstorff 1995; Vanhoozer 1998: 201–280; Ward 2002: 75–136; Horton 2002: 123–146.

[32] Schneider 1991: 27–29.

claim literally or as a sophisticated metaphor that picks up elements of a common feature of human existence in an attempt to explain how God relates himself to the creation?[33] A brief glance at the Bible itself reveals not only that the claim is more extensive than might first be thought, but that it is somewhat more complex as well.

There are very significant examples in Scripture of God's speech understood as God's own audible expression of his mind and purposes in words. The programmatic confrontation between God and the nation of Israel in the Old Testament is the meeting at Mount Sinai after the exodus from Egypt. Moses recalled those events for the second generation just prior to his death:

> And you came near and stood at the foot of the mountain, while the mountain burned with fire to the heart of heaven, wrapped in darkness, cloud, and gloom. Then the LORD spoke to you out of the midst of the fire. You heard the sound of words, but saw no form; there was only a voice.
>
> (Deut. 4:11–12)

There are none of the usual literary markers which would suggest that Moses is speaking metaphorically at this point. Those who were standing there before Mount Sinai that day did not just hear the threatening sound of thunder. They heard a voice and that voice was the voice of God. Indeed, the fact that God was heard rather than seen becomes an important plank in the argument against the idolatry that follows (Deut. 4:15–31). The faithful response to the God who speaks is to listen, to believe his promises and to obey his commands, not to seek some physical representation.

Similarly, there are three occasions during the ministry of Jesus when a voice is heard from the heavens, a voice that the Gospel narrative encourages us to identify as the voice of God. At his baptism this voice draws attention to him as the beloved Son with whom the Father is well pleased (Matt. 3:16–17). The voice from the cloud at the time of Jesus' transfiguration proclaims an identical message with the added words 'listen to him' (Matt. 17:5). Finally, in the days before the crucifixion, a voice is heard from heaven again, this time confirming that the Father has glorified his name up till now and will

---

[33] Karl Barth stands as one of those who insists that the claim must be taken literally (Barth 1932: 125–186 [*KD* I/1, 128–194 = *CD* I/1, 125–186]). See the illuminating discussion of Nicholas Wolterstorff (Wolterstorff 1995: 63–74) and further reflection by Timothy Ward (Ward 2002: 106–130).

glorify it again (John 12:27–30). On this last occasion the crowd, to be sure, draws various conclusions. Nevertheless, Jesus himself responds by saying, 'This voice has come for your sake, not mine'. In addition to these three instances of a voice from heaven, it should be noted that Jesus as God incarnate is a speaker. Indeed, his first public act is to proclaim the gospel of God (Mark 1:14) and he refuses to be deflected from a preaching ministry because 'that is why I came out' (Mark 1:38; my trans.). In a unique way, to hear the voice of Jesus is genuinely to hear the voice of God.

In such instances as these the analogy with human speech is clear. The relation between speaker and hearer is more or less direct: a voice is heard, the speaker's words are recognized as words and the process of understanding those words begins. Yet the Bible itself makes use of the basic terminology associated with speakers and speaking when referring to other less direct occurrences. Men and women did not always need to hear the voice of God audibly to recognize that what they did hear was in fact the word of the Lord, a series of words bearing no less authority than the words heard from the midst of the fire on the mountain. The most obvious example is the phenomenon of prophecy. The prophets of the Old Testament were those especially commissioned to speak on behalf of God and specifically authorized to announce particular messages as 'the word of the LORD'. The actual degree of superintendence in each instance may indeed vary: on occasion it could be said that God put these words into the mouth of the prophet (e.g. Jer. 1:9; Ezek. 3:10–11); at other times the prophet reports what he overhears in the heavenly court (e.g. Isa. 6; Ezek. 1); and there are still other occasions when the prophet appears to have made a more active contribution to the final form of the message (e.g. Jer. 36:32). Yet in all of these cases to reject or ignore the words of the prophet was to reject or ignore the word of the Lord, which ultimately meant rejecting or ignoring God himself. God has spoken.

Nicholas Wolterstorff finds little difficulty in including this phenomenon within a general analysis of speaking or discourse. He suggests that biblical prophecy best fits as a type of 'double-agency discourse'.[34] Commenting on Deuteronomy 18, he remarks:

> The prophet is one who speaks *in the name of* God. As a consequence, those who hear the prophet speaking, when he is

---

[34] Wolterstorff 1995: 37–54.

speaking in his prophetic capacity, are confronted with that which counts as God speaking; the utterances of the prophet are the medium of God's discourse . . . the biblical notion of the prophet blends the concept of one who is commissioned to communicate a message from someone with the concept of one who is deputized to speak in the name of someone.[35]

Wolterstorff applies the essential ingredients of this analysis to the apostles of the New Testament as well and concludes that, with the obvious Christological adjustments, we can speak of the line of the prophets as continued in the apostles.[36] They were commissioned to communicate what God said and did in Jesus Christ as well as to act in an important sense as his representatives, speaking 'in his name'. Paul, in particular, was conscious that he made his appeal 'on behalf of (*hyper*)' Christ (2 Cor. 5:20). It is this commission that explains why, with the aid of the Spirit, those who heard Paul's apostolic preaching were able to identify it too as 'the word of God' (1 Thess. 2:13).

The assumption that the living God speaks, then, is pervasive in both testaments.[37] As far as the Bible is concerned, God confronts his people, not with an inarticulate presence nor simply with actions that are somehow self-evidently significant, but with activity surrounded, as it were, by words. There is an eradicable verbal element to God's dealings with his people, indeed with the creation at large, which is not at all diminished by the personal reality of the incarnation. Personal presence does not do away with the need for words. Words are an entirely appropriate and effective medium for personal relationships.[38] They generate and sustain such relationships by expressing character, thoughts, emotions and intentions. They warn and beckon and explain. They enable the making of promises and covenants. In short, words can be intensely personal and it is not at all surprising that God should use words in his plan to draw men and women to himself. To say that God speaks is a shorthand way of saying that God is committed to personal relationships.

[35] Wolterstorff 1995: 48 (emphasis his).

[36] Wolterstorff 1995: 50–51, 288–295.

[37] Wolterstorff makes use of the category of 'appropriated discourse' to explain how biblical narrative, wisdom and poetry can also be understood as divine discourse (Wolterstorff 1995: 51–54). He goes on to use that same category to explain how the totality of the Christian Bible can be understood as God's book (53–54).

[38] See the exploration of the role of words in the divine–human relationship in Jensen 2002: 88–89; Knox 2000: 160–161.

Yet we can and must say more than this. The verbal character of God's self-revelation is not accidental in the Aristotelian sense. It is not simply a product of God's decision, the means he just happens to have chosen for the task, but one amongst many possibilities. God's activity of speaking is reflective of his character and eternal being. T. F. Torrance makes the point in his discussion of the knowledge of God in the thought of John Calvin:

> The Word of God which we hear in the Holy Scriptures derives from and reposes on the inner Being of the One God; and that is its objective ground, deep in the eternal Being of God, upon which our knowledge of God rests. In his own eternal Essence God is not mute or dumb, but Word communicating or speaking himself.[39]

Here the doctrine of the Trinity comes into the foreground again. We cannot claim to know much about the eternal self-communication of Father, Son and Holy Spirit, but the essentially other-centred nature of the intratrinitarian life is part of God's self-revelation. For example, Jesus spoke of his concern to obey and glorify the Father (John 4:34; 17:1). Though he is identified as the king of the kingdom, the beloved Son of the Father, and even the Word who eternally existed with God and as God, he does not seek his own advantage. Similarly, when the Spirit comes, Jesus explains, he will remind the disciples of what Jesus has said (John 14:26). Just as Jesus did not speak on his own authority (John 8:28), so the Spirit will not speak independently of the Son (John 16:12–15). It is surely significant that speaking features prominently in Jesus' comments about his relation to the Father and the Spirit. Nor should the fact that the pre-incarnate Christ is referred to as the Word be ignored in this connection. Words are not something alien to God, which only become significant when the Word becomes flesh and dwells amongst us. They are ingredients of the mutual self-giving of the divine persons to us.

It should be remembered that who God *is* cannot be separated from what God *does*. There is no gap between who he is and how he expresses himself towards us. This is reflected in a unique aspect of divine speech, one that distinguishes it from our own. There is an inevitable gap between ourselves and the words we use to express ourselves in one way or another. That gap is constituted both by our fin-

---

[39] Torrance 1965: 88. Cf. Webster 1998: 323–325.

itude and our sinfulness. Sometimes I cannot find the words to say precisely what I mean. At other times I can, but for one reason or another I choose to hide the truth rather than express it. And then there are all those times in between. However, no such incapacity or duplicity can be found in God. He is as he speaks of himself. Wolterstorff suggests that one of the rights acquired by speakers is the right to be taken at our word, other things being equal.[40] With God there is no need for the qualification.

God speaks, in various ways to be sure, but God speaks. Whenever he makes himself known to men and women, words are involved. Furthermore, God's use of words is intentional: they are meant to have an impact, meant to contribute to a true knowledge of God and his purposes.[41] One of the features of contemporary approaches to the philosophy of language is a heightened awareness of the way words do things.[42] Competent speakers use words purposefully with a variety of ends in mind. To use the jargon, our locutionary acts are also illocutionary acts. In the context of the gospel as the centrepiece of God's communicative activity, we can say that God uses words in the service of his intention to rescue men and women, drawing them into fellowship with him and preparing a new creation as an appropriate venue for the enjoyment of that fellowship. In other words, the knowledge of God that is the goal of God's speaking ought never to be separated from the centrepiece of Christian theology; namely, the salvation of sinners. As Colin Gunton put it, 'The centre is not divine self-identification but divine saving action.'[43]

## God and human words

A regular objection to such a picture of God and his dealings with creation is the prominence it affords to human language, which appears self-evidently as a creaturely phenomenon governed as much as anything else by social convention. Even if we can establish that God is a speaker, is there not some difficulty associated with his use of

[40] Wolterstorff 1995: 93–94.

[41] Isa. 55:10–11. God has been described as 'the determined communicator' (McQuilkin & Mullen 1997: 75).

[42] The source is usually recognized as the speech-act theories of Austin and Searle (Austin 1962; Searle 1969).

[43] Gunton 1995: 111. Robert Preus points out that this was in fact a concern of the orthodox Lutheran divines (Preus 1955: 170). That this divine saving action is co-ordinated with judgment may help to explain other features of God's speech and indeed of the biblical text, an observation to which we will return in the next chapter.

*our* words?[44] And the words that Scripture attributes to God *are* recognizably our words, human words. Furthermore, as we saw in chapter 1, it has often been argued that such words are inherently inadequate, open to mishearing and misinterpretation, prone to distortion and deception. Communication through words is difficult, all the more so when the communication is about transcendent realities.[45]

What is needed at this point is a theological perspective on human language.[46] It is in the end only partly true to insist that human language is a creaturely phenomenon. We are very definitely active in the shaping of language, expanding and shedding vocabulary, regularizing grammar and so on, but the phenomenon of human language has its origins in God's primeval address of the man and woman at the moment of creation. The first words spoken in Genesis are spoken by God and the narrative proceeds on the basis that these words can be – and are – understood by those God has so recently created. Human language should be viewed as a gift of God rather than as a human achievement. God is the first to speak in what would later be considered human words and by this first use he fashions those words as a fit instrument for his relationship with humanity. Richard Gaffin put it well:

> As our being itself is derived from God (we exist because he
> exists), and as our knowledge is an analogue of his knowledge
> (we know because he knows), so, too, our capacity for lan-
> guage and other forms of communication is derivative of his.
> We speak because God speaks, because he is a speaking God;
> that is his nature and so, derivatively, it is ours.[47]

Recognizing God as the speaker antecedent to all human speaking, and language as a gift given by him to his creatures, generates an entirely different perspective on the question we have been addressing. In the first place, it calls into question any suggestion that when

[44] Rachel Muers would also wish to call into question the way this picture 'privileges the speaker–hearer relationship' (Muers 2004: 119). Her answer, it seems to me, has been answered above by the link between the prominence of this dynamic in the economy and its eternal reality in God's own being.

[45] See above pp. 20, 24–25.

[46] For a more expansive version of what follows, see my forthcoming article 'The Transcendence of God and Finite Human Speech' (London: Latimer Trust).

[47] Gaffin 2004: 183. Michael Horton takes this a step further with his insistence that language is a divine construction, part of a 'Christian understanding of reality as a divinely constructed gift' (Horton 2002: 186).

God uses human words he is appropriating or 'commandeering' something that is in itself unsuitable for the task. Barth overstates the case when he says:

> The self-presentation of God in His Word is not comparable with any other self-presentation, for every other self-presentation that meets us is either direct communication or, if indirect, it is characterised by a certain similarity and correspondence between matter and form, a feature which makes it possible, as when a face is seen in a mirror, to dissolve the indirect into direct communication or knowledge. This is the very thing that is ruled out in the case of God's Word. Its form is not a suitable but an unsuitable medium for God's self-presentation. It does not correspond to the matter but contradicts it. It does not unveil it but veils it.[48]

Of course Barth's principal and proper concern is to preserve the freedom and 'mystery' (in a sense akin to otherness) of God. God is not containable in words and we can never say that the words we read, hear or repeat are themselves God. Barth will appeal in the small print that follows to Luther's theology of the cross and the idea of the *larva Dei* found in his 1535 commentary on Galatians. In that commentary Luther does state that in this life we cannot deal with God face to face but only in the veiled form in which he makes himself known, but his reference at this point is to the social position of individuals, which is a *mask* to be distinguished from God himself.[49] He does not suggest that human language or words are themselves masks behind which God conceals himself. Certainly, Luther does in a variety of places question the confident speculation of medieval theologians about the essence and attributes of God, but it is questionable whether he would ever have applied his theology of the cross to the language God uses to address men and women.[50] To suggest that God cannot be exhaustively known or contained within any conceptual or verbal system is one thing. To expose our general

[48] Barth 1932: 166 (*KD* I/1, 172 = *CD* I/1, 166). Similarly overstated is Bruce McCormack's suggestion that Barth is seeking to counter an unfortunate tendency to 'divinize' the human words of the prophets and apostles (McCormack 2004: 70).

[49] Luther 1535: 95 (*WA* XL-I, 173.24 – 174.3 = *LW* XXVI, 95). In the context of the Galatians commentary, Luther is actually referring to the social positions of men as the *mask* that must be distinguished from God himself and his work.

[50] E.g. Luther 1525: 138–140. See my discussion of this facet of Luther's theology in Thompson 2004: 103–112.

propensity for inept or deceitful use of language on this side of the fall is also entirely appropriate. However, if words are indeed the gift of God and if by creating men and women in his image he has made us fit speech partners for himself, then we must be careful in overextending Luther's insight.

The same applies to Calvin's concept of accommodation. In response to the foolishness of the Anthropomorphites, Calvin insists that there is language in Scripture that should not be taken literally, as when Scripture speaks of God's mouth or ears or eyes or hands.[51] Yet it is important that Calvin bases this observation of some accommodated language in Scripture on a truth he has established by other biblical statements that he considers to be clear and unambiguous, such as, in this case, the testimony that God is spirit (John 4:24). This is far from the contemporary suggestion that all talk about God must be metaphorical if it is not to be idolatrous.[52] Neither does it qualify him to be a prototype of 'the theological agnosticism of much post-Kantian Protestant theology'.[53] Recent research suggests that the term 'accommodation' was given expanded reference in later Reformed thought, perhaps with some influence from Socinius.[54] God's commitment to make himself known to men and women undoubtedly involves a measure of accommodation at certain points, but this ought not to be extended to the phenomenon of human language in general.

As we have seen, the gospel makes clear that God's overarching purpose is to be known, not hidden. His inexhaustibility and transcendence do not prevent this purpose from being realized. Indeed, genuinely knowing *God*, and not just some mask or representation of God accommodated to our weakness, is one important way in which Jesus himself speaks about eternal life (John 17:3). Here, there would seem, is a genuine parallel between God's address of men and women in human words and the incarnation of the Son as a truly human being. The fragile creatureliness of human language or of Jesus' human body does not so much conceal the truth about God as reveal it in a powerful way. The cross is not a representation of God's love but a demonstration of it. The language God uses to make himself known is not *always* and *necessarily* analogical, in the sense

[51] Calvin 1559: 121 (*Inst.* I.xiii.1).
[52] E.g. McFague 1983; Soskice 1985.
[53] This has been helpfully highlighted by Paul Helm's recent study of Calvin's thought (Helm 2004: 193).
[54] Klauber & Sunshine 1990.

of being indirectly related to reality.[55] God addresses himself to men and women directly in these words. He makes promises.[56]

The fragility of human language can be overstated. In reality, verbal communication succeeds most of the time, and when it doesn't, it is not at all clear that language itself is the problem. To quote Gaffin once more,

> we must be insistent that human language is not ultimately a human invention, but God's gift, a gift reflective of his own capacities as the Giver. That recognition engenders confidence, a confidence that needs to be focused negatively as well as positively. Our language is not innately ambiguous. Human language does not inherently veil and confuse as it seeks to communicate and disclose meaning. It does not inevitably create a distortion of the subject matter about which it speaks. Human language is not an intrinsically inadequate medium for communicating, for conveying meaning. Certainly our language, as we have seen, can confuse, veil, and distort. But this, we must remember, is directly attributable to our sin, to our varied misuse and deliberate abuse of language, not to any functional defect in our language itself.[57]

Even the reality of multiple languages and the necessity of translation do not prove an insuperable barrier to communication. It is true that the Bible itself presents this fracture in the unity of human language as something undesirable, the result of judgment upon human arrogance and self-assertion on the plains of Shinar (Gen. 11:1–9). It does make human cooperation more difficult. However, the call of Abram occurs *after* the disruption of Babel and there is not the slightest hint that God has found it more difficult to communicate his purpose to men and women because languages have multiplied across the face of the earth. Furthermore, whatever else may have been revealed on the Day of Pentecost, the spread of the gospel in a multilingual world is anticipated: 'we hear them telling in our own tongues

---

[55] At this point I would also wish to take issue with Jüngel's suggestion that 'basically all language forms of faith participate in the structure of parabolic language', even given his insistence that this is a 'higher level of directness' (Jüngel 1977: 293, 292 [see 289–298]). For the importance of at least some univocal language about God see Knox 1982: 67–69; Alston 1989; Helm 2004: 190; Williams 2005.

[56] An important question, which cannot be pursued here, is whether faith can be sustained without promises that are direct and univocal.

[57] Gaffin 2004: 191.

the mighty works of God' (Acts 2:11). Translation may not always be easy or straightforward (it may even multiply the opportunities for miscommunication), but it is a perfectly serviceable means of conveying meaning across language barriers. Where formal characteristics of the original language do not cross as easily, they are rarely critical for determining meaning and are almost always recoverable in large measure by commentary accompanying the translation.

## God and this text

God speaks and the words he uses are not part of some alien celestial language, but words that operate normally within our very human linguistic structures, structures that are themselves the gift of God to us. This simple fact cannot for a moment be separated from God's determination to be known by men and women. Human beings are addressed in human words that have their origin in God, in order that by repentance and faith in the promise of God we might be included in the salvation Jesus Christ has secured by his death and resurrection. Yet unlike those who stood at the base of Mount Sinai, or those who accompanied Jesus during his earthly ministry, or even those who first heard the prophets proclaim the word of the Lord or the apostles who preached as ambassadors for Christ, Christians in the twenty-first century have before them a book, a text. How does our starting point of God as he has revealed himself in the gospel shape our approach to this text and in particular its capacity to communicate clearly and effectively? Can we say that God is not only a speaker but an author?

There can be little doubt that for the vast majority of their history the Christian churches have considered the Bible to be the word of God.[58] That conviction can be traced to the attitude of Jesus himself and the earliest gospel preachers. For instance, I have already mentioned that Jesus counters each of the three temptations of Satan in the wilderness by citing the word of God (Matt. 4:1–11). God has something to say that unmasks each of the lies the ancient enemy is peddling. Yet at each point Jesus' citation is in fact of a verse from the

[58] Various attempts have been made to show otherwise, the most notorious of which has been the revisionist approach of Jack Rogers and Donald McKim (Rogers & McKim 1979). Yet even Alister McGrath suggests, with no evidence supplied, that the affirmation was variously understood at the time of the Reformation (McGrath 1999: 152). Precisely who amongst the mainstream Reformers of the sixteenth century believed Scripture *contained* rather than *is* the word of God? See Thompson 1998b.

book of Deuteronomy (8:3; 6:16; 6:13). Later, when Jesus is engaged in dispute with the Pharisees over the traditions of the elders, he points them to the commandment about honouring one's father and mother (found in Exod. 20:12) and says, 'So for the sake of your tradition you have made void the *word of God*' (Matt. 15:6; my emphasis). In John 10 another dispute with the Jews is recorded in which Jesus uses the expressions 'Law', 'Scripture' and 'word of God' almost as synonyms:

> Is it not written in your Law, 'I said, you are gods'? If he called them gods to whom the word of God came – and Scripture cannot be broken – do you say of him whom the Father consecrated and sent into the world, 'You are blaspheming', because I said, 'I am the Son of God'?
>
> (John 10:34–36)

Apart from these direct examples of Jesus using the expression 'word of God' with reference to texts from the Old Testament, his use of the Scriptures throughout his ministry confirms this identification.[59] He regularly appeals to the Scriptures as the final arbiter in his debates with the religious leaders. In an expression we will need to examine further in the next chapter, Jesus chides his adversaries with the question 'Have you not read . . .?' (Matt. 12:3, 5; 19:4; 22:31; Mark 12:10, 26). Of course they had read these things, yet they had not treated the text of Scripture anywhere near as seriously as it deserved. This, Jesus insists, is where the purposes of God are to be discovered.

This does not mean that Jesus ignores or even minimizes the human authorship of these texts. There is ample evidence that Jesus could just as easily refer to passages from the Old Testament as the words of Moses or David or the prophet Isaiah. In the Markan account of the encounter with the Pharisees about tradition (Mark 7:1–13), Jesus explicitly identifies Moses as the one who gave them the commandment about honouring their parents (v. 10), but this acknowledgment is surrounded by reference to 'the commandment of God' (v. 9) and, as we have seen, 'the word of God' (v. 13). Teaching in the temple, Jesus will refer to how 'David himself, in the Holy Spirit (*en tō pneumati tō hagiō*), declared . . .' (Mark 12:36). And on the road to Emmaus he simply chides his disciples with 'O foolish

---

[59] The most extensive treatment of Jesus' attitude towards the Old Testament in recent times remains that of John Wenham (Wenham 1993).

ones, and slow of heart to believe all that *the prophets* have spoken'
(Luke 24:25; my emphasis). A conviction that the words recorded in
the Hebrew Scriptures have their source in God and therefore that
they stand as the authoritative word of God does not for Jesus negate
the reality of genuine human authorship. It would seem that the phenomenon Wolterstorff describes as 'double agency discourse' fits
quite well with Jesus' own operating assumption about the Old
Testament.

It is not hard to find evidence of the same attitude in the apostolic
preaching and letters. The preaching of Peter on the Day of
Pentecost seeks to bring the prophecies of Joel 2, Psalm 16 and Psalm
110 to bear on the events they had all witnessed (Acts 2:14–41). What
God has promised, for instance, 'through (*dia*) the prophet Joel' is
now being fulfilled before their eyes. The prayer of the disciples after
the release of Peter and John from prison in Acts 4 makes use of
Psalm 2, introducing it with the words 'Sovereign Lord, who made
the heaven and the earth and the sea and everything in them, who
through the mouth of our father David, your servant, said by the
Holy Spirit . . .' (Acts 4:24–25). The point, it seems, is almost being
laboured. God has spoken, but the words were also the words of
David spoken by the Spirit. This is prima facie evidence at least that
this perspective was common amongst the earliest followers of Jesus.
That same perspective is expressed by Paul at the very beginning of
his letter to the Romans: Paul had been set apart for the gospel of
God which he, God, 'promised beforehand through his prophets in
the holy Scriptures' (Rom. 1:2). In this context the classic apostolic
statement on the origin and utility of Scripture does not appear at all
singular or surprising: 'All Scripture is breathed out by God and
profitable for teaching, for reproof, for correction, and for training in
righteousness, that the man of God may be competent, equipped for
every good work' (2 Tim. 3:16–17).

The extension of such a perspective to the apostolic writers is classically anchored in the promise of the Spirit given to them on the
night of Jesus' betrayal (John 14:25–26; 16:12–15) and the commission they received from Jesus prior to his ascension (Matt. 28:18–20).
Once again there is ample evidence that the preaching of the apostles
was properly understood as the word of God. Having prayed in Acts
4, the gathered disciples were 'all filled with the Holy Spirit and continued to speak the word of God with boldness' (Acts 4:31; cf. 6:7).
Paul explains to the Corinthians that he passes on the things freely
given to them by God 'in words not taught by human wisdom but

taught by the Spirit' (1 Cor. 2:13) and rejoices that the Thessalonians responded to his preaching amongst them by accepting it 'not as the word of men but as what it really is, the word of God, which is at work in you believers' (1 Thess. 2:13). Again it is not at all surprising that Peter should refer to the letters of Paul in the same breath as 'the other Scriptures' (2 Pet. 3:16).

Yet in the face of this cumulative evidence, the boldness of the claim that the Bible is the word of God written is still resisted, even by many who are engaged in constructive Christian dogmatics and who wish to take the Bible seriously as a normative source of their doctrine. So, in the Warfield Lectures for 1993, Colin Gunton wrote, 'We are confident that we have passed the stage when we any longer equate revelation and the actual words of Scripture.'[60] In the published version of his Scottish Journal of Theology Lectures for 2001, John Webster spoke of distortions that have occurred in the Christian doctrine of revelation during its long history: 'alongside the hypertrophy of revelation and its migration into epistemology, there develops a parallel process whereby revelation and Scripture are strictly identified'.[61] What is it that makes many theologians like this nervous about a 'direct identification' of Scripture and revelation, of the Bible and the word of God?

Much of this reticence (which in less conservative writers becomes outright denial) can be traced to the enormously influential treatment of the doctrine of the word of God by Karl Barth in the first two volumes of his *Kirchliche Dogmatik* (*Church Dogmatics*), though a much more radical separation of Scripture and the word of God had been a significant feature of mainstream Protestant liberal theology throughout the nineteenth century and remains so up to the present.[62] We have already noted that Barth himself provided the most significant challenge to such liberal theology, returning God and indeed the Bible to the centre of theological discussion. His massive and positive contribution should not be summarily dismissed. Unfortunately, his own long and stretching treatment of this topic has proven easy to caricature and just as easy to misappropriate, though a number of

[60] Gunton 1995: 6.

[61] Webster 2003a: 12; cf. Webster 1998: 330–331. That Webster still wishes to see the closest possible connection between these two phenomena is indicated by an earlier statement: 'the Bible as text is the *viva vox Dei* addressing the people of God and generating faith and obedience' (1998: 317).

[62] One should not underestimate either the influence of Emil Brunner, who in 1941 wrote of 'the fatal equation of revelation and the inspiration of the Scriptures' (Brunner 1941: 7).

more sophisticated and appreciative critiques have appeared in the last couple of years.[63] These have led to the recognition of two significant concerns that animate his presentation.[64]

The first of these we have already noted in connection with human language more generally: his concern to preserve the sovereign freedom of God with respect to all creaturely reality. God and God alone determines when and where he will speak and we can never bind him to our words either in oral or written form. He is not naturally accessible to human investigation for he is known only as he gives himself to be known. Barth explained that the consequence of treating 'inspiration' as a quality of the biblical text that guaranteed its character as the word of God was that such a move brought the Bible into the sphere of natural theology, 'that knowledge of God which man can have without the free grace of God, by his own power, and with direct insight and assurance'.[65] This he wished to avoid at all costs. As he insisted:

> That the Bible is the Word of God cannot mean that with other attributes the Bible has the attribute of being the Word of God. To say that would be to violate the Word of God which is God Himself – to violate the freedom and the sovereignty of God. God is not an attribute of something else, even if this something else is the Bible. God is the Subject, God is Lord. He is Lord even over the Bible and in the Bible.[66]

This statement from Barth leads naturally to his second concern, which helps to clarify it. For Barth, a direct equation of Scripture with revelation, an unqualified statement that the Bible is the Word of God, risks compromising the supremacy of Christ. For in the strictest sense, only Jesus Christ is the *logos*, the word of God. 'God's revelation is Jesus Christ, the Son of God.'[67] The Scriptures,

---

[63] Wolterstorff 1995: 63–74; Ward 2002: 106–130; McCormack 2004; Morrison 2004.

[64] Behind these two concerns, which he acknowledges, McCormack identifies the larger context of Barth's theological ontology. McCormack's article, while illuminating, has a certain apologetic flavour, accepts certain caricatures of classic orthodox doctrines of Scripture, and does not engage with the theological account of human language and the written text that I have sketched in this chapter (McCormack 2004).

[65] Barth 1938: 522–523 (*KD* I/2, 580 = *CD* I/2, 522–523).

[66] Barth 1938: 513 (*KD* I/2, 569 = *CD* I/2, 513). See further discussion of this point in Ward 2002: 107–110.

[67] Barth 1932: 137 (*KD* I/1, 141 = *CD* I/1, 137).

just like faithful contemporary preaching, do not draw attention to themselves: they witness to Jesus Christ. Not to do so would be to engage in just another form of idolatry. There is no qualification whatsoever when we speak about Jesus as the Word of God. He is so directly and, as Luther would put it, substantially.[68] In contrast, but Barth would insist without separation, the Bible's relation to revelation is indirect.[69] It is properly understood as a human witness to the Word, to Christ, which by virtue of its faithful witness and by the free and sovereign decision of God becomes the Word of God. In his words:

> Precisely in view of revelation, or on the basis of it, one may thus say of proclamation and the Bible that they are God's Word, that they continually become God's Word. But for this very reason one cannot say the same of revelation . . . Revelation is itself the divine decision which is taken in the Bible and proclamation, which makes use of them, which thus confirms, ratifies and fulfils them. It is itself the Word of God which the Bible and proclamation are as they become it.[70]

Or perhaps more simply:

> If we want to think of the Bible as a real witness of divine revelation, then clearly we have to keep two things constantly before us and give them their due weight: the limitation and the positive element, its distinctiveness from revelation, in so far as it is only a human word about it, and its unity with it, in so far as revelation is the basis, object and content of this word.[71]

This is not the place for a detailed engagement with Barth's doctrine of Scripture, though this is long overdue. Nevertheless, for our present purposes it is worth noting four things. First, for all the attractiveness of Barth's focus on Christ as God himself and so the content of God's self-revelation, it is difficult not to conclude that he has moved too quickly. There are significant 'linguistic aspects' to

---

[68] See Thompson 2004: 72.
[69] Barth 1938: 492 (*KD* I/2, 545 = *CD* I/2, 492).
[70] Barth 1932: 118 (*KD* I/1, 121 = *CD* I/1, 118).
[71] Barth 1938: 463 (*KD* I/2, 512 = *CD* I/2, 463). Cf. Barth 1932: 115 (*KD* I/1, 117–118 = *CD* I/1, 115).

God's revelation that are attested by Jesus himself.[72] God *spoke* by the prophets and has now spoken by his Son. A Christocentricity that does not reflect the textured nature of Jesus' own approach to the Old Testament runs the risk of being reductionist.[73] Second, while his serious attention to the genuine humanity of the biblical text is welcome (it is surely courting disaster ever to speak of the Bible as a 'divine text'), Barth appears to overplay the limitations of human language. If, as I have attempted to show, human language is a divine gift (not something commandeered by God despite its weakness and unsuitability, but initiated by God as a means of fellowship that remains effectual even on this side of the fall and the Tower of Babel), then the assumption that the Bible's genuine humanity must entail a capacity for error that extends to its religious or theological content (even if only 'within certain limits') is a dangerous miscalculation. If God speaks our words, not just as the incarnate Son but in the address of men and women throughout redemptive history, then these words *are* a suitable medium for revelation. God gave them in order that they might be so.[74] And if God himself initiates the move from oral to written speech, then why should the text be more frail than, say, the preaching of Jesus? Third, it is not at all clear why a recognition that this text finds its source in God, that the human authors are commissioned and enabled *by God* to write God's words in their words, should threaten the sovereign freedom of God. Wolterstorff has put it well:

> If it is indeed a limitation on God's freedom that God would commission a human being to speak 'in the name of' God, then perhaps we have to take seriously the possibility that God is willing on occasion to limit God's freedom in that way – or

[72] Ward 2002: 121, 136, who builds upon the observation of Vanhoozer 1994: 169.

[73] Similar things could be said about his stimulating allusion to Chalcedonian Christology as a way of speaking about the divine and human word in Scripture. Barth 1938: 499 (*KD* I/2, 553–554 = *CD* I/2, 499). The problem is exacerbated in the writing of one of Barth's students, Jacques de Senarclens, whose proposal has itself been influential for the recent work of John Webster (de Senarclens 1959: 267–297).

[74] Here I must register disagreement with John Webster's location of the notion of Holy Scripture within the broader category of sanctification, 'the act of God the Holy Spirit in hallowing creaturely processes'. While this is a stimulating and bold attempt to account for both a genuine humanity of the biblical text and its proper relation to God and his saving purpose, I cannot see that it ultimately avoids the charge of being adoptionist, a possibility Webster is aware of and that he seeks to avoid. More emphasis on words not merely as creaturely realities but as a divine initiative and gift seems warranted from the biblical evidence. See Webster 2003a: 17–30.

alternatively, consider the possibility that we are working with an alien and inapplicable concept of freedom.[75]

Fourth, the historical and exegetical anchors of Barth's conception are far from secure. For instance, it is true that Luther speaks of the threefold form of the Word of God (in his early Psalms lectures and again in Table Talk from 1540) but he does so with quite significant differences to Barth's approach and he does not say what Barth attributes to him; namely, that 'the Bible only holds, encloses, limits and surrounds' God's Word.[76] Likewise, Barth's exegetical comments, especially on 2 Timothy 3 and 2 Peter 1 are at points idiosyncratic and unconvincing. His concern to distinguish 'inspiration' from 'inspiredness' appears to distort the emphasis of the biblical texts themselves.

Having said all of this, Barth's powerful insistence that the Spirit's involvement with this text is not complete once the Scriptures have been written helpfully points us to one final feature of the relationship between God and the Bible. Unlike any other text we might name, the biblical text never leaves the presence of its ultimate author. God attends not only the production but the reception of this text. Paul was not just given a message to proclaim but his proclamation of that message was accompanied by the convicting work of the Spirit of God. This is what he rejoices in when writing to the Thessalonians, the word coming 'in power and in the Holy Spirit and with full conviction' (1 Thess. 1:6). The word of God is not simply a product of the Spirit of God: it is the sword of the Spirit (Eph. 6:17).

In classic Reformed theology this continuing work of the Spirit, especially as it is associated with reading and proclaiming the text of Scripture, is described as 'illumination' and Barth was right to bring this into the closest possible relation with revelation, even if he risks collapsing the former into the latter.[77] John Webster has emphasized the presence of God as the proper context of a faithful reading of

[75] Wolterstorff 1995: 74. T. F. Torrance's development of Barth's objection amounts to little less than a caricature: 'The practical and the epistemological effect of a fundamentalism of this kind is to give an infallible Bible and a set of rigid evangelical beliefs primacy over God's self-revelation which is mediated to us through the Bible. This effect is only reinforced by the regular fundamentalist identification of biblical statements about truth with the truth itself to which they refer. Here undoubtedly we find a marked failure to acknowledge the unique Reality of God in its transcendent authority and majesty over all the contingent media employed by God in his self-revelation to mankind' (Torrance 1982: 17).

[76] Barth 1938: 492 (*KD* I/2, 545 = *CD* I/2, 492). See Thompson 2004: 71–72, 88–89.

[77] The observation of many, including Helm 1982: 42; Wolterstorff 1995: 72–73; Ward 2002: 120.

Scripture as well as talking about God. In his words, 'To read is to be caught up by the truth-bestowing Spirit of God.'[78] To use the imagery I have employed in this chapter, if God's speaking is an intentional communicative act and if the biblical text is caught up in that act, then God himself ensures that his purpose (whether for salvation or for judgment) will be accomplished. God has not only spoken. In this text he still speaks.

## The clarity of Scripture and the character of God

I have been seeking to provide a theological framework for an evangelical affirmation of the clarity of Scripture, conscious that evangelical theology is at its heart talk about God, the God of the gospel. There is nothing essentially novel about this approach. Classic treatments of Scripture's clarity have regularly emphasized the theological dimensions of the subject. Irenaeus spoke of God's desire to be known and his ability to effect it through the Scriptures.[79] Martin Luther, challenged by Erasmus about the obscurity of Scripture, insisted 'the Holy Spirit [note, not the Bible] is no sceptic'.[80] Heinrich Bullinger placed his discussion of how Scripture is to be read firmly in the context of a history of the word of God.[81] Even Charles Hodge, for all his alleged indebtedness to Common Sense Realism, refuses to separate the clarity of Scripture from the personal activity of the Spirit.[82]

Christian doctrine is not essentially rational, mechanistic or impersonal, but is relational at its very core because God in his eternal being is relational and determines all reality. A Christian doctrine of

---

[78] Webster 2003a: 95. In contrast T. F. Torrance insists that 'Apart from the Spirit [Holy Scripture's] cognitive and linguistic forms are quite opaque, but through the Spirit they are made to direct us away from them to God himself (Torrance 1965: 94). But (1) Has Torrance confused meaning and reference or even meaning and salvific impact? (2) When is the Scripture ever 'apart from the Spirit'? (3) Has Torrance left room for God's purposes of judgment as well as salvation?

[79] Irenaeus 189: 398–399, 466, 468 (*Adversus haereses* II.xxvii.2–5; IV.v.1; IV.vi.4; *PG* VII, 802–804, 983–984, 988–989 = *ANF* I, 398–399, 466, 468]).

[80] Luther 1525: 24 (*WA* XVIII, 605.32 = *LW* XXXIII, 24). Similarly, the *Leiden synopsis purioris theologiae* (1588) declared, 'we say that Scripture is its own interpreter, or rather God, speaking in the Scriptures and through the Scriptures. In the clearer and essential passages He openly indicates His will to believers . . . In obscure passages He more and more confirms the same will of His for them by comparison of them with clearer passages' (excerpted in Heppe 1861: 35).

[81] Bullinger 1549: 36–80. I am indebted to John Webster for pointing me in the direction of Bullinger.

[82] Hodge 1871: 187.

Scripture must speak of Scripture as it is related to God, and this will of necessity draw attention to the person, work and words of Jesus Christ, the one who is genuinely and without reduction both God and human. Scripture exists by and within the purpose of God to be known by men and women, those he is determined to rescue for himself. It is properly understood as an integral part of the purposeful communicative activity of God.

Here are the beginnings of an answer to the suggestion that God as transcendent mystery challenges any notion of Scripture's clarity, for the transcendent God who cannot be contained by our thoughts and words lovingly chooses to be known. He has spoken in many and various ways through the prophets and in the last days through his Son. The transcendence of God should not be played off against this determination on God's part to be known and to use the capacity for language that he has given us as a vehicle for a true knowledge of him. If God chooses to speak to us personally, in his Son and through those he has commissioned and enabled to write his words for us, then it is no transgression of his majesty to take him at his word.

Here too, as we have seen, is an answer to the charge that human language, spoken or written, is inadequate to express in a direct way the truth about God, since language, like humanity itself, is a fragile creature of the dust. God is the primeval speaker, the originator not just of language in some vague or celestial sense, but of language addressed to and understood by human beings. It is his gift to us, a means of relationship that he is the first to use, not something alien that he commandeers or appropriates for this purpose. Furthermore, the transition from oral to written word is not something done in his absence but at his direction, and, like Joshua, faithful men and women today are called to read and meditate on the written word in the presence of God.

Yet to say all this is to raise the stakes enormously when it comes to the issue of Scripture's clarity, for the lines of connection run both ways. If Scripture is not clear, not generally accessible to faithful men and women who prayerfully read, seeking to know the mind of God, what are we then saying about God? As one contemporary writer asks, 'What kind of God would reveal his love and redemption in terms so technical and concepts so profound that only an elite corps of professional scholars could understand them?'[83] If communication is generally possible between human beings, as common experience

---

[83] Sproul 1977: 16.

confirms, then what kind of arrogance (Luther would say blasphemy) will suggest that this is beyond God? Of course there is more to be said. We need to examine Scripture's own testimony about its clarity and indeed those instances where clarity is hard won. We need to respond to the challenges thrown up by contemporary hermeneutics. But let this truth stand over all those attempts: the living God is an effective communicator.

Chapter Three

# It is not beyond you: The accessible word of the living God

'It is not too hard for you'

The critical test for any Christian doctrine is whether it accords with the teaching of the Bible. This remains the case when the doctrine under review is an aspect of our doctrine of Scripture itself – perhaps we should say it is even more especially the case. There is always the possibility that we might claim more for the Bible than the Bible claims for itself, that a priori theologizing might lead us to conclusions that do not fit the Bible we actually have. Coleridge once protested about those who would 'lie for God', by which he meant those who would claim more for Scripture than accords with reason.[1] We might want to quarrel with the naivety of his appeal to reason; after all on this side of the fall it is not in such a pristine condition as to be able infallibly to judge what is in fact a lie or an error or a slip of the pen. Yet, in broader terms, which of us wants to be found fighting to the death for something God himself would not recognize as an article of faith?

A recent polemical piece has described the doctrine of the clarity of Scripture as 'a conviction brought to the Bible rather than an article of faith drawn from the Bible'.[2] There is a measure of truth in this statement. Our confidence in the Bible God has given us is anchored in our understanding of the character of the God who has given it to us. Yet we know the character of God supremely in the gospel and we have access to the gospel, the authentic gospel, that is, only in the pages of Scripture. We expect to be able to understand the Bible because we know that God is committed to

[1] Coleridge 1840: 42.
[2] When published, the polemical tone of the article was muted somewhat with this line appearing as, 'The clarity of scripture, then, is at least as much a conviction brought to the Bible as an article of faith drawn from the Bible' (Cowdell 2004: 122).

81

our welfare and there can be no impediment to the fulfilment of his plans for us.[3]

Yet the challenge to show that this expectation is consistent with what teaching the Bible does provide about itself remains. Indeed, as we saw in chapter one, this challenge has been advanced by those who have opposed the doctrine of *claritas scripturae* down through the ages. It is a challenge that has been answered often enough, and the response that follows owes much to classical defences of the doctrine in centuries past.

# The phenomenon of Scripture according to Jesus and the apostles

## *Jesus and the Old Testament*

James Callahan has recently written that 'there is no direct statement in Christian Scripture that says that it is clear and not obscure'.[4] This, he insists, is not the end of the matter. There are metaphorical expressions that make the point without much room for ambiguity. However, rather than begin at this point, the theological priorities I outlined in the last chapter suggest that we approach the biblical witness from its centre in the person, work and words of Jesus Christ. What does his attitude towards the Scriptures in existence in the early first century teach us about the clarity of Scripture?

The four Gospels are full of quotations of and allusions to passages from the Old Testament and the vast majority of these are found on the lips of Jesus himself.[5] These quotations serve a range of purposes. Some point to promises or pictures in the Old Testament that, Jesus claims, have now been fulfilled in his person and his activity (e.g. Matt. 10:35–36; Luke 4:18–19; John 13:18; 15:25). Others are proffered as

---

[3] There is always a certain circularity to any Christian doctrine of Scripture; yet this need not be vicious, since its fundamental reference point is external (in particular, Jesus' death and resurrection as real rather than merely textual events), and the active presence of God with the text of Scripture means that the activity of seeking to understand that text on any topic is undertaken in the presence rather than the absence of God. On non-vicious circularity from another angle, that of general hermeneutics, see Ricœur 1981: 212–213.

[4] Callahan 2001: 33.

[5] The precise numbers vary depending upon how multiple and combined quotations are treated. One count suggests 70 out of 112 direct quotations of the Old Testament in the Gospels are actually attributed to Jesus himself. In most individual Gospels the ratio is roughly 2:1, the exception being the Gospel of John where of the 14 direct quotations, only 4 are found on Jesus' lips.

evidence that what he is teaching is true (e.g. Matt. 21: 42–44; Mark 10:4–9; John 10:34–35). Still others are employed in the midst of controversy with the Jewish religious establishment, unmasking its failure to conform itself to what all recognize to be the authoritative word of God (e.g. Matt. 21:13; Mark 7:6–7, 10). What is common to all of these (and the other uses of biblical quotation by Jesus as well) is a confidence that appeal to the text of the Old Testament is decisive: it settles the matter. Jesus' ministry is validated, not only by the miracles he has performed but by the testimony to him embedded in the Law, the Prophets and the Psalms (Luke 24:44). Equally, it seems, Jesus makes such an appeal not only with the expectation that this testimony will be accepted by faithful Jewish men and women, but that it will be intelligible to them. What use would there be in quoting texts no-one was able to understand? And in most cases in the Gospels the quotation stands alone without gloss or embellishment.

A number of quotations and allusions play a highly significant role in providing an interpretative framework for what is happening or is about to happen in Jesus' life and ministry. These occur throughout the Gospels, and the most critical are those surrounding his arrest and crucifixion. Jesus had given his disciples many of the most important categories for understanding these events long before: his use of the image of ransom in Mark 10:45, the parable of the wicked tenants (which in Matthew's Gospel at least follows immediately from Jesus' discussion with the chief priests and scribes about their rejection of John the Baptist, Matt. 21:23–46) and the apocalyptic discourse of Matthew 24. Yet on the night of his arrest, still in the upper room with his disciples, he draws their attention to one of the most enduring reference points for a Christian explanation of these events: the suffering servant of Isaiah 53. 'For I tell you', Jesus says, 'this Scripture must be fulfilled in me: "And he was numbered with the transgressors." For what is written about me has its fulfilment' (Luke 22:37).

Jesus' arrest and execution, between two criminals, via an instrument usually reserved for insurrectionists and disturbers of the imperial peace, was not all it seemed, just as the suffering and death of the Servant in Isaiah 53 was not all it seemed. Jesus appears to trade on the intelligibility of this image as a way of helping those closest to him to make sense of what is about to happen. If not immediately to make sense of it amidst the trauma of the next few hours, then certainly later when the Spirit brings back to their remembrance all he has said to them (John 14:27). The key to understanding the disturbing chain of events that leads up to his death is to be found in the Old Testament, in places such as Isaiah 53. In the language of contemporary Christian theology, Jesus' death is substitutionary.

On the way from Pilate to the place of execution, Jesus passes through a crowd including wailing, lamenting women. He calls on them to weep, not for him, but 'for yourselves and for your children' (Luke 23:28). The language of extremity he uses includes a quotation of Hosea 10:8:

> and they shall say to the mountains, Cover us,
> and to the hills, Fall on us.

Such language resonates with the crisis of this hour. The great judgment that awaited the idolatrous nation of greater Israel now stands before those who will do something like this when the Father's beloved Son has come amongst them. The events these women are witnessing make such a judgment inevitable. A day has now been fixed. Jesus' death is to be understood in such a context. His substitution, his being numbered amongst the transgressors, his ransom for many, is inextricably bound to the judgment to come. It has an indispensable forensic or penal element. Of course the weeping women on the side of the road out of Jerusalem that day might not have made all the connections. That would be left to other women and men in the years that followed. But that Jesus had employed language from the paramount crisis of Israel's history, the loss of the kingdom of David and his line, that he had used this language to present his own death as a crisis (not for himself but for them!), that much ought to have been obvious. Jesus seems to expect that the images of this Old Testament text would be both recognizable and intelligible.

On a number of other occasions, most notably the famous 'antitheses' of the Sermon on the Mount, Jesus' quotation from the Old Testament is a launching point for his own teaching. Six times in Matthew 5:21–48 Jesus tells his disciples, 'You have heard that it was said . . . But I say to you . . .' In each of these instances Jesus does not call into question the teaching of the Old Testament, since in the immediately preceding verses he insists, 'I have not come to abolish (*katalysai*) them [the Law or the Prophets] but to fulfil (*plērōsai*) them' (v. 17). The antitheses are properly understood as illustrative of this fulfilment.[6] The Old Testament law, the Torah, remains sacrosanct (he

---

[6] Harrington 1991: 90.

is not here dealing with certain laws regarding ceremonial or dietary matters, which are addressed elsewhere). With regard to the laws quoted by Jesus at this point, the coming of the Messiah calls for a righteousness that takes seriously the 'direction' of the Torah as well as its letter. Jesus intends to show how the greater righteousness he is talking about, the righteousness that 'exceeds that of the scribes and Pharisees', surpasses the demands of the Torah without contradicting or overthrowing it. In other words, he both exposes and opposes a casuistic or legalist approach to the teaching of the Old Testament.[7] In this way the antitheses lead up to their conclusion in verse 48: 'You therefore must be perfect, as your heavenly Father is perfect.' It is evident that Jesus' use of the Old Testament texts in this connection relies upon an understanding and indeed a basic agreement with them.

A further interesting case in point is found four chapters later, in Matthew 9. The Pharisees have complained to Jesus' disciples that he eats with tax collectors and sinners, and when Jesus hears about it he addresses them with the words 'Those who are well have no need of a physician, but those who are sick. Go and learn what this means (*poreuthentes de mathete ti estin*), "I desire mercy, and not sacrifice." For I came not to call the righteous, but sinners' (Matt. 9:12–13).

Is this an instance where the meaning of the Old Testament text had eluded its readers? Is Jesus suggesting that the Pharisees do not know what these words mean? Such a conclusion would not fit either with the context or with the picture of the Pharisees in the rest of Matthew's Gospel. Their problem is not an ignorance of the Old Testament Scriptures but rather a failure to modify their own prejudices and behaviour in the light of them. 'They cannot see how the words, "I desire mercy, and not sacrifice", justify Jesus' outreach to sinners.'[8] Nor could they see how this text should shape their response to genuine human need, even if that need manifests itself on the Sabbath (Matt. 12:1–8). Intellectual apprehension is one thing; living in the light of what you know is quite another. Something more than a clear text is needed at this point and that something is a repentant and faithful heart.

This is also what lies behind the rhetorical question 'Have you not [have you never] read . . .' that Jesus asks six times in Matthew's Gospel.[9] There may be echoes here of a standard rabbinic teaching

---

[7] Davies & Allison 1988–97: I, 508.

[8] Davies & Allison 1988–97: II, 104. This is somewhat more than the 'lack of imagination' that Davies and Allison suggest.

[9] Matt. 12:3, 5; 19:4; 21:16, 42; 22:31.

device,[10] but the force of the question as asked by Jesus lies in the assumption that of course those he addresses have read the passages in question. Of course the Pharisees had read the account of David in 1 Samuel 21 and the laws regarding the priests in Numbers 28 and the account of creation in Genesis 1 and 2. The problem is that while they may have understood the meaning of these Old Testament texts, they do not demonstrate that they have grasped their significance; that is, how the perspective these texts provide should transform their own attitudes and behaviour. This is not to suggest that meaning and significance are entirely separable, but that is an issue we will return to in a later chapter.

Must we then conclude that Jesus' general confidence in the accessibility of meaning in the Old Testament extends to every part of it without qualification? We need to exercise caution at this point. Perhaps the most enigmatic saying of Jesus in this connection is his injunction to 'let the reader understand' with reference to the 'abomination that causes desolation' in Matthew 24 and its parallels. The larger context is the application of the apocalyptic language of the Old Testament, in this particular case from the prophet Daniel, to events that will occur before this generation passes away (v. 34). In such a context this injunction would appear to be an aside by Jesus that draws the attention of all those who read Daniel to the significance of Daniel's words, most particularly that these words are about to be fulfilled.[11] The diversity of interpretations that have accompanied this passage over the past two thousand years would seem to indicate that no claim for its clarity can be maintained. No consensus has yet been reached about the referent of 'the abomination that causes desolation' (v. 15).[12] Furthermore, it is very likely that this expression originally referred to something or someone in or just outside the Old Testament period and that Jesus now relates this typologically to the events soon to come. Jesus, it would appear, is encouraging the readers of Daniel to think again about the words the prophet was given. There is more to these words than many may have

[10] Daube 1956: 433. Daube suggests this device could be paraphrased, 'Surely you have read this or that text, so you ought to understand its import' or 'but you do not seem to understand its import'.

[11] Bolt 2004: 100 n. 35.

[12] Amongst others, possible referents include Caligula's intention to set up an altar in the temple in AD 40, the destruction of Jerusalem in AD 70 and the return of Christ at the end of human history. For a particularly stimulating treatment of this passage as it appears in Mark's Gospel, which sees the referent as the cataclysmic event of the crucifixion, see Bolt 2004: 85–103.

seen. Their fullest meaning can be grasped only in the light of what is about to happen 'in this generation'.

Jesus appears to operate on the assumption that when the words of Scripture are read or heard, they will be understood, at least well enough understood to warrant an acknowledgment that he is who he says he is and that his words are true. Yet this overarching confidence does not exclude the possibility that an individual passage might prove difficult, such that the exhortation 'let the reader understand' is appropriate. He is not suggesting that every text is transparent, that understanding is always and in every case automatic or simple. Nevertheless, in general terms the Scriptures can only operate the way they do in Jesus' teaching ministry because they are assumed to make sense as they stand. This assumption enables him to hold accountable those who claim to know the Scriptures but fail to respond to him with repentance and faith (John 5:36–47).

## The apostolic appeal to the Old Testament

A similar pattern can be found in the ministry of the apostles. Their preaching and writing is characterized by engagement with the text of the Old Testament in the light of the events of Jesus' life, death and resurrection. We have already noted this in the sermon of Peter on the Day of Pentecost and the introduction of Paul's letter to the Christians at Rome. An appeal to the Scriptures is important to the fundamental argument that Jesus and the events surrounding him are the climax of God's eternal purposes. In an important sense Jesus and the Old Testament Scriptures interpret each other. The Old Testament provides the basic categories of thought for a proper understanding of who Jesus is and what he has done. At the same time it is Jesus who, as it were, opens up the Old Testament as he did for the disciples on the Emmaus road. So, on the Day of Pentecost, Peter can cite Psalm 16 with its statement 'you will not abandon my soul to Sheol or let your holy one see corruption' (v. 10) and then immediately draw attention to the fact that David, the author of the psalm, both died and was buried, and his tomb in Jerusalem is available for Peter's listeners to visit (Acts 2:25–29). In that light, this psalm cannot be talking about David. Yet Peter goes on, 'Being therefore a prophet, and knowing that God had sworn an oath to him that he would set one of his descendants on his throne, he foresaw and spoke about the resurrection of the Christ, that he was not abandoned to Hades, nor did his flesh see corruption' (Acts 2:30–31). Jesus' resurrection is the fulfilment of Old Testament prophecy and that prophecy can be seen for what it is by the resurrection of Jesus. Strictly speaking, the psalm was perfectly clear prior to Peter's explanation: God will not let death triumph over his holy one. Yet the true referent of that statement (the identity of this 'holy one') is now revealed by the resurrection. And Peter, as a commissioned witness of the resurrection, allows this Old Testament text to be seen as a prophecy about the Christ.

A striking feature of the apostolic appeal to the Old Testament is that it is not reserved for Jewish audiences where some familiarity with the Scriptures, even if at the most basic level, might fairly be assumed. Paul's ministry to the Gentiles is no less characterized by appeal to the Old Testament than Peter's ministry to the Jews.[13] True, his ministry strategy does involve first seeking out the Jews in each district and only then turning to the Gentiles, in line with certain of his most basic theological commitments (Rom. 1:16; 9 – 11).[14] Yet his epistles anticipate both Jewish and Gentile readers. He expects all to recognize the authority of the prophetic writings and to understand them at least to such an extent that their endorsement of his exposition of the gospel and its implications is acknowledged. Once again this is not to suggest that the texts Paul cites are necessarily transparent, that a recognition of their meaning and significance was always immediate or spontaneous, as we will see in a moment. Yet neither did Paul feel constrained to engage in sustained exposition of each text he cited, even in epistles such as those to the Galatians and Ephesians with their demonstrable focus on Gentile Christians.[15] When the gospel concerning God's Son is accepted, along with its anchorage in God's ancient promises through the prophets, an interpretative framework is provided that enables productive engagement with the text of the Old Testament, even by young Gentile Christians.

Paul's exposition of his gospel in his letter to the Romans contains the greatest concentration of Old Testament quotation and allusion of all his letters. It appears to be critical for his apostolic and evangelistic purpose in this letter that he demonstrate the consistency of his message with that of the Scriptures.[16] The tone is in fact set in the opening greeting: the gospel of God is that which God promised

---

[13] In spite of the fact that explicit quotations appear almost exclusively in the *Hauptbriefe* (Romans; 1–2 Corinthians; and Galatians) (Silva 1993: 638).

[14] Köstenberger & O'Brien 2001: 185–191, 258–260.

[15] Silva 1993: 639. On the likely focus on Gentile Christians in these epistles see Bruce 1982: 31–32 and O'Brien 1999: 50.

[16] Silva 1993: 638.

beforehand through his prophets in the holy Scriptures (1:2; cf. 3:21).
Paul's use of the Old Testament in this epistle and elsewhere is sophisticated and varied and we must be careful not to suggest that we have
said all that needs to be said in this connection.[17] Nevertheless, for
our purposes, two particular ways in which he appeals to Scripture
stand out: first, as the climactic or decisive proof that substantiates
the point he has been making; and second, as a starting point for an
argument, citing the text and then unpacking its implications in a way
that leads directly to a gospel idea or practice. An example of the first
is found in the programmatic verses in the middle of Romans 1:

> For I am not ashamed of the gospel, for it is the power of God
> for salvation to everyone who believes, to the Jew first and also
> to the Greek. For in it the righteousness of God is revealed from
> faith for faith, as it is written, 'The righteous shall live by faith.'
>                                                         (Rom. 1:16–17)

Habakkuk 2:4 is the textual justification for the point Paul has been
making; namely, that the gospel is the power of God for the salvation
of everyone who believes. In other words, Paul's confidence in the
gospel as God's way of saving people is justified by this prophetic reference to the life of faith. The text appears unadorned in any way. Paul
does not expound Habakkuk 2. Rather, in common with other examples of this type of use of the Old Testament in Romans, the text is
simply introduced with the words 'as it is written (*kathōs gegraptai*)'.[18]
A key example of the second way in which Paul employs the Old
Testament in Romans is his appeal to Genesis 15:6 in chapter 4:

> What then shall we say was gained by Abraham, our forefather
> according to the flesh? For if Abraham was justified by works,
> he has something to boast about, but not before God. For
> what does the Scripture say? 'Abraham believed God, and it
> was counted to him as righteousness.' Now to the one who
> works, his wages are not counted as a gift but as his due. And
> to the one who does not work but trusts him who justifies the
> ungodly, his faith is counted as righteousness . . .
>                                                         (Rom. 4:1–6)

---

[17] See Ellis 1957; Longenecker 1975: 104–132; Hays 1989; Silva 1993; O'Brien 2004:
375–390; Enns 2005: 113–165.
[18] Rom. 1:17; 2:24; 3:4, 10; 4:17; 8:36; 9:13, 33; 10:15; 11:8, 26; 15:3, 9, 21. Cf. 4:18;
9:9, 15, 17, 25, 27, 29; 10:5, 11, 16, 18, 19, 20, 21; 11: 9; 12:19; 14:11; 15:10, 11, 12.

The quotation from Genesis does not appear unannounced. The point established by this appeal to the Old Testament has in fact already been made in the preceding chapter: 'we hold that one is justified by faith apart from works of the law' (Rom. 3:28). In one sense Paul's reference to Abraham is to justify that point and to demonstrate that this has always been God's way of dealing with men and women (i.e. the first use we mentioned above). However, the rest of chapter 4 is a reflection on this quotation and its implications for Paul and his readers with his conclusion that 'the words "it was counted to him" were not written for his sake alone, but for ours also' (Rom. 4:23–24). This is a case where Paul seems engaged in the exposition of an Old Testament text, explaining its meaning and drawing out its implications for a response to the salvation Jesus has provided. In the verses that follow, he explores both the idea of imputation (faith is not a wage that is earned, but a gift that is given, vv. 4–5) and the nature of faith (a trust in the promise of God that is misunderstood when it is redefined as a response of obedience to the Law, vv. 9–22). In the process Paul integrates the teaching of this verse with the wider Abraham story and indeed the pattern of God's dealings with his people (hence the comparison with Ps. 32:1–2).

An application of this text (Gen. 15:6) to his readers' situation is manifestly justified, but why does Paul engage in such a sustained exposition? What might Paul's sense of the necessity for such an exposition say about the clarity of the text itself? It is not at all difficult to establish that the example of Abraham played an important role in the controversial exchanges between Jesus and the Jewish establishment.[19] There is also abundant evidence that Genesis 15:6 itself was a key text in the continuing debates with Judaism in the first century. It was, after all, an important text for the self-understanding of Paul's Jewish contemporaries.[20] It was, in that sense, well known and its meaning well established. However, Paul was seeking to correct what he understood to be a misreading of this text. Jewish scholars of his day tended to read these words in the light of Genesis 22 and Abraham's obedience on Mount Moriah. This allowed them to understand faith as itself meritorious, itself a righteous act well-pleasing to God.[21] Paul takes the time to show that this is not what the text means. The immediate context of

---

[19] See e.g. John 8:31–59.
[20] O'Brien 2004: 376, 378.
[21] See O'Brien 2004: 378–380 and the Jewish texts he cites.

Genesis 15:6 should not be violated by a headlong rush to connect it to Genesis 22. Abraham's righteousness before God was established *before* he had either been circumcised (Gen. 17) or taken Isaac to the mountain (Gen. 22).

The intricacies of the argument Paul makes have been discussed at length by others.[22] Yet from the prima facie realities of Romans 4 we may confirm that, just as we found in the case of Jesus himself, Paul's general confidence in the accessible meaning of the Old Testament does not preclude the possibility of difficulty with certain texts or indeed the reality of misunderstanding. Yet the way he responds to this reality demonstrates that these problems are not seen by him as insurmountable. The text is not surrounded by impenetrable darkness. Rather, further careful engagement with the text itself, attention to its context, and responsible integration of that text into what we might call a broader biblical theology (i.e. responsible in that it does not let one text overturn the meaning of another) proceeds with the expectation that misreadings can be shown to be just that and the real import of such texts can be known.

In two places in particular Paul speaks directly about the usefulness of the Old Testament Scriptures for Christians living in the new situation brought about by Christ. The first of these is further on in Paul's letter to the Romans. In chapter 15, having appealed to his readers to take seriously their responsibility to their 'neighbour (*plēsios*)', Paul cites the example of Jesus' own lack of self-interest. Where we might then have expected him to illustrate this selflessness with an incident from Jesus' life, he instead quotes Psalm 69:9, 'the reproaches of those who reproached you fell on me', and he quotes it without comment (Rom. 15:1–3). Once again it is evident that for Paul an appeal to the Old Testament settles the matter: Jesus' fulfilment of these words in his own willingness to endure the perverse hostility of human beings towards God is more than sufficient ground to call on the strong at Rome to 'bear with the failings of the weak' (v. 1). Paul then continues,

> For whatever was written in former days was written for our instruction, that through endurance and through the encouragement of the Scriptures we might have hope. May the God of endurance and encouragement grant you to live in such harmony with one another, in accord with Christ Jesus, that

---

[22] O'Brien 2004: 376–390; Carson 2004: 55–68.

together you may with one voice glorify the God and Father of our Lord Jesus Christ.

(Rom. 15:4–6)

We should not miss the parallel between endurance and the encouragement of the Scriptures in verse 4 and the God of endurance and encouragement in verse 5. The usefulness of the Scriptures is not abstracted in any way from the activity of God; yet at the same time Paul can speak unambiguously of 'the encouragement of the Scriptures'.[23] It is hard to see how Paul could have spoken in this way if he did not assume the basic accessibility of Scripture's meaning to those who read it with faith in Christ. There is a real encouragement to be gained from reading the Scriptures. Hope is fed by that encouragement and by the endurance of those who read.

The second passage is found in Paul's second letter to Timothy, a passage we have touched upon previously.[24] 'All Scripture is breathed out by God and profitable for teaching, for reproof, for correction, and for training in righteousness, that the man of God may be competent, equipped for every good work' (2 Tim. 3:16–17).

Here again we should notice that the usefulness of Scripture cannot be separated from the activity of God: all Scripture is both 'God-breathed (*theopneustos*)' and 'profitable (*ōphelimos*)'.[25] Paul's encouragement to Timothy to continue in the things he has learned, to remain in close contact with those sacred writings that 'are able to make you wise for salvation through faith in Jesus Christ' (v. 15), is a particular application of this general principle. So too is the instruction in his first letter that Timothy should devote himself to '[public] reading' (1 Tim. 4:13). Yet what sense would any of this make without a general assumption that Timothy, and indeed any believer, can understand these texts as they stand?[26] Certainly, Paul encourages his young apprentice to exercise care, to rightly handle (*orthotomeō*) 'the word of truth' (2 Tim. 2:15). It is indeed a serious responsibility that

[23] Schreiner 1998: 749.

[24] I do not propose any defence of Pauline authorship of the Pastorals. The burden of proof remains on those who would dismiss the express attribution of 1 Tim. 1:1; 2 Tim 1:1; and Tit. 1:1. For helpful discussion see Guthrie 1962; Prior 1989: 13–59; Duff 1998; Ellis 1999: 322–324.

[25] 'Only its divine origin secures and explains its human profit' (Stott 1973: 102). 'The writer declares that the Scriptures are inspired, as a datum with which his readers would agree, and uses this as a basis for the point that he wants to stress: whatever is divinely inspired is therefore useful' (Marshall 1999: 795).

[26] For the argument about whether *ho tou theou anthrōpos* refers to all believers or more specifically those engaged in leadership roles see Marshall 1999: 796.

Timothy has been given. Just as clearly, this careful, sober handling of the word of truth that Paul is advocating is contrasted with the reality of false teaching: enticing but self-serving and completely at odds with the faith as Timothy has learned it. Yet Paul would have none of this undermine Timothy's conviction that a faithful reading of the Scriptures equips the believer 'for every good work'. It is not as if any fundamental ambiguity or obscurity of the Old Testament has produced such a challenging context for ministry in the last days. It is rather the result of a refusal to endure sound teaching (4:3).

Much of this apostolic perspective could just as easily have been established from the epistles of Peter. He too appeals to the Old Testament without elaboration as the reason for accepting what he has been saying (e.g. 1 Pet. 1:22–25; 3:8–12). He too is confident that Scripture provides a solid warrant for the life of faith, describing 'the prophetic word' as 'a lamp shining in a dark place' (2 Pet. 1:19). He too acknowledges the reality of false teaching, the origin of which he traces to a 'twisting (*strebloō*)' of the Scriptures by 'the ignorant and unstable' (2 Pet. 3:15–16). Paul's confidence is not simply the product of his rabbinic training or a facet of his personality. It is something he shared with the other apostolic writers as well. In short, the extensive use of quotations from and allusions to the Old Testament in the writings of the apostles, as in the ministry of Jesus himself, is built upon an assumption that those quotations will be understood and those allusions identified.

There is more to be said from the Gospels and from the literary legacy of the apostles of Jesus Christ. In particular, there are still three alleged counter-examples to which we will return in a moment. However, given the relationship between the person, work and words of Jesus on the one hand and the prophetic writings of the Old Testament on the other, we may well ask whether the Old Testament can be spoken of as in any sense clear prior to the coming of Jesus. Put another way, is this attitude of Jesus and the apostles reflected in the Old Testament texts themselves?

# The Old Testament and the clarity of Scripture: The classic texts

Traditional accounts of the clarity of Scripture, from Whitaker's detailed response to attacks on the doctrine in the sixteenth century and Turretin's defence of it in the seventeenth, back further to those more incidental comments on clarity and obscurity in the writings of the early church Fathers, have all regularly drawn attention to four main lines of evidence in the Old Testament.

## Moses and the accessible Book of the Law

As Moses concludes his farewell to the Israelites in Deuteronomy, calling for them to choose obedience and blessing rather than rebellion and curse, he speaks of the important role that the 'Book of the Law (*sēper hattôrâ*)' is to play in their future as the nation chosen by God.

> For the LORD will again take delight in prospering you, as he took delight in your fathers, when you obey the voice of the LORD your God, to keep his commandments and his statutes that are written in this Book of the Law, when you turn to the LORD your God with all your heart and with all your soul. For this commandment that I command you today is not too hard for you, neither is it far off. It is not in heaven, that you should say, 'Who will ascend to heaven for us and bring it to us, that we may hear it and do it?' Neither is it beyond the sea, that you should say, 'Who will go over the sea for us and bring it to us, that we may hear it and do it?' But the word is very near you. It is in your mouth and in your heart, so that you can do it.
>
> (Deut. 30:9b–14)

Moses is addressing the nation, not just some educated elite within it. His concern throughout this sermon is to encourage the entire nation to embrace a commitment to live under this law. Parents are to teach it diligently to their children. Indeed, the law is to be integrated into the very fabric of everyday life (Deut. 6:7). In the next chapter, Moses will instruct the entire nation to gather once every seven years to hear the Book of the Law read publicly: 'Assemble the people,' he says, 'men, women, and little ones, and the sojourner within your towns, that they may hear and learn to fear the LORD your God, and be careful to do all the words of this law . . .' (Deut. 31:12). Moses expects a very wide range of people to benefit from hearing the law read to them, and in Deuteronomy 30 this expectation is anchored in a conviction that the commandment was 'not too hard (*lo' niplē't*)' and 'not far off (*lo' rĕḥōqâ*)'.[27] As one contemporary

---

[27] This is an image the New Testament will later pick up and apply to the 'word of faith' (Rom. 10:6–9).

Jewish commentator puts it, 'God's instruction is not unintelligible or esoteric (v. 11), nor is it inaccessible and unknown (vv. 12–14). It has already been imparted to Israel by Moses, permitting Israel to learn it, meditate on it, and carry it out.'[28] In choosing obedience and life the Israelites were not wandering into an uncertain future with little sure knowledge of the demands of God. Nor were they committing themselves to a set of commands they were physically incapable of keeping (whether they were morally capable of keeping them is another matter). God had made his mind known, not concealed his will from them; and he had made it known in a way that could be grasped. When in the mid-sixteenth century Roberto Bellarmino insisted that Deuteronomy 30 referred only to fulfilling the commandments, not to understanding them, William Whitaker replied, 'one cannot possibly do that which he does not understand'.[29]

In such a context the words of the Lord to Joshua after the death of Moses are not something novel or extraordinary. As the new leader of God's people he is to exemplify the confidence and obedience that come from a serious engagement with the law God has given:

> This Book of the Law shall not depart from your mouth, but you shall meditate on it day and night, so that you may be careful to do according to all that is written in it. For then you will make your way prosperous, and then you will have good success. Have I not commanded you? Be strong and courageous. Do not be frightened, and do not be dismayed, for the LORD your God is with you wherever you go.
>
> (Josh. 1:8–9)

Joshua's leadership of the people of Israel was very different in certain respects from that of his predecessor. He would not be the mouthpiece of God in quite the same way as Moses was over those forty years in the wilderness. Rather, Joshua is, just like the people he leads, bound to the words Moses has written at the direction of God. In the new situation following Moses' death, the Lord will rule his

---

[28] Tigay 1996: 286. '[T]he commandment is not inaccessible, nor does it require some specially qualified person to make it clear' (Christensen 2002: 742–743). '[I]t is nothing abstruse or incomprehensible, like the complicated structure of the human frame (Ps. 139:6; cf. 131:1; Pr. 30:18); it is nothing recondite, which can be reached only by laborious and protracted study' (Driver 1895: 331). Cf. Craigie 1976: 364–365.

[29] Whitaker 1588: 382.

people through this man *and* through the 'Book of the Law'. But for that to work this book must not only be clear and accessible. It must be read as well. It can be read, these verses suggest, in the expectation that it will be understood. For just as the Book of the Law must not depart from Joshua's mouth, so too he has the promise of God: 'I will not leave you or forsake you' (Josh. 1:5). Joshua will never read the words of God's law in God's absence.

## The light of the Psalms

Perhaps the most commonly quoted text in connection with the clarity of Scripture is Psalm 119:105:

> Your word is a lamp to my feet
> and a light to my path.

On occasion another verse (v. 130) from the same psalm is put alongside it:

> The unfolding of your words gives light;
> it imparts understanding to the simple.

The import of the metaphor seems straightforward enough. God's word enables the faithful pilgrim to see clearly. It dispels the darkness so characteristic of life on this side of the fall and so keeps the faithful one from stumbling. It gives guidance. It sets direction.

Once again, as the wider context of the psalter reminds us, this light of God's word can never be opposed to or separated from the light of God's person. So in Psalm 36 there is a meditation on the joy of a relationship with the living God in just these terms:

> How precious is your steadfast love, O God!
> The children of mankind take refuge in the shadow of
> your wings.
> They feast on the abundance of your house,
> and you give them drink from the river of your delights.
> For with you is the fountain of life;
> in your light do we see light (*bĕʾôrĕkā nirʾeh ʾôr*).
>
> (Ps. 36:7–9)

The light of God's word is not something abstract or impersonal. It is God's own light that comes to the reader in the word of God. God himself is at work in and through his word to dispel darkness, to prevent stumbling, to give guidance and to set direction (Ps. 43:3). This point has been made emphatically in our own time by John Webster:

> Holy Scripture is clear because God is light and therefore the one in whose light we see light. God is himself light . . . It scarcely needs to be said that this divine radiance by which all things are illuminated is no impersonal state of affairs. It is the presence of God the revealer. To speak of the light of God is to speak of a personal action and mode of relation, the free self-disposing of the Lord of all things existing towards and with his creatures. God's radiance is not a simple metaphysical formula but a matter of fellowship between himself and those whom he enlightens by manifesting himself, showing them the light of his presence.[30]

This much is certainly true and a necessary response to caricatures of Scripture's clarity explained in terms of a so-called 'static' and 'impersonal' attribute of the text. Yet at the same time this consideration must not obscure the verbal or linguistic edge in verses such as Psalm 119:105. Precisely because God is light, the words he has spoken through and by means of the creaturely activity of his servants are 'a lamp to my feet and a light to my path'.[31]

This appeal to Psalm 119:105 and similar verses was also dismissed by classical opponents of the doctrine of the clarity of Scripture. Bellarmino argued that it was simply a reference to the way Scripture enlightens the believer when it is understood (i.e. a description of its impact on the reader after certain implicit conditions are met), not an indication of its own clarity (i.e. a description of the text). After all, this illumination is precisely what is on view in verse 130 and in other places such as Psalm 19:9. Whitaker, in his response, refused to play one of these aspects off against the other. 'Then the scripture is called *lucid*, he argued, 'not only because it hath light in itself, but because it illuminates us, dispels the darkness of our minds, and brings us new light, which is what no lamps can do.' Nevertheless, even when such illumination manifestly does not take place, he insisted that the

---

[30] Webster 2005: 40. See also similar reflections with a closer and more explicit tie to the teaching of this psalm in Brown 2002: 198.

[31] Note the similarities between Pss. 119:105 and 18:28. See too Ps. 27:1.

description of Scripture as a lamp and a light remains valid: 'A lamp hath light in itself, whether men look upon that light or not: so also the scripture is clear and perspicuous, whether men be illuminated by it, or receive from it no light whatever.'[32] There might, after all, be other reasons why individuals were not illuminated by a luminous text. They may have wilfully turned their eyes away from the light.[33]

## Understanding against the odds

A third line of evidence in the Old Testament, to which classic defences of the doctrine often appeal, are those examples of a biblical text being understood, even in circumstances remote from when it was first written. Two of these will suffice for our purposes. The first surrounds the recovery of the Book of the Law by Josiah in 2 Kings 22.[34] In the long, dark years of Manasseh's reign and the brief interlude in which his son Amon was on the throne, both king and people had abandoned faith and morality. Few, if any, remembered any other way of life. Yet the new young king turned it all around. Whilst still a minor, Josiah 'began to seek the God of David his father' (2 Chr. 34:3). Upon reaching maturity he began a six-year purge, removing all the apparatus of idolatry from the land. He next turned his attention to the temple, instructing money to be collected and repairs to begin. It was during those repairs that Hilkiah the priest found 'the Book of the Law'. He gave it to the king's secretary, Shaphan, and he brought it and read it before the king. And then we are told, 'When the king heard the words of the Book of the Law, he tore his clothes' (v. 11). Josiah immediately understood that he and the nation stood under the judgment of God, the curses of which Moses had spoken in the book of Deuteronomy.[35] He needed no scholars to make this plain to him. As he tells the working group he gathers soon after hearing these words read, 'great is the wrath of the LORD that is kindled against us, because our fathers have not obeyed the words of this book, to do according to all that is written concerning us' (v. 13). Whatever may have changed since the time of Moses (and much had changed in political and social terms at least), this much was clear: the nation of Judah had broken its covenant with the living God. In

---

[32] Whitaker 1588: 384.

[33] Whitaker 1588: 383.

[34] Cf. 2 Chr. 34.

[35] For the argument that the book found by Hilkiah was the book of Deuteronomy see the reference in 2 Chr. 34:14 to 'the Book of the Law of the lord given through Moses' (*sēper tôrat-yhwh bĕyad-mōšeh*). See also Robinson 1951.

such a context, the mission to Huldah the prophetess was not an attempt to seek an explanation of the text, but rather to ask when the expected judgment would fall (vv. 14–20).

The second example is Ezra's reading of the Book of the Law to the returned exiles after Jerusalem's wall had been rebuilt:

> And they told Ezra the scribe to bring the Book of the Law of Moses that the LORD had commanded Israel. So Ezra the priest brought the Law before the assembly, both men and women and all who could understand what they heard, on the first day of the seventh month. And he read from it facing the square before the Water Gate from early morning until midday, in the presence of the men and the women and those who could understand . . . Also Jeshua, Bani, Sherebiah, Jamin, Akkub, Shabbethai, Hodiah, Maaseiah, Kelita, Azariah, Jozabad, Hanan, Pelaiah, the Levites, helped the people to understand the Law, while the people remained in their places. They read from the book, from the Law of God, clearly, and they gave the meaning, so that the people understood the reading.
>
> (Neh. 8:1b–3, 7–8)

The context seems to suggest that the people did not know this text well. It is uncertain what access these returnees might have had to it during the years of exile in Babylon. Yet it is read publicly, before 'all who could understand what they heard'. In this case the Levites have a special role in facilitating that understanding. Later Jewish tradition saw this activity as the origin of the scriptural Targum.[36] More recent studies have not been so sure. The Levites may have translated from Hebrew to Aramaic, ensured exact pronunciation, intonation and phrasing, or have gone beyond all these to instruct the people on the basis of what had been read to them.[37] That help was provided and that it resulted in all the people understanding what was read is certain. What form that help took remains a matter of debate.

Traditional appeals to this text usually emphasize the result: 'the people understood the reading' (v. 8). Here is evidence that whatever barriers may have existed between the returned exiles and this text from centuries before, they were not insuperable. God ensured

[36] Blenkinsopp 1988: 288.
[37] Allison 1995: 211; Williamson 1985: 290; Blenkinsopp 1988: 288; Davies 1999: 113; Duggan 2001: 115.

that his word was understood. Yet many have also turned to this passage as an illustration of the way the clarity of the text does not do away with the need for exposition. Heinrich Bullinger, writing in 1549, pointed to the way the Levites not only read the Book of the Law but also expounded it as support for his insistence that the word of God 'refuses not a godly or holy exposition'.[38] The text of Scripture is not shrouded in mystery or difficulty, but neither is the apprehension of meaning always immediate or intuitive, as it appears to have been in the case of Josiah. The clarity of Scripture does not render all exposition unnecessary. Yet for Luther, Bullinger, Whitaker and the classical exponents of this doctrine, the reverse is also true: a real place for exposition does not undermine all affirmation of the clarity of Scripture. In fact, exposition can proceed only on the assumption that the text is clear, that its meaning can be grasped and its significance for the lives of the hearers can be appreciated, since all expositions are to be tested by reference to the text itself.

## The guarantee of God: His words will never fail

A fourth and final line of evidence gathers those statements throughout the Old Testament (and the New Testament as well) where God speaks of the effectiveness of his word. The most well known of these is undoubtedly Isaiah 55:10–11:

> For as the rain and the snow come down from heaven
>     and do not return there but water the earth,
> making it bring forth and sprout,
>     giving seed to the sower and bread to the eater,
> so shall my word be that goes out from my mouth;
>     it shall not return to me empty,
> but it shall accomplish that which I purpose,
>     and shall succeed in the thing for which I sent it.

God does not speak aimlessly. His words are not confused, tangled or ineffectual. When God speaks, his purpose is certainly fulfilled. As Westermann put it, 'God's word is a word that does things. When God speaks, something comes about.'[39] Just as there was no cosmic

---

[38] Bullinger 1549: 72.
[39] Westermann 1966: 289. Note he wrote this before speech-act theory came into vogue!

resistance when the words 'Let there be light' were uttered at the beginning of time, nothing thwarts or even retards his intention whenever he speaks. With the word of God there is certainty and that certainty entails clarity. Yet there is an important context to this powerful reassurance about the efficacy of God's word. In the immediately preceding verses, God calls on his people to repent (vv. 6–7). This call is then grounded in the greatness of God's purpose:

> My thoughts are not your thoughts,
>> neither are your ways my ways, declares the LORD.
> For as the heavens are higher than the earth,
>> so are my ways higher than your ways
>> and my thoughts than your thoughts.
>
> (vv. 8–9)

The efficacy of God's word, the certain accomplishment of the purpose for which God sent it, does not mean that by means of it God is somehow captured or comprehended. It still stands over against the rebellion of his people, warning them of the need to repent. The word God speaks is his personal determination, not something that can ever be used to manipulate him.[40]

This determination of God is directly related to the written word as well. After the defeat of the Amalekites at Rephidim, Moses is told, 'Write this as a memorial in a book and recite it in the ears of Joshua, that I will utterly blot out the memory of Amalek from under heaven' (Exod. 17:14). Inscribing the intention of God does not make it any more certain. Yet it does act as a reminder to Joshua and the people of the settled purpose of God. The written word will last and it will be vindicated. Similarly, Jeremiah is told to record the promise of God to his people: 'Write in a book all the words that I have spoken to you. For behold, days are coming, declares the LORD, when I will restore the fortunes of my people, Israel and Judah, says the LORD, and I will bring them back to the land that I gave to their fathers, and they shall take possession of it' (Jer. 30:2–3). God's word will be fulfilled. It is sure and certain. Yet a natural corollary of this is that it must be clear. What comfort would a clouded or confused word be to Joshua or to exiles in Babylon?

The classic appeal to certain Old Testament texts to establish Scripture's own testimony to its clarity is sometimes caricatured. Yet

---

[40] 'The word of God is the unfailing agent of the will of God' (Motyer 1993: 458).

a careful contextual examination of each of those texts confirms the appropriateness of that appeal. The expectation of Jesus and the apostles that the Old Testament can be understood, that in general terms its meaning is clear even if there are some passages more diffi-cult to understand than others, is reflected in the Old Testament itself. Much still awaits the coming of the Christ. There is a restless-ness in the Old Testament that keeps driving the reader forward, looking for the seed of the woman (Gen. 3:15), wondering about the eternal king from David's line (2 Sam. 7:12–13), asking who it is that will bear 'the iniquity of us all' (Isa. 53:6). Yet on its own terms the Old Testament makes sense and later parts are able to quote and allude to earlier parts with confidence that those who hear or read will understand.

# Clarity hard won: Scripture acknowledges its own difficulty

Often when the Bible's testimony concerning its own clarity is consid-ered, a number of texts are cited as counter-evidence. Those who present them, as did Bellarmino in the sixteenth century and many others since, argue that they show the difficulty of understanding Scripture. In one sense, as his opponents made clear, Bellarmino's knockout punch was merely a swing in the air. No serious defence of *claritas scripturae* has ever denied that there are difficulties in Scripture. Clarity is not the same as uniform simplicity or even trans-parency. In some cases the clear meaning of a passage is hard won, often because of factors that have little to do with a problem in the text itself. Nevertheless, such opponents have often pressed their case, insisting that the Bible in general requires an externally validated, authoritative interpretation. For this reason it is worth considering the three main cases that are usually cited.

## *The parables: Teaching to prevent understanding?*

Jesus is rightly understood as the master teacher. He knew how to communicate effectively with the highly educated scribe or lawyer as well as with the fisherman, soldier or harlot. His parables are a won-derful case in point, taking everyday images and using them to make known the truth about God and his purposes. The parable of the sower acts as a kind of gateway into the parables in Mark's Gospel. It is the parable that provides a key to all parables. Yet in connection with this parable, Jesus quoted a passage from the prophet Isaiah which demonstrates that the practice of teaching in this way had at least a double purpose.[41]

> And when he was alone, those around him with the twelve asked him about the parables. And he said to them, 'To you has been given the secret of the kingdom of God, but for those outside everything is in parables, so that "they may indeed see but not perceive, and may indeed hear but not understand, lest they should turn and be forgiven".'
>
> (Mark 4:10–12)

The quotation is from Isaiah 6 and speaks of the judgment of God on the apostate kingdom of Judah. The prophet Isaiah is sent to the people of the southern kingdom in the knowledge that his words will make no difference; if anything, they will only harden these people in their resolve to rebel against the rightful rule of God: 'Make the heart of this people dull', says the Lord to Isaiah, 'and their ears heavy, and blind their eyes' (Isa. 6:10). In this way his words of warning will themselves stand as an indictment on the spiritual deadness of his audience. Instead of drawing near to God, the people are moving further and further away. The prophet not only speaks of judgment; his speaking is itself part of the judgment.

These are the words Jesus applies to what he does when he preaches in parables. In what has been termed one of the most controversial passages in Mark's Gospel, he differentiates between those who have sought him out and 'those outside (*tois exō*)', going on to suggest that the purpose of the parables (*hina*) is to prevent this second group from understanding.[42] In other words, whatever we might say about their productive illustrative function in other contexts, the parables also operate as instruments of judgment.[43] The secret of the kingdom has been made known (it is no longer a secret), but only for some. The same preaching that fosters understanding in his disciples (although,

---

[41] Robert Stein, for one, finds three purposes in the parables: (1) to conceal Jesus' teaching from those outside (particularly those who were seeking a way to accuse him); (2) to reveal and illustrate his message to both his followers and outsiders; (3) to disarm his listeners (Stein 1981: 33–35).

[42] Guelich 1989: 212.

[43] In some circles the suggestion that the parables might be intended to prevent insight has faced powerful opposition as being theologically objectionable. T. W. Manson described the suggestion that the parables are intended to prevent insight as 'absurd' (Manson 1931: 76); Vincent Taylor rejected it as 'intolerable' (Taylor 1952: 257).

as the following verses show, even their understanding is faltering and incomplete) closes out those who will not follow him.[44] Understanding is not finally separable from faith.

Here, critics of the doctrine of scriptural clarity argue, is a repudiation of the accessibility of at least the New Testament from the mouth of Jesus himself. What is more, the use of Isaiah 6 highlights a similar phenomenon at work from time to time in the Old Testament. What sense does it make to speak of scriptural clarity in the light of these words from Jesus?[45] In the seventeenth century, the Socinians raised this question in their rejection of the doctrine.[46] Yet the issue in Mark 4 is not one of intentional ambiguity or a deliberate lack of clarity, but the condition of those who hear. That is, after all, the leading feature of the parable Jesus has just told them, the parable of the sower or the soils. There is nothing wrong with the seed sown, but not all soil is the same. And not all who hear the parables are the same either. The parables are intricately interwoven with Jesus' person and his mission. Those who refuse to come in, who remain on the outside, have removed themselves from the proper context for understanding the parables. Those who have come to Jesus hear, in this case, not just the parable but its explanation. Indeed to them he 'explained everything' (v. 34).

The Christian doctrine of the clarity of Scripture takes seriously not only the benevolence and power of the God whose word this is, and not only the text itself (after all, it is and remains the clarity *of Scripture*), but also the condition of those who read. It is no companion to a naive universalism. The clarity of Scripture does not guarantee that all who read will truly grasp its meaning. The light of the Scriptures shines in the midst of darkness. But in the perversity of our sin, human beings, apart from the regenerative work of God's Spirit, love darkness rather than light (John 3:19).[47]

---

[44] Vaughan Roberts of St Ebbe's Church, Oxford, explained this phenomenon very simply: The parables are like automatic doors in a shopping centre. If you move towards them, they open up; if you move away, they slide shut. As you come to Jesus, the parables open up; if you refuse to come, you are shut out from their meaning.

[45] Robert Fowler suggests that Jesus' words are an example of verbal irony, but I find his argument unconvincing (Fowler 1991: 168–170).

[46] See the discussion of the seventeenth-century debate between Abraham Calov and the Socinians in Preus 1955: 162–163.

[47] A similar line of argument is developed by Paul when talking about the importance of faith in Christ for properly understanding Moses (the Old Covenant) (2 Cor. 3:12 – 4:6).

## *The Ethiopian: Seeking understanding in a clear text?*

The second case is perhaps the most obvious one. The great persecution that followed the martyrdom of Stephen scattered many of the followers of Jesus, including Philip, one of the seven so-called 'deacons' of Acts 6. Instructed by an angel of the Lord, Philip takes the road from Jerusalem to Gaza and is brought into contact with an Ethiopian eunuch. This court official is reading Isaiah 53 as he travels along, so, overhearing him, Philip asks, 'Do you understand (*ginōskeis*) what you are reading?' The eunuch's response has attracted the attention of many in the debates about the clarity of Scripture: 'How can I, unless someone guides (*hodēgēsei*) me?' (Acts 8:30–31). Here, it seems, is a confession that an authoritative interpreter is indispensable. The eunuch's problem is the problem of every reader. Here is a pious man, reading the Scriptures seeking understanding, but without Philip's assistance he is lost in a sea of possibilities. That is why he asks Philip, 'About whom, I ask you, does the prophet say this, about himself or about someone else?' (v. 34).

Philip undoubtedly provides a model for the way in which others assist in the process of understanding. Faithful teachers within the Christian community are resources provided by God to enable men and women to understand his word (Eph. 4:11; 2 Tim. 2:1–2), and in this narrative the point is made again and again that Philip has been provided by God in order to help the Ethiopian official. The initiative lies neither with Philip nor with the Ethiopian.[48] Here is an indication of that legitimate, God-given, corporate dimension to a Christian reading of the Bible that need not be seen to compromise the accessibility or intelligibility of the text. Indeed, it is possible to misuse the doctrine of the clarity of Scripture in the interests of an individualism that owes more to seventeenth- and eighteenth-century philosophy than any biblical concept of Christian freedom. This sometimes happens when the clarity of Scripture is defined in terms of 'the right of private judgment'.[49] Even the Reformers, insistent as they were that the Bible should not be shackled to any ecclesiastical authority, made frequent use of the writings of others (the church Fathers and medieval exegetes as well) as they sought to explain the Bible's teaching. Hearing God's word is something done in the midst of the communion of saints.

[48] 'The conversion of the Ethiopian was planned not by Philip but by God . . .' (Barrett 1994: I, 422).
[49] This is the critical weakness in Charles Hodge's defence of the doctrine. His defence is constructed in terms of 'the right of private judgment', which he then associates with civil liberty (Hodge 1871: 186).

Yet, as many have also pointed out, it is somewhat of an exaggeration to suggest that the eunuch was 'lost in a sea of possibilities'. Is it actually the case that he was striving to understand an obscure text?[50] His real problem seems rather to be one of reference. Given all that this passage says about this extraordinary figure, the Servant of the Lord who bears the iniquity of us all and pours out his soul to death, who bears this humiliation in silence despite monumental injustice, the passage does not identify him by name. The Ethiopian is concerned to know whom this text is speaking about). What he lacks is a knowledge of how these words have been fulfilled in the life and ministry of Jesus, something Philip has been commissioned to provide.

In the unfolding narrative of the book of Acts, the Ethiopian is one more example of those who need to be brought from the fringes of the Old Covenant directly into the heart of the New Covenant. He had, at best, an outsider's view of the promises of God.[51] Yet, as we have seen, even for the insider under the Old Covenant the gospel is necessary as the proper interpretative framework for understanding those promises. Perhaps it is no accident that Luke describes the assistance Philip provided for the eunuch in terms reminiscent of Jesus' ministry to the disciples on the Emmaus road:

> Then Philip opened his mouth, and beginning with this Scripture he told him the good news about Jesus.
>
> (Acts 8:35)

> And beginning with Moses and all the Prophets, he [Jesus] interpreted to them in all the Scriptures the things concerning himself.
>
> (Luke 24:27)

## Paul: A theologian on steroids?

The third classic case often presented against any suggestion that the Bible affirms its own clarity is the comment made by the apostle Peter about some of the things in Paul's letters. It comes amidst Peter's

---

[50] His is 'a confession of personal inadequacy to be remedied by someone with [a] better grasp of Scripture's content, not an assertion of the essential obscurity of the subject matter' (Carson 1997: 98).

[51] Barrett points out that he was not a Jew by birth and neither could he become a proselyte, since he was a eunuch. 'He was thus a stage more remote from the people of God than Cornelius, whose story follows in ch. 10 . . .' (Barrett 1994: 420).

encouragement to persevere in hope and holiness while 'waiting for and hastening the coming of the day of God' (2 Pet. 3:12). There is, after all, a reason to be urgent as you wait for the promised new heavens and new earth 'in which righteousness dwells' (v. 13).

> Therefore, beloved, since you are waiting for these, be diligent to be found by him without spot or blemish, and at peace. And count the patience of our Lord as salvation, just as our beloved brother Paul also wrote to you according to the wisdom given him, as he does in all his letters when he speaks in them of these matters. There are some things in them that are hard to understand, which the ignorant and unstable twist to their own destruction, as they do the other Scriptures.
>
> (2 Pet. 3:14–16)

These words are tremendously significant for a number of reasons. Here is an apostolic recognition that Paul's letters are to be considered alongside 'the other scriptures (*tas loipas graphas*)'. Contrary to some suggestions, this recognition did not take centuries to develop. Even in the first century Paul's letters were acknowledged to have this special status.[52] Also important is the reference to 'as he does in all his letters (*hōs kai en pasais epistolais*)'. It appears that a 'nascent Pauline collection' was known to both Peter and his audience.[53]

Yet for our purposes the most significant comment is Peter's observation that in Paul's letters there are 'some things hard to understand (*dysnoēta tina*)'. The term he uses is rare,[54] but there is little doubt

---

[52] So too 1 Clement, usually dated around AD 95 or 96, refers to Paul's first letter to the Corinthians as written under the influence of the Spirit: '1. Take up the epistle of the blessed Paul the Apostle. 2. What did he first write to you at the beginning of his preaching? 3. With true inspiration (*ep' alēthias pneumatikōs*) he charged you concerning himself and Cephas and Apollos, because even then you had made yourself partisans' (1 Clement xlvii.3).

[53] Kraftchick 2002: 172. In this regard Paul's encouragement for the Christians at Colossae and Laodicea to exchange the letters he has sent them (Col. 4:16) is most probably the earliest stage in the process of collection.

[54] Two occurrences in the classical literature are usually identified. In Lucian's account of Alexander the false prophet, he records how Alexander provided eight responses to a question put to him, each of which 'had no connection with earth or heaven, but were silly and nonsensical (*anoētous de kai dysnoētous*) . . .' (Lucian, *Alexander* 54; Loeb trans.). Diogenes Laertius, in his life of the philosopher Heraclitus, reports a letter sent to the philosopher from King Darius, which began, 'You are the author of a treatise *On Nature* which is hard to understand and hard to interpret (*dysnoēton de kai dysexēgēton*) . . .' (Diogenes Laertius, *Vitae philosophorum* ix.13; Loeb trans.).

about what Peter is saying at this point. He may have endorsed Paul's letters in the highest terms, but he is not going to pretend that reading them is always easy. On the one hand, they are not so difficult that they should be put aside. After all, he has just made an appeal to them in support of what he has been saying, which presumably indicates that he understood what Paul was saying at some point. It is not that their meaning *cannot* be discerned, that they are *beyond understanding* (*anoēta*). Rather, he is acknowledging that reading Paul, particularly at certain points, is going to take concentrated attention.[55]

That attention is all the more necessary because some, described here as 'the ignorant and unstable', actually twist the words of Paul. To make such an observation, let alone to warn people against being carried away by the result of such a perverse manipulation of Paul's words, carries with it a number of assumptions. It assumes that what these people do is not restricted to the epistles of Paul: this is also what they do to 'the other Scriptures'. It also assumes that the proper meaning of Paul's words can be identified and contrasted with what these people are suggesting. Furthermore, Peter seems to assume that the recipients of his letter are in a position to make this identification and draw this contrast. How else could they avoid the error?

It has often been noted that it is in this same letter that Peter describes the prophetic word as 'a lamp shining in a dark place'. Peter evidently does not see darkness or obscurity as something characteristic of Scripture as a whole. He does not even think it is characteristic of everything Paul writes, only *some* things.[56] Nevertheless, the presence of Scripture in the world of fallen men and women exposes it to the possibility of abuse and misappropriation. A clear text does not do away with the need for diligence. In those cases where the clarity might be hard won, confidence need not be abandoned – but we need to be alert to the reality of self-interested abuse of God's good gift.

---

[55] In his discussion of this text in the context of a treatment of the doctrine of perspicuity, François Turretin highlighted four contrasts: 'hard to understand' vs. 'unintelligible'; 'some things' vs. 'all things'; 'Paul's manner' vs. 'the things delivered'; and 'the unlearned and unstable' vs. 'believers' (Turretin 1679–85: 146).

[56] Paul himself insisted that at least in writing to the errant Corinthians, 'we are not writing to you anything other than what you read and understand' (2 Cor. 1:13, esv margin).

# Confidence and concentrated attention: The textures of biblical clarity

If biblical authority is to be taken seriously as something arising from the ultimate origin of this text in God's self-expression, then this inspired text must direct our discussion of the contours and content of its own clarity. Our doctrine of the clarity of Scripture must reflect the text we actually have. It must be consistent with both the phenomena and the express statements of the written word of God. All the more so when one of the classic charges against this doctrine is that it is in fact at odds with Scripture's self-testimony.

Our investigation of the teaching of Scripture bearing upon this topic has been necessarily brief. Once again there is much more that could be said. We have hardly touched upon Scripture's manifest concern for intelligibility as demonstrated by the New Testament practice of translating Hebrew and Aramaic terms (e.g. Matt. 1:23; Mark 5:41; 15:34; John 20:16). We will have reason to reflect upon the common eschatological positioning of the text and the twenty-first-century reader in the next chapter, but it is worth noting at this point that this too has implications for our expectation that the text meaningfully intersects with the lives of its distant readers.[57] Nevertheless, through a series of contextualized affirmations (and not simply isolated proof texts) we have been able to see both the coherence and the texture of the biblical picture of scriptural clarity.

Jesus and the apostles approach the Old Testament, the Scripture of their day, with the general assumption that when the words of Scripture are read or heard, they will be understood. Their confidence that an appeal to a passage from the Old Testament is sufficient to settle a dispute, without gloss or exposition, is built upon that assumption. The theological framework we investigated in a previous chapter, the effectiveness of God as a communicator and his benevolent intentions towards his people finds practical expression in this confident use of the biblical text. Furthermore, a brief examination of four commonly cited features of the Old Testament itself confirms that the intelligibility of its own words is assumed even prior to their critical fulfilment in the person, work and words of Jesus Christ. The charge that the Bible itself displays no knowledge of this notion of clarity cannot be sustained in the light of the evidence we have examined.

---

[57] See also Thompson 2000: 373–374.

Nevertheless, this does not suggest a uniform simplicity across the entire Old Testament any more than that, in due course, this assumption will lead to claims for an absolute and unvaried transparency of the emerging New Testament writings. Understanding is not always automatic or simple. There remains room for explanation and application. And even then there are occasions when the clear meaning of a particular text will be hard won. The most important expositions of Scripture's clarity from the early centuries through to the present have all recognized that the clarity of Scripture must not be trivialized or used as an excuse for superficiality or exegetical laziness. God has placed both heights and depths in Scripture, given us passages so simple a child can understand them and others so intriguing they engage the ablest minds over many years.[58]

The clarity of Scripture can be affirmed on the basis of Scripture's own teaching. The biblical text can be approached with confidence by the believer who seeks to know God and his purposes. God has been good to us in giving us the Scripture we have. Here, in this cradle as Luther would put it, you will find the Christ.[59] What is more, God has given us resources to help us as we read: his Spirit who has never abandoned his word, the fuller context of the whole Bible, and a fellowship of readers not only in our own time but stretching back to the time when these words were first written. The struggle between light and darkness remains the context of all our reading of Scripture in the last days. Yet the confidence of the apostle Peter continues to be echoed at the beginning of this third millennium: 'we have something more sure, the prophetic word, to which you will do well to pay attention as to a lamp shining in a dark place, until the day dawns and the morning star rises in your hearts' (2 Pet. 1:19).

---

[58] See classic statements in this regard by Augustine and Gregory the Great. 'The Holy Spirit, therefore, has generously and advantageously planned Holy Scripture in such a way that in the easier passages He relieves our hunger; in the more obscure He drives away our pride. Practically nothing is dug out from those obscure texts which is not discovered to be said very plainly in another place' (Augustine 426: 537, *De doctrina christiana* II.6 (8) [*CCSL*, XXXII, 36 = *NPNF*, 1st Series, II, 537]). 'For indeed, just as the divine discourse exercises the wise by means of mysteries, so it usually revives the simple by means of what lies on the surface. It holds in the open that by which little ones may be nourished [and] keeps hidden that by which those of lofty intellect might stand in wonder. It is, so to speak, a kind of river, if I may so liken it, which is both shallow and deep, in which both the lamb may find a footing and the elephant swim' (Gregory 583–590: 9, *Moralia in Iob*, ad Leander Iv [*CCSL*, CXLIII, 6]).

[59] Luther 1522: 122 (*WA* X-I/1, 15.1–10 = *LW* XXXV, 122).

# Chapter Four

# Engaging the hermeneutical challenge

'Let the reader understand'

The Christian confession of the clarity of Scripture is an aspect of faith in God. Christians approach this text with confidence that its meaning is accessible to the ploughboy as well as the scholar, because the God who is able to make himself known, and is determined to do so, has given them both this text. Without reservation we acknowledge that this book is genuinely the work of those human authors who in various ways produced it. It is always and ever a piece of human communication, using all the structures and conventions of human written discourse. Its origins can properly be traced to particular historical situations or locations. Yet at the same time, without compromise in either direction, these texts come to us as divine discourse, as the word of God. These words are themselves God's self-revelation in the world. In them *he* presents his Son to us. By them *he* gathers his people and brings about his ancient intention. God's self-communication is no more distorted by its expression in human words than his compassion is distorted by its expression in human flesh. To put this another way, the ultimate guarantee that God's word will be heard and understood, that it will achieve the purpose for which it was spoken and written, is the power and goodness of God himself. In this sense, a conviction that Scripture is clear is something believers bring *to* their reading of the Bible.

Yet, as we saw in the last chapter, this is not an alien imposition on the text. It just as powerfully arises *from* the pages of Scripture. In the Gospels, Jesus exhibits precisely this confidence as he quotes from and alludes to passages of the Old Testament. Certainly, there are difficult passages, those that require explanation or reflection ('let the reader understand'). Certainly, a refusal to come to him in faith makes understanding, at least at the level of appreciating the text's significance, fraught with additional difficulty. Certainly, misunderstanding and wilful misuse of biblical texts remains a possibility.

Clarity is not the same thing as simplicity or uniform transparency. Nevertheless, consistently throughout his ministry Jesus appeals to the Old Testament as the arbiter of issues in dispute and as the definitive proof that in himself and in what he has come to do, the long-standing purpose of God is being fulfilled. This confidence in handling the Old Testament features just as prominently in the ministry of his commissioned witnesses, the apostles. What is more, there is evidence that as the apostolic writings themselves begin to be placed alongside the Old Testament, they too are treated as clear in this sense: they are accessible, intelligible and are to be treated responsibly and with care.

The theological framework of this doctrine has been a feature of most classical treatments, though this is rarely acknowledged by its critics. Likewise, while it is true that not all appeals to the teaching of Scripture have paid due attention to the context of each statement, it is not often recognized that there have also been genuine attempts to ensure that nothing is claimed for Scripture that does not arise from its own teaching, and that teaching understood in much more than a superficial way. However, in our contemporary climate, attacks upon this doctrine most often accuse it of hermeneutical naivety. Our knowledge of texts and how they function, as well as deep reflection upon the complex activity that is reading or interpretation, leads us to be suspicious of any straightforward appeal to the 'meaning' of a text – any text, let alone the Bible. Refusal to engage with contemporary hermeneutical concerns appears to be like stubbornly maintaining a geocentric view of the universe, even in the face of the work of Copernicus and Galileo.

Hermeneutics is everywhere. 'Ours', it has been said, 'is a hyper-hermeneutical age.'[1] Since the 1980s or longer it has been the vogue subject in theological curricula the world over. Weighty tomes have been written examining every facet of 'the hermeneutical task' and new treatments keep pouring off the presses. It has generated its own vocabulary, which has become commonplace in theological discussion. Undoubtedly, there have been many gains from our contemporary fascination with this subject. It has highlighted once more the genuine literary qualities of the Bible, which need to be taken seriously. It has called on us to recognize that absolute objectivity in dealing with the text of Scripture is both unattainable and undesirable. Furthermore, it has raised a series of important questions about

---

[1] Gaffin 2004: 191.

the way Scripture functions in the lives of Christian readers generally and in Christian congregations more particularly. A doctrine of common grace might lead us to expect that even outside the community of faith those who have reflected upon the discipline of reading might have useful things to say to us.

Yet the volume and the complexity of much writing in this area also produces a level of anxiety in many. Hermeneutics, one significant writer in the field acknowledges, is often a 'troublesome and intimidating word'.[2] It suggests that reading is neither natural nor simple and that meaning is a somewhat illusive goal, an achievement rather than a gift. How can I hope to understand the Bible unless I have mastered the appropriate hermeneutic? Worse still, hermeneutical theory, especially in its most avant-garde forms, can be explicitly anti-Christian. I have already mentioned the most notorious example of this: Roland Barthes's call for the 'anti-theological activity' of refusing meaning and so refusing 'God and his hypostases – reason, science, law'.[3] In such a context anxiety can quickly transform into repudiation. Do we really need all this talk about hermeneutics?[4]

Decidedly too much writing in this area has in fact served to generate doubt and hesitation rather than confidence, obedience and faith. Indeed, until quite recently, reflection upon hermeneutics from the perspective of faith in the God who speaks was, if not non-existent, certainly rare. Hermeneutical discussion generally has taken place with a determined anthropological orientation. Reading for understanding is a human activity, pure and simple. Almost inevitably agnosticism and doubt have taken over in many quarters as a result. Meaning cannot be sustained by anthropological considerations alone. As one contemporary German philosopher has put it, 'the core of hermeneutics is scepticism and the important form of scepticism today is hermeneutics'.[5] Understanding seems a more remote possibility than ever, and some suspect that this is not entirely an accident. More than a century and a half ago Søren Kierkegaard voiced his concern about this preoccupation with interpretation in a characteristically forthright way:

---

[2] Wood 1981: 9. Aidan Nichols observes that 'Hermeneutics has become a bogey with which to frighten the children' (Nichols 2002: 181).

[3] Barthes 1968: 129.

[4] Odo Marquard voices this complaint in an ironic way at the beginning of his stimulating article on hermeneutics: 'Hermeneutics is the art of getting out of a text what is not in it. Otherwise – since after all we have the text – what would we need it for?' (Marquard 1981: 9).

[5] Marquard 1981: 9.

And now God's Word! 'My house is a house of prayer, but you have changed it into a den of thieves'. And God's Word – what is it according to its purpose, and into what have we changed it? All this interpretation and interpretation and science and new science is produced on the solemn, grave principle that it is for rightly understanding God's Word. Look more closely, and you will see that it is to defend itself against God's Word.[6]

We should acknowledge at once that recent years have seen considerable highly sophisticated engagement with contemporary hermeneutical theory from a determinedly theological perspective.[7] Furthermore, there is no *necessary* connection between an interest in hermeneutics and an evasion of the truth and authority of the Bible. We need to recognize that it is all too possible to treat Scripture in a way that dishonours God rather than honours him. Flippant, superficial and mischievous readings of the text do great harm in the end. Rigorous study and research are not the enemies of faith. At the beginning of this new century, especially in the face of enduring controversy within the churches and the theological fraternity, reflection upon what makes for a faithful and responsible reading of Scripture would seem entirely appropriate.

Nevertheless, a series of questions remain. Can the ancient Christian affirmation of Scripture's clarity survive this new hermeneutical awareness? Must confidence in and enthusiasm for the written word of God be restrained by concern to put in place all the appropriate hermeneutical apparatus? There may well still be a meaning in this text, but how many detours must we take before we find it? Is the best we can hope for the clarity of hermeneutics?[8]

Our task in this chapter is to explore the hermeneutical challenge in the light of the theological and biblical work we have already done. Such an enterprise is not without its own hazards. However, there is

[6] Kierkegaard 1851: 37.

[7] I think particularly of Kevin Vanhoozer's *tour de force*, his 'systematic and trinitarian theology of interpretation that promotes the importance of Christian doctrine for the project of textual understanding' (Vanhoozer 1998: 9). However, the work of Anthony Thiselton in this area has been highly significant (Thiselton 1980, 1992).

[8] 'Objectifying the manner of understanding texts – a central, if not the central contemporary hermeneutical task – can be easily substituted for what a text itself supposedly means. That is, the perspicuity of hermeneutics is often a substitute for the perspicuity of Scripture' (Callahan 2001: 248).

no need to adopt a defensive posture as we approach this exploration. We need not be fearful that those who write on the subject of hermeneutics are all trying to lead us astray. We might, instead, take our cue from Augustine, who in AD 391 wrote about the proper way to approach the writings of others with whom we suspect we might finally disagree: 'I do not think that the character of an author has much to do with the task of sifting truth. It is most honourable to believe that an author was a good man, whose writings were intended to benefit the human race and posterity.'[9]

A little naive? Perhaps. Yet this stance encourages us to seek understanding first rather than to anticipate a hidden but fatal flaw. It allows us to take authors at their word and is itself one preliminary defence against the evils of caricature. After all, we should expect that there is much to learn, even from those who oppose us most vehemently. So we do well to pay careful attention to the various questions and concerns posed by contemporary writers in this field. But first we should take time to consider hermeneutics as a discipline and its relation to Christian theology.

## Theology and the shape of contemporary hermeneutics

At one level the present fascination with hermeneutical questions appears to be a relatively recent development. The 'linguistic turn' in philosophy is usually associated with people like Bertrand Russell and Ludwig Wittgenstein in the middle of the twentieth century.[10] Suddenly everything became a matter of language and how we use it. More specifically, though biblical hermeneutics seemed to have entered a new phase with Schleiermacher's lectures on the subject, it too gained a new prominence in the mid-twentieth century. This was largely due first to the New Hermeneutic associated with Ernst Fuchs and Gerhard Ebeling, later to the embrace of literary criticism more generally as a rich resource for biblical interpretation (e.g. structuralism), and most recently to the impact of post-structuralist and deconstructionist approaches of various kinds.

However, questions concerning how we understand each other, and especially how written communication is understood, have in

[9] Augustine 391: 300 (*De utilitate credendi* V.11 [*NPNF*, 1st Series, III, 352]).

[10] It has been widely observed that the rise of hermeneutics parallels the decline of epistemology (e.g. Vanhoozer 1998: 19).

fact an ancient pedigree. Treatments of textual understanding, with special attention to the text of the Bible, have been a feature of the Christian tradition throughout its history. Augustine's *De doctrina christiana* (*Concerning Christian Doctrine*) is in large part a discussion of interpretative principles. In fact, his discussion of signification (the way words relate to the things they describe) has had a monumental influence on the Western literary tradition. He also cites seven 'rules' for understanding figurative language in Scripture, rules suggested originally by Tichonius the Donatist.[11] Moving forwards, amongst the many treatises devoted to the principles of biblical interpretation in the medieval period, three have proven to be influential (in different ways) in the centuries that followed. Hugh of St Victor's *De scripturis et scriptoribus sacris* (*Concerning Holy Scripture and its Authors*) dates from the twelfth century,[12] while Nicholas of Lyra's *Postilla litteralis super totum bibliam* (*Homilies on the Literal Sense of the Whole Bible*) and John Wyclif's *De veritate sacrae scripturae* (*On the Truth of Holy Scripture*) both date from the fourteenth century.

Further, it is well known that many of the Reformers' writings contain extended comments on how to read and understand the Scriptures 'according to their true meaning'. We can also draw attention to a number of pieces written specifically on the topic, including Luther's *Ein Unterrichtung wie sich die Christen ynn Mose sollen schicken* (*An Instruction on how Christians Should Regard Moses*) and *Ein kleyn Unterricht, was man ynn den Euangelijs suchen und gewartten soll* (*A Brief Instruction on what to Look for and Expect in the Gospels*). In the next generation Matthias Flacius Illyricus would produce what some have considered the real beginnings of the discipline as we know it, his *Clavis scripturae sacrae* (*Key to the Holy Scriptures*). In short, there has been no shortage of specifically Christian reflection on responsible reading of the biblical text over the past two thousand years.

Yet in both biblical hermeneutics and in hermeneutics more generally, a significant shift is discernable from the time of the Enlightenment. Some have argued that this shift was, in some measure at least, a response to the religious wars of the sixteenth and seventeenth cen-

---

[11] Augustine 426: 568–573 (*De doctrina christiana* III.30 (42) – III.37 (56) [*CCSL* XXXII, 102–116 = *NPNF*, 1st Series, II, 568–573]).

[12] Attention is usually drawn to Hugh's *Didascalicon* in this connection. For an argument that *De scripturis* should be treated as his key contribution to the area of biblical study, see Zinn 1997.

turies. Underlying those conflicts, according to this argument, is 'the hermeneutical civil war over the absolute text'.[13] Both sides (whether Catholic or Protestant, Lutheran or Calvinist) claimed to be defending the truth of God expressed in Scripture, and transforming their dogmatic positions into interpretative ones was a means of diffusing the conflict. The groundwork was thus laid for a new stance towards interpretative plurality.[14] Others have explained the shift more in terms of developments in philosophy, particularly those in the field of epistemology, developments associated with Descartes in the first instance and that came to full flower in the writings of Immanuel Kant.[15] There is some truth in both aetiologies, yet the net effect is the same: as Colin Gunton observed, in the post-Kantian era readers have seen themselves more and more as judges of what they read rather than pupils.[16] Understanding has been gradually transformed into overstanding.

Paul Ricœur has given us another productive way of viewing the general trends in hermeneutics over the past two hundred years. He suggests two basic 'movements': (1) from regional hermeneutics to general hermeneutics (deregionalization) – special fields of hermeneutical endeavour (e.g. biblical hermeneutics, legal hermeneutics) became subsumed under more general principles; and (2) from epistemology to ontology (radicalization) – hermeneutics came to be seen not merely as something we do with texts, but rather as a fundamental category of human existence.[17] The classic instance of the first movement is Benjamin Jowett's insistence that we should 'read Scripture like any other book'.[18] The most obvious example of the second is the way Gadamer develops the later work of Wilhelm Dilthey: 'Life interprets itself. Life itself has

[13] Marquard 1981: 21–22. See also his observation 'The dogmatic quality of the claim to truth that is made by the unambiguous interpretation of the absolute text can be deadly' (22).

[14] Whether this was a deliberate strategy in the seventeenth and eighteenth centuries or not, it is one widely in evidence three to four hundred years later.

[15] Gadamer's famous article on hermeneutics made this connection between 'the origins of the modern concept of method and of science (*der Entstehung des modernen Methoden- und Wissenschaftsbegriffs*)' and hermeneutics in the sense it is used today (Gadamer 1974: 1062).

[16] Gunton 1985: 112. He appeals to the words of Kant himself: 'Reason . . . must approach nature in order to be taught by it . . . It must not, however, do so in the character of a pupil who listens to everything that the teacher chooses to say, but of an appointed judge who compels the witnesses to answer questions which he has himself formulated' (Kant 1781: 20).

[17] Ricœur 1981: 43–44.

[18] Jowett 1860: 338.

a hermeneutical structure.'[19] By both routes contemporary hermeneutics distances itself from the classic hermeneutical stance of the
Christian tradition. Not only is the interpreter's role seen as more
constructive and determinative, but classic Christian categories
such as faith, repentance and obedience are deemed inadmissible
– these are inextricable from pre-modern notions of authority and
the fallacy of authorial intention. As one contemporary theological analysis concludes, Christian convictions such as the clarity of
Scripture have been eclipsed by 'the prominence of a strand of
hermeneutical theory which seeks to secularize and deabsolutize
Scripture'.[20]

Of course not all hermeneutics in the modern or postmodern
mode is a-theological. In fact, it is striking how often Christian
vocabulary and theological categories are employed even by those
concerned with hermeneutics in its widest sense. Yet even in those
discussions the real controls are provided by disciplines other than
Christian theology.[21] What we are given so often is 'a general theory
about texts, readers and reading communities developed in relative
isolation from theological considerations'.[22] The Christian reading
of the Bible is then construed by some as just one instance of this
more general phenomenon. Little attention is paid to the *sui generis*
(unique) character of Scripture. Jowett's fundamental premise was,
after all, reductionist – reading the Bible is like reading any other
book, *but not entirely*.[23] The basics of grammar and syntax, of genre
and context, of style and vocabulary are as important in reading the
biblical text as in reading other texts. Yet, unlike other texts, this text
with all its variety and texture finds its ultimate origin in God, it is
read in his presence, and by means of these words God makes himself
known. The otherness of the Bible demands respect too. John
Webster puts it this way:

[19] Gadamer 1984: 226. '[T]he world is full of interpreters; it is impossible to live in
it without repeated, if minimal, acts of interpretation; and a great many people obviously do much more than the minimum. Interpretation is the principal concern of their
waking lives' (Kermode 1979: 49). 'For human beings, to exist is to interpret' (Wallace,
Ross & Davies 2003: 593).

[20] Webster 2005: 34.

[21] One of the most insistent protests at this weakness in contemporary hermeneutical theory, even much that claims to be theological in orientation, has come from
the pen of John Webster, now of the University of Aberdeen. Much that follows in
this section is indebted to his writing on the subject (Webster 1998; 2003a: 68–106;
2005: 34).

[22] Webster 2005: 35. See also Webster 1998: 309–317.

[23] Watson 1994: 2.

Successful description of the hermeneutical situation cannot be accomplished by eliminating all its secondary or contingent characteristics. The self-definitions of the participants, their professed goals, their use of this particular text and not some other, their language of 'listening to the Word of God' and so forth, cannot be eliminated or transcended in describing the situation, for in eliminating them we eliminate the situation, or at least so distort it by theory that it becomes blurred, losing its contours. When the only purchase we have on the situation is thinking about it critically (in terms of its conditions of possibility) rather than descriptively, then it simply recedes from our grasp . . . A Christian depiction of the Christian hermeneutical situation will thus be a depiction determined all along the line by the priority of the Word of God.[24]

The debate about the necessity or otherwise for special hermeneutics, in the face of proposals for a more general hermeneutic, has been raging in certain quarters for some time.[25] However, the recent call for a *theological* construal of biblical hermeneutics appears to be gathering momentum.[26] Such a call is itself multilayered. At its most basic it is a call to reinstate the theological controls of God's nature, character and purpose.[27] Reading this text should not be considered in isolation from God's intention to make himself known and his capacity to realize that intention. Beyond this, the call also includes a recognition that Christian doctrine does in itself constitute a hermeneutic.

[24] Webster 1998: 319, 320. Note an earlier, but similar, protest by Helmut Thielicke: 'Wherever a non-Biblical principle derived from contemporary secular thought is applied to the interpretation of the Bible, the Bible's *facultas se ipsum interpretandi* is violated, with fatal results. This is what happened in Kant's philosophy, and again in theological idealism. It is happening with Bultmann too. By adopting Heidegger's conception of understanding he is surrendering to the sovereignty of an intellectual world view, which deprives him of any feeling for the distinctiveness of the Bible' (Thielicke 1948: 149–50). So too Colin Gunton's protest from 1985 that in biblical studies there have been 'increasingly desperate attempts to impose upon the text methods derived from supposedly "objective" disciplines [which] have made it impossible to understand the texts for what they are' (Gunton 1985: 146).

[25] Karl Barth argued against the need for a special hermeneutic, since the humanity of Scripture was real and should be respected. Yet he insisted that the starting point for a valid general hermeneutic was learning to listen to the Bible as the witness of revelation (Barth 1938: 463–466 [*KD* I/2, 512–516 = *CD* I/2, 463–466]).

[26] Wood 1981: 21, 26; Jeanrond 1991; Watson 1994; Fowl 1998; and the texts by Gunton and Webster cited above.

[27] 'If the primary genre of the biblical texts is considered to be theological because all of these texts reflect on the nature of God and on God's relationship with humankind, then these texts ultimately demand a theological reading' (Jeanrond 1993: 95).

'The relation between exegesis and theology', as Francis Watson puts it, 'is, in fact, a manifestation of the hermeneutical circle or spiral, in which the whole and parts are dialectically related.'[28] A third level at which this call is made is an insistence that the reading of Scripture has a specific context; namely, God's activity of rescuing, gathering and ruling his people by his word. To cite Webster again, the act of reading this text is not something that should be analysed apart from the divine economy.[29] In the haste to ensure that the churches do not *control* the biblical text, imposing an authorized interpretation that cannot be questioned even from the text itself, too little attention has been given to the churches as a proper *context* for reading Scripture. The corporate address of so much of the New Testament, for instance, demands to be taken seriously. Private reading of the Scriptures is certainly encouraged – with considerable biblical precedent – yet there is an important sense in which such reading is derivative of the public reading and proclamation of the word of God.

All of this is highly significant as we consider the challenges presented to the doctrine of Scripture's clarity by contemporary hermeneutical concerns. We might expect that reinstating the theological character of biblical hermeneutics will cast many of those concerns in significantly different shape. Some that seemed so urgent will fade from view when the otherness of the biblical text, and the relation to God and his purposes which constitutes that otherness, is acknowledged. Others will remain as legitimate and pressing concerns, perhaps even heightened in their relevance by a fresh appreciation of the uniqueness of Scripture. Still others will draw attention to neglected features of the Christian interpretative tradition, revealing our blind spots and calling on us to take the clarity of Scripture more, not less, seriously. In other words, elements of this challenge will need to be accepted, while others will need to be answered.

## Taking Scripture and its readers seriously

Contemporary biblical hermeneutics at its best is a challenge to take the text of Scripture and the responsible reading of that text with the utmost seriousness. It constitutes a determination to avoid misuse of the text by careful attention to what we actually have in front of us, and a heightened self-awareness that recognizes what we bring to the

[28] Watson 1994: 222.
[29] Webster 2005: 36, 59.

task of reading and understanding. Those who write in this area aim to serve the Christian reading community by providing an account of what good readers already do.[30] Their exhortations are not intended to complicate the process of understanding, but to prevent it from going awry. I will draw attention to five of these as challenges we need to accept.

1. *The form of Scripture is not a dispensable shell.* Many recent books on biblical interpretation call on us to respect the literary features of the text we are examining. They remind us that the cognitive content of a text is not disembodied. The text's meaning cannot finally be isolated from the form in which that meaning comes to us. Attempts to bypass the particularities of the text under consideration risk doing violence to that text. Content and form are inseparable. Seeking to penetrate behind the text, to reconstruct its setting or to determine externally the intention of its author occurs too often and to the neglect of the text itself. If it really is *this text* we are trying to understand, then we must direct our attention there.

To recast this complaint in theological terms and sharpen our focus on the Bible, we might say that we need to be grateful to God for the Scripture he has given us. His word has not come to us as a series of unadorned doctrinal propositions. The form in which each part comes to us is not incidental or unimportant. That we have been given not a treatise about Jesus or a prototype of the Chalcedonian Definition, but instead four Gospels together with the apostolic preaching and teaching, is something we may well recognize but sometimes do not fully appreciate. Truths about God's ultimate self-expression and the fulfilment of his ancient purposes are prone to distortion if we abstract them in any way from the historical particulars of this man and his activity in early first-century Palestine.[31] The combination of Gospel and apostle in the New Testament reminds us that to talk about the eternal Son, the Logos, the suffering and exalted Servant, is to talk about this Man, who he is and what he has done. Indeed, it binds our talk *about* Jesus inextricably with a testimony *to* Jesus. Consideration of the form will aid our understanding of the content. All God's acts are purposeful and the Bible we have is one of the most

[30] Vanhoozer 1998: 338. Vanhoozer's work is a thorough and edifying treatment of many of the issues in this section. See also the volumes produced by the 'Scripture and Hermeneutics Seminar' and edited by Craig Bartholomew.

[31] See Barth's appreciation of Martin Kähler's critique of the quest for the historical Jesus, which similarly avoided the text we have in search of historical nuggets from which a life of Jesus could be reconstructed (Barth 1938: 64–65 [*KD* I/2, 71 = *CD* I/2, 64–65]).

important aids to understanding the Bible we have.[32] Put another way, we might say that the form of Scripture is itself part of the content of Scripture.

One significant aspect of this form is its essentially narrative structure. Even those parts of Scripture that do not quite fit the category of narrative have nevertheless been placed within an overarching story, which for convenience we might label 'redemptive history'. Since around the mid-1970s, the insistence that this narrative structure of Scripture is not incidental and that it deserves more detailed attention has been fuelled by the important work of Hans Frei, not least his *The Eclipse of Biblical Narrative*. In this book he describes the way in which scholarship of the eighteenth and nineteenth centuries marginalized the biblical narrative.

According to Frei, the rise of historical studies in this period deflected attention from the text itself to 'some reconstructive context to which the text "really" refers and which renders it intelligible'.[33] The particular reconstructive context that was the real focus of attention might well be different in each case. Some sought the historical situation that lay behind the story. Others pursued the ancient perspective on reality that they believed was given expression by the story. Theologians, it might be argued, were still often caught up in the search for a timeless kernel of universal truth within the story. Yet these were all but variations on a theme and that theme was a reluctance to take the text on its own terms, to understand it first and foremost as a literary entity in which meaning arises from an interaction of character and plot. Frei's analysis is penetrating and productive and his warning against pursuing the meaning of Scripture without due consideration of the form of Scripture is one that bears regular repetition. He also had something to say to contemporary theorists: 'the theoretical devices we use to make our readings more alert, appropriate, and intelligent ought to be designed to leave the story as unencumbered as possible'.[34]

This concern to do justice to the narrative structure of much of Scripture fits neatly within a larger concern to be responsive to the varieties of biblical genre. A genre is, according to one theorist, a 'family resemblance' between texts. These resemblances are produced

[32] I have already argued (ch. 2 above) that reading Scripture takes place in the presence of God and that God himself is the ultimate guarantor of effective communication in and through this text.

[33] Frei 1974: 135.

[34] Frei 1975: xv.

by a literary tradition: 'a sequence of influence and imitation and inherited codes connecting works in the genre'.[35] What is more, identifying the literary genre to which any particular text belongs has significant bearing upon how that text is read. Competent readers recognize the difference between a political commentary and a Greek tragedy and intuitively adjust their expectations and their mode of reading accordingly. Perhaps more obviously, few would read a piece of personal correspondence from a loved one and an extract from *Halsbury's Laws of England* in quite the same manner. A genre is a literary convention that provides 'room' for the author to write in and clues for the reader at the same time.[36] As Kevin Vanhoozer puts it, 'to invoke the notion of genre is to acknowledge a tacit agreement on how a text should be written and how it should be read'.[37] It is at least part of the answer to the Derridean concept of the indeterminacy of meaning, since it reveals a relatively stable literary context that remains despite the variety of personal and social contexts in which the text might be read.[38] Not everything is in flux.

The Christian Bible contains a stunning variety of literary genre. Historical narrative is certainly prominent in both testaments. Yet we might also readily identify legal material, poetry, prophecy, wisdom literature, epistle, exhortation and apocalyptic. Responsible reading takes into account the differences between these various types of literature, recognizing those features within the text itself that position it in one category or another.[39] The genre gives the reader the most basic clues about what is being done in this text, what intention has been enacted in following these conventional procedures.[40] In this way it can be seen as an aid to the text's presentation of its own meaning.

There is another aspect of the form of the biblical text that should not be neglected. On the larger scale, the canonical shape of the Bible is the form in which it comes to us. The significance of the canon for biblical interpretation is a point made most persuasively in the late twentieth century by Brevard Childs.[41] That significance operates on

[35] Fowler 1982: 41–42.
[36] Fowler 1982: 31. Werner Jeanrond suggests that text genres demand appropriate 'reading genres' (Jeanrond 1986: 94–119).
[37] Vanhoozer 1998: 342.
[38] 'Literary genre holds communicative freedom and determinism in constructive tension' (Vanhoozer 1998: 339).
[39] 'The rules that govern a particular literary genre are not extrinsic to the text but are rather embodied within it' (Vanhoozer 1998: 338).
[40] Vanhoozer 1998: 340.
[41] Childs 1979.

two levels. First, as Childs argued, 'the theological function of [the] canon lies in its affirmation that the authoritative norm lies in the literature itself'.[42] In other words, the recognition that a specific text resides within the Christian canon is an aid in properly orienting the reader to this text. It is inadequate and inappropriate to treat the Bible or any of its parts simply as 'a classic of human aspirations' or 'a noble monument to the potential of creative imagination'.[43] It is nowhere near as innocuous as that. By means of this collection of writings and through his Spirit God rules his people and confronts our world. The claim to authority is not something made later and by others on behalf of this text. It is intrinsic to the text itself and its very character as the word of God written. It stands over against us as a given with which we are not at liberty to meddle. What Oliver O'Donovan calls 'the "cunning" project of outwitting the text' is seen for what it is when the canonical status of these documents is appreciated.[44]

The second level on which the significance of the canon operates has more to do with its Christian 'shape'. The Bible we actually have comes to us as a unique collection of documents shaped into two testaments and finding 'its architectonic centre of gravity in the Gospels'.[45] Each of its parts is located within this whole, but located specifically within this whole. There is a trajectory from Genesis through to Revelation. There is, as is well known, a different principle of arrangement between the Hebrew Bible and the Christian Old Testament. Yet both arrangements are intelligible in general terms and both provide insight into the larger-scale function of each book. Most importantly, the coordination of Old and New Testaments makes a significant contribution to the interpretation of passages in both. In particular, the prophetic writings of the Old Testament strain forward towards their fulfilment in the New, and Jesus' life, death and resurrection in the New Testament are explained 'in accordance with the Scriptures' (1 Cor. 15:3). There is also a sense in which the canon itself provides a *sensus plenior*, 'fuller meaning' (e.g. Eph. 3:4–12; 1 Pet. 1:10–12).

At the micro and macro levels, then, the form of Scripture assists rather than retards an understanding of its content. Put the other way around, the clarity of Scripture does not come through ignoring the form of Scripture.

---

[42] Childs 1992: 71.
[43] Childs 1992: 726.
[44] O'Donovan 2002: 65.
[45] The phrase belongs to Oliver O'Donovan (O'Donovan 1996: 22; 2002: 66).

2. *The words of Scripture may refer but reference does not exhaust their function.* While the text itself and neither the background nor the foreground is the primary carrier of meaning, Christians have nevertheless insisted that Scripture does refer beyond itself to speak of God and his dealings with the world.[46] This insistence has become all the more determined in the face of Derrida's denial of textual reference (the deconstruction of the transcendental signified) and Ricœur's suggestion that ostensive reference should be suspended in the interests of entering the world generated by the text.[47] The words of Scripture properly describe the reality we inhabit, the actual world in which we live. They point us to the God who is there. While there are indeed many instances of figurative language of one kind or another in the Bible, the text itself makes clear that these are figurative by markers provided at the macro and micro level. The details of biblical poems and parables, for instance, are not to be pressed beyond the demands of the context (though this has in fact been done repeatedly: witness Augustine's allegorization of the parable of the good Samaritan). However, the correspondence between what is taught in Scripture and the actual state of affairs in the world God has made is crucial. The apostle Paul famously remarked to the Corinthian Christians that if Christ had not in fact been raised from the dead, then their faith was futile and they were still as lost they had ever been (1 Cor. 15:17).

Very sophisticated defences of this referential aspect of biblical language have been produced since the 1960s, not least amongst them T. F. Torrance's exposition of Christian critical realism.[48] It is surely right to warn that 'fixation on the biblical text *divorced from the referent that the text itself demands* is a kind of idolatry'.[49] Contemporary 'hyper-textuality' (what Ricœur calls 'the ideology of absolute texts') can, after all, have its own false piety.[50] However, no matter how determined our commitment to the notion of reference, it should be plain that the words of Scripture, like words generally, do more than refer. They do not *only* provide a faithful description or

---

[46] We have already noted Augustine's influential exposition of signification in *De doctrina christiana*.

[47] Derrida 1967a: 44–65 (esp. 49–50); Ricœur 1981: 148–149.

[48] This is a slight stretch for, strictly speaking, Torrance has defended the truthfulness of theological statements rather than specifically biblical language (Torrance 1969: 173–202). He would wish to distance himself from suggestions that the words of Scripture are themselves infallible or inerrant.

[49] Carson 1996: 172 (emphasis his).

[50] Ricœur 1976: 36.

representation of reality. Speech-act theorists have subjected this self-evident fact to detailed analysis, identifying locutionary, illocutionary and perlocutionary aspects of human discourse. The locution is simply the set of words spoken or written with a particular meaning. The illocution, which theorist John Searle once described as 'the minimal unit of linguistic communication', is the act performed by those words, such as warning, promising, arguing and so on.[51] The perlocution is the effect the speech act is designed to accomplish, such as alerting people, comforting or persuading them. Words certainly do describe reality – and they do that effectively – but they also command, warn, promise, and express emotion.

This simple fact of life is of considerable importance for understanding and explaining biblical texts. Undoubtedly, the words of Scripture describe or explain reality, both natural and spiritual. Yet the words we are examining at any point may have a quite different purpose or function. In the mouth of the serpent the words of Genesis 3 are calculated to deceive. So too are the words of the lying prophet in 1 Kings 22. The words of God to Abraham in Genesis 12, on the other hand, are promises that generate and nourish a relationship of trust. Further back in Genesis the words of God are creative, bringing into existence an entire universe where there was once nothing but formlessness and void (Gen. 1).

This flexibility in verbal communication, whether spoken or written, is a factor of common human experience. Speakers and readers pick up clues about the illocutionary stance of a particular locution from the context, the genre and the specific details of the discourse. The issue is that this aspect of the text can be compromised by a zealous apologetic stance towards textual reference. In the interests of defending historical reliability, for instance, the other functions of biblical language can be glossed over, resulting in tenuous and idiosyncratic interpretations. In the final analysis, paying attention to what is in fact being done by the words is just another facet of taking those words (and their context) seriously.

3. *Reading takes place in a context (and so does hermeneutical theorizing!)*. Reading of the ordinary, everyday variety is multidimensional. When we read a text, we not only recognize the words on the page, but we integrate those words and their message with a pre-existent body of knowledge. Indeed, to varying extents and in various ways, this pre-existent knowledge (our presuppositional stance,

[51] Searle 1996: 110.

if you like) shapes our approach to the text we read. We are predisposed to read the latest J. K. Rowling novel in a certain way by our knowledge of earlier volumes in the series, by our views about children's literature, by concerns or otherwise about the prominence of magical themes in contemporary culture, and a whole host of other things besides. In some cases, the step of integrating what we read with our pre-existent knowledge involves serious reflection or meditation. Some degree of evaluation may be involved and perhaps also a resolution to appropriate the message or the impact of this text in a certain way.[52] The total communicative activity may well involve the author, the text itself, the reader and even the community of which the reader is a part. None of this is a creation of contemporary hermeneutical theory – competent readers do these things almost intuitively.

The warning contemporary hermeneutics has sounded is that a failure to recognize that our reading is influenced by more than just the text can lead to unrealistic claims of absolute objectivity and moral neutrality. We are so much better at identifying the influence of presuppositions and cultural location on the readings of others than we are at acknowledging our own prior commitments. *We* just read the text; *they* impose an interpretation. Yet our own pristine objectivity is an illusion. Furthermore, the influence of a reader's forejudgments and predispositions (our own and anyone else's) need not be vicious. Gadamer and others have called on us to reject the Enlightenment's 'prejudice against prejudice'.[53] Philosophers such as Michael Polanyi have reminded us that all knowledge is personal, with its own tacit dimensions, rather than strictly and absolutely objective.[54] This phenomenon need be no more distorting when it comes to the reading of texts than it is in the observation of the natural world. Christian readers of the Scriptures need not be embarrassed by their expectations arising out of a robust faith in God. The insistence in some quarters that serious scholarship requires you to lay aside your personal investment in the teaching of Scripture is naive and to some degree disingenuous. Such a manoeuvre is not able to safeguard objectivity and the integrity of interpretative judgments. It simply cloaks presuppositions of a different kind.

[52] Karl Barth spoke of three basic steps when it comes to reading the Bible: observation (*explicatio*), reflection (*meditatio*) and appropriation (*applicatio*) (Barth 1938: 722–740 [*KD* I/2, 810–830 = *CD* I/2, 722–740]).

[53] Gadamer 1984: 271.

[54] Polanyi 1962, 1966.

An associated warning is that neglect of the community in which we read is also problematic. Particularly when it comes to reading the Bible, we do not read alone. The communion of saints, stretching across the centuries and including those whose cultural and intellectual context is considerably different from our own, is an important check on idiosyncratic or self-interested readings. The Reformation principle of *sola scriptura* did not mean an abandonment of the exegetical tradition. Luther, Calvin, Zwingli, Cranmer and the other mainstream Reformers studied the Scriptures in conversation with those who preceded them, especially the early Fathers. To be sure, they resisted imposition of an institutional arbiter of interpretative disputes. The church must not circumvent the ordinary Christian's engagement with the Bible. Luther insisted upon this in the strongest terms in his *An den christlichen Adel deutscher Nation*.[55] Yet Luther and the rest all still read the Bible *in the church*. What is more, to acknowledge this corporate dimension to Christian reading of the Bible was not taken by any of them as to call into question the clarity of Scripture.

It is, however, possible to stress the contribution of readers and reading communities to the detriment of the text being read. Umberto Eco has written of his impression that in much recent writing on the subject, 'the rights of interpreters' have been overstressed and 'the rights of texts' neglected.[56] The reader effectively supplants the author and plays havoc with the text. When it comes to reading the Bible, we need to be aware that our prior commitments may operate as a filter that prevents its challenge from being heard. They need not do so of necessity, but they *may* do so.[57] Likewise, the community in which we read may itself need to be challenged rather than simply confirmed in its convictions and patterns of reading. We have our own issues and interests and we can just as easily read these into the text as heed its call to repent of them. God's word might not be far from us, but it always confronts us as a word *outside* us, God's address of us rather than simply the echo of our own perspectives and cultural preoccupations. Seen in this light, the strangeness of the Bible is in fact part of its clarity rather than an obstacle to be overcome.[58]

4. *Critical methods have brought significant gains but at a cost*. It would be foolish and petulant, not to mention untrue, to suggest we

---

[55] Luther 1520a: 133–136 (*WA* VI, 411.8 – 412.38 = *LW* XLIV, 133–136).
[56] Eco 1992: 23.
[57] Jensen 2002: 221.
[58] Jensen 2002: 203; Barth 1917.

have received nothing worthwhile from the hands of critical scholars. In large measure as a result of their labours, we undoubtedly know more about the biblical text, more about the languages in which it comes to us and more about the culture in which it emerged than ever before. One simple and obvious example is the way critical studies have highlighted the distinctive presentation of Jesus in each Gospel. They have encouraged us to resist the temptation to harmonize the accounts too quickly, without first appreciating the realistic contours that emerge from a fourfold testimony rather than a single testimony repeated verbatim three times. Yet the indirect gains have perhaps been even greater. By asking hard questions about the text, critical scholarship has stimulated others to return to the Scriptures to see if these things are indeed so. Responsible evangelical scholars have in this sense been well served by their more critical colleagues. Many penetrating insights have been the result of this interaction.

Criticism, like other exercises of human reason, need not be the enemy of faith. It is possible to construct an agenda for biblical criticism that actually promotes the perspective and the interests of the text. If criticism understands itself as an aid to good reading, if, as Peter Jensen suggests, critics remember their moral obligations and respect the personhood of the author and the reader, enabling them 'to see what may be seen' as the text is read, then criticism may be an act of service to the Christian reading community rather than an assault upon it. But only when all concerned remember that 'the first task of the critic is respectfully to discern and accept the actual nature of what he or she is reading' – in the case of Scripture this is the word of God.[59]

There is certainly room for appreciation of the critical enterprise, especially when it is conducted on terms such as these, but we must admit that, until recently, this appreciation too often has taken the form of veneration and that the conclusions of critical scholars have regularly gone unchallenged. It is, after all, possible to overstate the gains that have been made. Oliver O'Donovan goes so far as to say:

Out of the vast quantity of intellectual detritus left behind by the historical-critical project, a few (remarkably few) penetrating insights survive the test of time and impose themselves –

---

[59] Jensen 2002: 206–209. In a similar vein Kevin Vanhoozer suggests that 'the first hermeneutical reflex . . . should be charity towards the author' (Vanhoozer 1998: 32).

A CLEAR AND PRESENT WORD

simply by virtue of shedding such light on the text that when
one reads the text one feels it would be doing violence to read
it apart from that light.[60]

The continuing enthusiasm of many biblical scholars needs to be
tempered by a healthy dose of realism. There has been a lot of dross
as well as gold.

Furthermore, we cannot hide from the fact that a great deal of historical-critical scholarship in particular has tended to evade the biblical text's intrinsic claim to authority.[61] It has not often approached
Scripture on its own terms as Scripture or adopted the appropriate
posture of a disciple, that of faith and a genuine repentance of mind
and heart. Instead, it has remained captive to the trajectory installed
in modern thinking by Kant: 'Reason is by nature free and admits of
no command to hold something as true (no imperative "Believe!" but
only a free *credo*).'[62] At his insistence the critic refuses to be a pupil
of the text: he or she stands over it as judge.[63]

5. *The misuse of Scripture in the interests of personal or corporate
power is not simply hypothetical.* We have mentioned more than once
the protest associated with Michel Foucault that claims to truth are
in reality exercises of power.[64] While the protest is no doubt overdone
and does not consider the difference between human claims to true
knowledge and God's gift of truth in the Son who came to die, the
point is still well made. We have learnt to be suspicious of words,
especially words that claim to be true. Authoritative interpretations
make us nervous. Religious warfare may have revitalized scepticism
in the seventeenth century. Fundamentalist terrorism has handed it
an easy victory at the beginning of the twenty-first century. What is
more, thanks to the wonder of television documentary, the spectre of
the Nazi propaganda machine has not entirely faded from memory.

[60] O'Donovan 2002: 66. Recent appreciation of so-called precritical exegesis provides yet another reason to temper our enthusiasm for the gains of critical scholarship
(Steinmetz 1980).

[61] Gunton 1985: 115.

[62] Kant 1798: 249. John Webster quotes these words of Kant and then contrasts
them with 'a Christian theological account of reason' that 'will want to disengage the
exercise of reason from its associations with indeterminate liberty and the act of judgement' (Webster 2003a: 125).

[63] Kant 1781: 20.

[64] Rowan Williams has decried the tendency towards 'intellectual totalitarianism',
arguing it is essential 'that theologians become aware of how theology has worked and
continues to work in the interests of this or that system of power' (Williams 1991: 8 [cf.
4–6]).

Abusive appeals to authority are not beyond our imagination; for too many they are not beyond our experience.

Awareness of the way an authoritative text, or appeal to the clear meaning of an authoritative text, can be used to coerce or manipulate others adds a sombre note to the practice of biblical interpretation. The Bible has been repeatedly misused in the interests of power over the past two thousand years. There have been sub-Christian understandings of biblical authority, which have led to torture, murder and forced conversions. The refrain 'this is the word of the Lord' is meant to provoke thanksgiving, yet it can also be used as a weapon to bludgeon people into conformity, to shortcut the process of Christian persuasion. We cannot afford to close our eyes to our own history – even, perhaps especially, evangelical history. Yet the answer is not to jettison the text or to locate real authority elsewhere. This *is* the word of the Lord. It is his gift to us and by this means he rules his people. Believers seek to be shaped in thinking and behaviour by God's revelation of himself and his purposes. The problem is not with the word God has given, but with the use made of it by sinful men and women. Hard questions need to be asked about just whose interests are being served by our explanation of a particular biblical text. Are we prepared to have those interests challenged by the text? This does not mean surrendering at the first sign questions such as these are asked by those who oppose what we might be saying. After all, the claim that a particular interpretation is in reality a covert exercise of power may turn out to be itself a covert exercise of power.[65] What it does mean is that we should be asking those questions of ourselves.

In at least these five ways the challenge of contemporary literary studies and hermeneutical theory needs to be heard and accepted. In our theory of reading and our explanations of the text's meaning we must be careful not to sidestep the text of Scripture itself, the Bible as it comes to us. We do well to remember that the referential function of words and texts is not their only function, and to cultivate a sensitivity to what is being done with the words at any point. Our reading is well served by an appropriate awareness of both our own predisposition and that of the community in which we read. After all, our reading does not occur in a vacuum nor in isolation from other readers. There are benefits to be enjoyed from the exegetical and

---

[65] It is also just possible that in some cases the claim could conceal a far more serious problem: unbelief.

interpretative labours of even the most critical scholars, but naive veneration of the 'assumed results of scholarship' or 'the scholarly consensus' is a danger to be avoided. Finally, the possibility of misusing the biblical text in our own interests, or those of the particular community to which we belong, calls for care. The Bible is *God's* word addressed to us, not a weapon we use against others.

We have certainly not exhausted the benefits of recent hermeneutical discussion with these five observations. Nor have we said all that could be said about the way they might be embraced by Christian readers and reading communities. Nevertheless, enough has been said to show that aspects of this discussion promote rather than discourage serious attention to Scripture, and that a more sober assessment of our own integrity as readers is called for. The clarity of Scripture need not be compromised by any of these insights. In large measure, though, this is because its viability does not ultimately depend upon the skill of the interpreter.

## The theological protest at the contemporary hermeneutical agenda

For all the insight and assistance afforded by contemporary hermeneutics, theologians and many ordinary readers of Scripture have expressed a lingering unease about its profile. In the words of one influential evangelical theologian, 'In our culture we are making heavy weather of the business of reading.'[66] Having escaped the clutches of the priests, to some it seems as if today the Bible is being sequestered by the academic guild under the guise of hermeneutical sophistication. Not all that has been written is helpful or compatible with faith in God. There are aspects of the hermeneutical challenge that need to be answered rather than accepted and the theological framework that supports doctrines such as the clarity of Scripture provides the most fruitful response.

1. *But God . . .* We have already noted the resistance of some to invoking the person and character of God in our explanation of the very human activity of reading. Yet Christian theology cannot succumb to such an abstraction. God is not absent from his world, certainly not absent from his people, and least of all absent from those who come to the Scriptures in faith, seeking to read and understand the word of God. Many contemporary treatments are decid-

[66] Jensen 2002: 228.

edly reductionist at this point. It is undoubtedly true that reading is a creaturely activity. At this level, it is perfectly appropriate to subject it to the kind of analysis that features so prominently in the writing of literary theorists. Nevertheless, our existence as creatures and all our creaturely activity has a theological context, whether this is acknowledged or not. Creatures live and move and have their being in the context of God's creative activity, his saving purpose and his continuous providential involvement with all created life.[67] When the focus is narrowed to the reading of Scripture, we can affirm that this is more than a creaturely activity, though certainly not less. God involves himself as we take and read.

Kevin Vanhoozer has extensively defended the relevance of the author to the task of reading.[68] 'The death of the author' is in the end a convenient fiction, notwithstanding the legitimate concerns of those who fear the intentional fallacy (assuming that a text means what its author meant it to mean). It has not secured respect for the text despite the best efforts of the New Critics, structuralists and narrative theorists. Too often the only interests secured are those of the reader. Particularly, in the case of the Bible this idea has too often justified a refusal to attend to the text's own claim to present God's perspective and to speak with God's authority. Appeal to 'the death of the author' is in fact the ultimate power play: it dethrones God, privileges the present and recasts these words as dim echoes of past experiences.[69] Yet the divine author has not relinquished this text. The apostles and prophets may be long dead, but the word of God that comes to expression in and as their words remains the sword of the Spirit (Eph. 6:17). To speak of the vulnerability of the written word, adrift on a sea of interpretations, is a strangely romantic notion when the word concerned is the word of God. The Bible is not merely the record of God's activity long ago in human history; it is the means by which, through the illuminating and convicting work of the Spirit, God directly and personally addresses his people and the world today. Contemporary reading of Scripture is not simply a recollection of redemptive history, but itself exists within that redemptive history in which God is continuously active and never absent.

---

[67] John Webster suggests that it is 'at just this point – the theological specification of creatures and their acts – that much hermeneutical theology (like much moral theology) is decidedly attenuated' (Webster 2003a: 92).

[68] Vanhoozer 1998: 201–280.

[69] The hermeneutical project has often been 'suspected of ambitions to justify and insure the reader's present against the text's past' (O'Donovan 2002: 68).

The real presence of God in the reading of his word dramatically redraws the content of appropriate hermeneutical theory. First, the question of authority cannot be ignored or deferred. As I have already suggested, the claim to authority is intrinsic rather than extrinsic to the Bible. To suspend engagement with that claim is not to take the text on its own terms. More seriously, it amounts to an act of defiance, since the context of our reading is God's own sovereign presence. Such defiance is the deep flaw that mars the human condition. The Enlightenment insistence on the autonomy of human reason was, perhaps before all else, a revolt against all 'authorities'. The postmodern recognition that reason has its limits has not brought that revolt to an end. Instead it has given it a different dress, the inviolability of personal perspective: no-one has the right to say I am wrong. Yet the call to repent will not be silenced as the Scriptures are read. Ricœur's search for a 'non-heteronomous dependence' (a way of relating to the testimony of Scripture as a stimulus to imagination rather than 'rule by another') is hard to sustain in the personal presence of the God who has spoken.[70] By these words God equips his people. By these words he cuts through the pretence of our self-sufficiency.

Second, in line with what I have already said, prayer must assume a profile that it lacks in much writing on hermeneutical theory. The doctrine of the clarity of Scripture is not a claim that the meaning of every passage is obvious or that the process of understanding is always simple or transparent. There are difficulties in Scripture. In the language used in earlier chapters, sometimes clarity is hard won. Yet we must beware of what some have described as 'hermeneutical Pelagianism'.[71] The knowledge of God is a gift, not an achievement. Understanding in the fullest sense is not merely a matter of technical proficiency. We remain as dependent upon God in the matter of reading, understanding and appropriating the words of Scripture as we do in all other areas of life. When we recognize that reading Scripture cannot be extracted from the economy of salvation, that the struggle between light and darkness, faith and rebellion, bears directly upon our approach to the biblical text, the importance of prayer becomes even clearer. This was at least part of the reason why medieval centres of biblical learning, such as the Abbey of St Victor outside Paris, sought to blend academic study with devotional

---

[70] Ricœur 1977: 37.
[71] Webster 2003a: 100.

models such as the *lectio divina*.[72] Only a determined blindness can ignore God as the Scriptures are being read.

Third, as mentioned in an earlier chapter, the nature of God's dealings with his people generates confidence rather than confusion. God does not delight in tormenting his children with the promise of understanding forever held just out of reach. He desires to be known and he will be known. He is able to reveal himself to men and women in a way that is both accommodated to our understanding and unfailingly true. When the Scriptures are portrayed primarily as a puzzle to be solved, a code to be cracked or a mystery to be unravelled, the risk is that God's benevolence, his loving self-giving, will be forgotten or obscured. Christian reading of the Bible is bold and confident, not because of an overweening sense of human capacity, but because this activity is part of life lived in the presence of the good and gracious God.

2. *The Bible is not just another text.* This is the corollary of what we have just observed. The protest against subsuming biblical hermeneutics under more general principles, against subordinating the particulars of this text to a universal human phenomenon, needs to be heard. Of course the Bible is still a written document and reading is still reading. Yet the Bible does not fit neatly and without remainder in such categories. There is a decidedly Procrustean feel to some writing about biblical interpretation.[73] The relationship between author and text is not the same as that in other texts. The relationship between author and reader (any reader) is different in the case of the Bible to any other text. In other words, the *sui generis* character of this text needs to be respected.

As an historical document, the Bible encourages the exploration of the situation of its writers and original readers. It contains explicit claims to present things as they actually are, to record events as they actually happened, and in fact encourages those claims to be tested (e.g. 1 Cor. 15:3–8; Acts 17:10–12). As a literary artefact, the Bible is patient of analysis in terms of genre, structure, language and literary device. There is much to appreciate in the way in which Scripture has been constructed as literature. Yet neither historical nor literary analysis is sufficient when it comes to the study of the Bible. The same is true of that branch of social anthropology that seeks to examine how

---

[72] 'The Victorine canons endeavoured to be both monks and academics with a remarkable degree of success' (Evans 1984: 29).

[73] Procrustes was the mythical figure who ensured his guests fitted neatly into the bed he supplied by either stretching them or removing their limbs.

the Bible functions within various religious communities.[74] Christian engagement with the Bible cannot forget, ignore or suspend for the sake of some higher goal, the identification of this text as the written word of God. It cannot condone any attempt to give the reader some kind of priority over the text. As Karl Barth put it:

> Precisely in order that he may really appropriate what Scripture has to say, the reader and hearer must be willing to transpose the centre of his attention from himself, from the system of his own concerns and questions (even if he thinks he can give them the character of concerns and questions typical of his whole epoch) to the scriptural word itself. He must allow himself to be lifted out of himself into this word and its concerns and questions. It is only from this that light can ever fall upon his own life, and therewith the help that he needs for his life.[75]

'The help that he needs for his life' hints at one significant and distinctive feature of the Bible and our reading of the Bible: its relationship to God's purposes in salvation. Discussion of biblical interpretation has too often been isolated from soteriology. As Paul wrote to Timothy, the holy Scriptures 'are able to make you wise for salvation through faith in Christ Jesus' (2 Tim. 3:15). The Bible functions within the divine economy of salvation. It presents the promise of God that generates saving faith in God. Its exposition of the human condition, its illustration of that condition within its history of Israel and the early church, and above all its testimony to Jesus Christ as the crucified and risen one, all serve this end. It is the sovereign desire of the living God to make himself known and to restore to himself those who, through their own rebellion, have separated themselves from him. This soteriological focus has sometimes been obscured by the rush to ask other questions of this text. One cannot avoid the conclusion that on too many occasions the Bible has been abused by the attempt to make something out of it other than what it actually is. Yet the richest and most lasting engagement with the Scriptures does not neglect their own proper concern.

There are few texts, if any, that have been produced over such an extended period as the Christian Bible, incorporating as it does the Hebrew Scriptures and the apostolic testimony to Jesus. Massive

---

[74] E.g. Malley 2004.
[75] Barth 1938: 739 (*KD* I/2, 828–829 = *CD* I/2, 739).

differences of culture, language and sociopolitical reality across this period all find expression in the text as we have it. Yet, despite this, and notwithstanding differences of perspective and emphasis between the individual documents that make up the canon, there is an extraordinary cohesion to Scripture, which is highlighted by a rich 'intertextuality' (to use Julia Kristeva's term). The theological explanation of this cohesion lies both in the ultimate source of the canonical documents, in the one God's activity of self-revelation and in its critical and determinative centre; namely, a rich testimony to the person and work of Jesus Christ.

In the theological tradition, the unique authority of this text and its fundamental unity have been reflected in a distinctive interpretative approach. From the earliest days, Christians have insisted that Scripture should be compared with Scripture. Recourse to this 'analogy of Scripture (*analogia scripturae*)' can be found in the work of Irenaeus, Augustine and many others.[76] This is what Luther had in mind when he insisted that 'Scripture is its own interpreter'.[77] By means of this principle, Scripture itself was allowed to shed light on those particular parts of it that might initially seem obscure – the difficult passages are explained by the easier ones. In addition, an interpretative control was thus provided that did not jeopardize Scripture as itself the final authority in faith and life. Idiosyncratic interpretation could be checked by an insistence, in the language of the *Thirty-nine Articles of Religion*, that no one place of Scripture may be so expounded 'that it be repugnant to another' (Article 20). In other words, passages of Scripture are to be compared with each other in such a way that the meaning of no individual text is overturned but rather all are treated seriously and in the context of the whole counsel of God. Prior convictions about the nature of this text, in particular an identification of the canon in its entirety as the word of God, meant no contradiction or conflict between individual passages could be admitted on principle. Where such appeared to be the case, more work was needed.

3. *The most important location of the reader is the eschatological location of the reader.* Much is often made of the historical and social location of the Christian reader of Scripture, and in particular the distance between that location and the location of the biblical text and its author. Hermeneutical principles are sometimes presented as

---

[76] Irenaeus 189: 400 (*Adversus haereses* II.xxviii.3 [*PG* VII, 806 = *ANF* I, 400]); Augustine 426: 539 (*De doctrina christiana* II.9 (14) [*CCSL* XXXII, 40–41 = *NPNF*, 1st Series, II, 539]). See Blocher 1987.

[77] 'Scriptura . . . sui ipsius interpres' (Luther 1520b: 97 [*WA* VII, 97.23]).

a way to 'bridge the gap' between the text and its contemporary readership, between 'what it meant' and 'what it means'. Undoubtedly, the world of the twenty-first century would have been inconceivable in the first. Social structures are so markedly different as to be almost unrecognizable. The languages have developed, political regimes have come and gone, and powerful intellectual movements have shaped even those who know nothing about them. In the light of such a thoroughgoing transformation of the conditions of everyday life, the idea that a text of the first century might be relevant on its own terms today seems hardly credible. At one simple level, today's reader brings a dramatically different interpretative grid to the biblical text than that of his or her counterpart in first-century Rome or Corinth or Ephesus. How much greater must we consider the gap between the reader of today and the faithful scribe in the time of Solomon or the priests in the time of Moses?

The historical, cultural and intellectual location of the biblical writers, the text they produced, and their original readership is an important part of the otherness of Scripture that, as I have already argued, demands respect. For instance, to impose the canons of contemporary historiography on the writer of 2 Kings is recognizably anachronistic. The Gospels do not equate with the biographies of our time, or even the hagiography of the nineteenth century. Nevertheless, as we saw in a previous chapter, the historical gap between human author and reader was not considered an insuperable barrier within the Bible itself. Texts originally located in the time of the wilderness wanderings or the ancient amphictyony still spoke to Judaeans crushed under the heel of imperial Rome. There were certain 'constants' that rendered the ancient text intelligible even in a markedly different context.

The most significant of these is the character and purpose of God himself. God has not changed and he remains determined to accomplish his ancient purpose. Though more may be known of God under the new covenant than under the old (after all, the incarnate Son has now made the Father known), God has not changed, grown or developed, since he has always been perfect. He has always been intensely relational to the core of his own being. His unchangeability is not due to some alien static notion of divinity, but rather to his fully dynamic nature that admits of no unrealized potential.[78] He keeps his promises

---

[78] For an exploration of this idea from the perspective of contemporary Thomism see Weinandy 2000: 113–146.

and his sovereign control of all things has not waned with the passage of time. Whether during the wanderings of Abraham, the reign of Solomon, the exile, the ministry of Jesus or the era of gospel mission, God can be relied upon and both his power and love remain constant.

The second constant is God's assessment of the human predicament. The most pressing need of men and women, whether in the eighth century BC, the fifth century AD, or the present day, is the forgiveness of sins and new life in fellowship with God. No matter how technologically advanced, how intellectually sophisticated or how culturally developed humans are, the dire situation brought about by our own sinfulness is the most critical truth about our race. The apostolic preaching emphasized the universal scope of this human predicament as a critical starting point for its call to repentance and faith, a call that from the start was made across significant cultural barriers (e.g. Acts 17:29–31; Rom. 1:18–3:26).

Since the time of the resurrection, however, one particular constant binds all Christian readers across the centuries: we are those upon whom the end of the ages has come (1 Cor. 10:11). In terms of the divine eschatology, the location of all between the resurrection and the parousia is the same. That is not to say that there are no differences or that the first century seamlessly merges into the twenty-first. The historical distinctives of each remain significant. Yet there is an underlying unity to the interim. The new age of grace, forgiveness and the Spirit has broken in on the old age of the Law, sin and death. Brokenness and blessing now exist side by side. An eschatological overlap, a tension between 'now' and 'not yet' is a powerfully relevant feature of Christian living throughout the last days. Nineteen and a half centuries may have passed since Paul wrote to the Roman churches about life in the Spirit during the last days, but the basic grammar of Christian experience remains the same: waiting in hope and the intercession of the Spirit while we wait (Rom. 8:18–39).

A determinedly theological framework for the Christian activity of reading Scripture raises questions about significant aspects of the current hermeneutical endeavour. When the reading of Scripture is placed in the context of God's active and saving presence, when the *sui generis* character of the Bible is taken into account, and when several genuine constants are acknowledged, all talk about a gap between the biblical texts and the contemporary Christian appears inadequate and one-sided. The hermeneutical emperor is certainly not naked, but we might say he is not properly attired for a meeting with the word of the living God.

# The hermeneutics of a clear text in the hands of a good God

We can anticipate further fruitful developments in the field of biblical hermeneutics. It may well be that writers in this field will rescue general hermeneutics from its own self-destructive tendencies. Yet throughout this chapter I have preferred to speak of *reading* rather than of *interpreting* or *hermeneutical practice*. Reading appears less pretentious and, as John Webster puts it, is less overlain with the complexities of the theorists.[79] After all, good reading has never been dependent upon a grasp of the theory behind it.[80] Furthermore, there is cause for serious concern if a discipline designed to encourage the responsible reading of Scripture results in less reading of Scripture due to a fear that the Bible's meaning is not really clear or that it may lie beyond the grasp of the ordinary Christian.

As a matter of fact, the challenges posed to the doctrine of Scripture's clarity by contemporary theories of reading are nowhere near as serious as may first appear. There are certainly bold and aggressive ways of presenting the challenge. The words 'naive' and 'unsophisticated' do get thrown about from time to time. Nevertheless, the Christian's confidence in turning to the Bible has very secure warrant in the character and activity of God, in the singular identity of this text as God's word, and in the experience of the communion of saints down through the centuries. It is worth pointing out that in far too much of contemporary hermeneutical discussion (even the discussion of biblical hermeneutics) God is ignored, the self-testimony of the text is prematurely dismissed as tainted, and almost all attention is focused upon the autonomous reader, whose context is restricted to the present.

There is an ethical dimension to reading that includes respect for the author as well as careful attention to what has in fact been written and the form in which it has been written. Yet reading the word of God in the presence of God demands more than these more general courtesies. In this case, the very human activity of reading takes on a new importance as a vital element of the life of faith. The suggestion that we approach the text with a 'hermeneutic of suspicion', or that we must 'master the text lest the text master us', is, quite frankly, incom-

---

[79] Webster 2003a: 83. He goes on to say, '"reading" is more fitting in view of the self-presenting or self-explicating character of the divine revelation which Scripture serves'.

[80] 'In itself, the business of reading requires no special justification, training or analysis by the reader' (Jensen 2002: 206).

patible with faith in the goodness of God. It cannot but lead to a distortion of Scripture's meaning and the elevation of our own interests above the express will of the one who made us and redeemed us.

In short, hermeneutics is like everything else in the world outside Eden. It is an area of scholarly activity that can be an avenue for faithful service or an opportunity for human self-assertion.

> The act of interpretation repeats the basic motif of Christian existence, which is being drawn out of the darkness of sin and turned to the light of the gospel. Holy Scripture is clear; but because its matter is that to which we must be reconciled, readers can only discern its clarity if *their* darkness is illuminated . . . Interpretation of the clear Word of God is therefore not first of all an act of clarification but the event of being clarified. Reading, therefore, always includes a humbling of the reader, the breaking of the will in which there is acted out the struggle to detach our apprehension of the text from the idolatrous schemas which we inevitably take to it, and by which we seek to command or suppress it or render it convenient to us.[81]

---

[81] Webster 2005: 63–64 (emphasis mine).

# Chapter Five

# The sharp double-edged sword: Restating the clarity of Scripture today

'Which are able to make you wise for salvation'

## The classic exposition

### The scholar and the monk

In 1524 Desiderius Erasmus of Rotterdam finally succumbed to the pressure that had been applied to him for almost seven years. In that year this literary giant, one of the truly great figures of the Northern Renaissance, declared himself against the theology of Martin Luther, publishing his famous *De libero arbitrio diatribē sive collatio* (Diatribe or Conference concerning Free Will). Erasmus himself was in no doubt about the significance of the moment and of the subject he had chosen. He wrote to Henry VIII on 6 September to say, 'The die is cast. The little book on free will has seen the light of day.'[1] What he did not know was that he would provoke one of the true classics of the Christian theological tradition, famous amongst other things for its brief but rich exposition of the clarity of Scripture.[2]

Erasmus had taken aim at what he saw as a dangerous threat to the humanist program of reform, which he and others had engaged in for some time. He recoiled from Luther's pessimistic anthropology, his insistence that human beings were incapable of reforming themselves in line with reason, believing that this teaching, like some of the teaching of Augustine, would open 'a window to impiety' to the populace in general.[3] However, in the book's preface, Erasmus had also attacked Luther's bold way of doing theology, his use of assertions

---

[1] Erasmus 1524b: 373 (*Epistola* 1493).
[2] Thompson 2004: 191–247. For a thorough account of the dispute and surrounding events, see Brecht 1986: 213–238.
[3] Erasmus 1524a: 41.

and his appeal to the clear teaching of Scripture. He even confessed a preference for the opinion of the Sceptics over what he saw as Luther's dogmatism. His explicit starting point was Luther's *Assertio omnium articulorum* (Assertion of All the Articles) of 1520, in which the Reformer had insisted, 'The meaning of Scripture is, in and of itself, so certain, accessible and clear that Scripture interprets itself and tests, judges and illuminates everything else.'[4] Luther himself, it seems, had placed the clarity of Scripture close to the centre of his disagreement with the church of Rome. Erasmus countered by listing those matters in Scripture where clarity could not be expected or at least had not been achieved:

> there are some secret places in the Holy Scriptures into which God has not wished us to penetrate more deeply and, if we try to do so, then the deeper we go, the darker and darker it becomes, by which means we are led to acknowledge the unsearchable majesty of the divine wisdom, and the weakness of the human mind.[5]
>
> Many things are reserved for that time when we shall no longer see through a glass darkly or in a riddle, but in which we shall contemplate the glory of the Lord when his face shall be revealed.[6]
>
> And then there are certain things of which God has willed us to be completely ignorant – such as the hour of death or the Day of Judgment . . .[7]
>
> There are some things which God has willed that we should contemplate, as we venerate himself, in mystic silence; and, moreover, there are many passages in the sacred volumes about which many commentators have made guesses, but no one has finally cleared up their obscurity: as the distinction between the divine persons, the conjunction of the divine and human nature in Christ, the unforgivable sin; yet there are other things which God has willed to be most plainly evident, and such are the precepts for the good life.[8]

---

[4] '[H]oc est, ut sit ipsa per sese certissima, facillima, apertissima, sui ipsius interpres, omnium omnia probans, iudicans et illuminans . . .' (Luther 1520b: 97 [*WA* VII, 97.19–24]).

[5] Erasmus 1524a: 38.

[6] Erasmus 1524a: 39.

[7] Erasmus 1524a: 39.

[8] Erasmus 1524a: 39–40.

In these few pages, Erasmus provided the broad contours for much later writing against the clarity of Scripture. Such a notion, he insisted, takes little account of the transcendent majesty of God, the imperfection of our knowledge this side of the parousia, the will of God to conceal certain matters, and the lack of consensus amongst students of the Bible at a significant number of points. Yet Erasmus' own preference for morality over doctrine, for practical piety over theological speculation and controversy, is never far from the surface. Even if Luther were right on this matter of human inability, it would not be right to broadcast this to 'the common herd'. Given our 'incurable propensity toward all manner of evil', Erasmus argued, 'there is no need to add fuel to the furnace'.[9] Some things are better left unsaid.

Erasmus was able to subpoena an impressive list of witnesses in support of his argument. Yet he insisted that he was not seeking to evade the *authority* of Scripture; rather, he was simply appealing to the writings of the Fathers and Doctors of the church in order to establish the *meaning* of Scripture.

> I confess that it is right that the sole authority of Holy Scripture should outweigh all the votes of all mortal men. But the authority of the Scripture is not here in dispute. The same Scriptures are acknowledged and venerated by either side. Our battle is about the meaning of Scripture.[10]

Erasmus knew he had aimed well. However, it seems that he did not quite anticipate the overpowering reply that thundered from Wittenberg some sixteen months later, Luther's *De servo arbitrio* (The Bondage of the Will).[11] The delay in its appearance was not due to indifference on Luther's part. Other factors such as the Peasants' Revolt and Luther's own marriage had intervened along the way. As the months dragged on, though, rumours abounded about Luther's imminent reply to the great scholar. When it came, the tone was sharp and the arguments seemed irrefutable.

---

[9] Erasmus 1524a: 41.

[10] Erasmus 1524a: 43.

[11] For a stimulating treatment of this work, its reception and its use within the Lutheran tradition see Kolb 2005. Luther's understanding of the clarity of Scripture has been the subject of detailed attention, often with special reference to *De servo arbitrio*. See Beisser 1966; Rothen 1990; and Thompson 2004: 192 and the work cited there.

Luther mounted a stunning array of arguments for maintaining the clarity of Scripture. In the first place, he argued that Erasmus' appeal to the impenetrable depth of God's greatness (that God is so great that we ought to expect Scripture to be difficult at points) involved a confusion of two distinct things:

> God and the Scripture of God are two things, no less than the Creator and the creature are two things. That in God are many things hidden, of which we are ignorant, no one doubts . . . But that in Scripture there are some things abstruse, and everything is not plain – this is an idea put about by the ungodly Sophists . . .[12]

In other words, to say that those things revealed in Scripture are meant to be understood is not to say that everything has been revealed in Scripture. Some things, such as the exact timing of the parousia, simply have not been given to us to know. Yet what has been given to us can be approached with confidence. Luther was not saying there are no difficulties in Scripture. Just a few lines later he would admit there were many texts (*multa loca*) in the Scriptures that remain obscure. However, the explanation for this obscurity lay, not with some deficiency in the Scriptures themselves, nor with 'the majesty of their subject matter' but with 'our ignorance of their vocabulary and grammar'. The problem is with us, the readers, not with the text of Scripture. Furthermore, those currently difficult texts 'in no way hinder a knowledge of all the subject matter (*omnium rerum*) of Scripture'.[13]

Luther was able to say this because he subscribed to the ancient principle of the analogy of Scripture.[14] When Scripture is compared with Scripture, the clear passages enable us to make progress with those less clear.

> The subject matter of the Scriptures, therefore, is all quite accessible, even though some texts are still obscure owing to our ignorance of their terms. Truly it is stupid and impious, when we know the subject matter of Scripture has all been placed in the clearest light, to call it obscure on account of a few obscure words. If the words are obscure in one place, yet

---

[12] Luther 1525: 25 (*WA* XVIII, 606.11–13, 16–17 = *LW* 33, 25).
[13] Luther 1525: 25 (*WA* XVIII, 606.22–24 = *LW* 33, 25).
[14] Blocher 1987.

they are plain in another; and it is one and the same theme, published quite openly to the whole world, which in the Scriptures is sometimes expressed in plain words, and sometimes lies as yet hidden in obscure words.[15]

Yet at the same time Luther does not see this as a licence to divide Scripture into those parts that are clear and those that are obscure. To create such categories is to neglect the provisional and contingent nature of the difficulty with some texts. They are not meant to be obscure or to stay obscure. The Christian can approach them with the expectation that a growing familiarity with the Scriptures as a whole, greater facility with biblical languages, further engagement with Christ as its subject matter, will open up their meaning.

> in opposition to you I say with respect to the whole Scripture, I will not have any part of it called obscure. What we have cited from Peter holds good here, that the word of God is for us 'a lamp shining in a dark place'. But if part of this lamp does not shine, it will be a part of the dark place rather than of the lamp itself. Christ has not so enlightened us as deliberately to leave some part of his word obscure while commanding us to give heed to it, for he commands us in vain to give heed if it does not give light.[16]

The very phenomenon of commands in Scripture requires its clarity.

Luther will not isolate his discussion of Scripture from its theological context. I have previously mentioned his response to Erasmus' express preference for the arguments of the Sceptics over Luther's brash dogmatism: 'the *Holy Spirit* is no Skeptic'.[17] Later on in the book Luther asks, 'if Scripture is obscure or ambiguous, what point is there in God giving it to us? Are we not obscure and ambiguous enough without having our [own] obscurity, ambiguity, and darkness augmented for us from heaven?'[18] To make such a claim about Scripture is to impugn the character and purpose of God. That is why Luther can describe it as both 'impudent and blasphemous'.[19] It was one thing to appeal, as Erasmus did, to the *perfect knowledge* of the

[15] Luther 1525: 26 (*WA* XVIII, 606.30–35 = *LW* 33, 26).
[16] Luther 1525: 94–95 (*WA* XVIII, 656.15–21 = *LW* 33, 94–95).
[17] Luther 1525: 24 (*WA* XVIII, 605.32 = *LW* 33, 24; my emphasis).
[18] Luther 1525: 93–94 (*WA* XVIII, 655.25–27 = *LW* 33, 93–94).
[19] Luther 1525: 94 (*WA* XVIII, 656.6 = *LW* 33, 94).

end; it was another to neglect the *certain knowledge* that comes this side of the resurrection. Christ, the key to all the Scriptures, has been given to us and he dispels all darkness.[20]

Luther cited a myriad of biblical texts in support of this argument. The classic references to Scripture as light (Ps. 119:105, 130; 2 Pet. 1:19) were connected by him with Jesus' own words that he is 'the light of the world' (John 8:12; 9:5). He drew attention to the way Scripture is presented as the standard against which all teaching and behaviour is to be measured (Deut. 17:8). Encouragements to read the Scriptures themselves imply it can be understood and will prove fruitful for life before God (John 5:39; Acts 17:11; 2 Tim. 3:16–17). As significant as any other piece of biblical evidence for this conviction, in Luther's eyes, is the gospel appeal to the Old Testament (e.g. Rom. 1:2; 3:21). The person and work of Jesus, the Saviour in whom we must place our trust, is understood in the New Testament as the fulfilment of God's Old Testament promise. The Law and the prophets testify to the salvation he has brought. All he has done is 'according to the Scriptures'.

Luther did not avoid Erasmus' complaint that diverse and conflicting interpretations are evidence that Scripture is not clear. First, he reminded Erasmus that all explanations of Scripture, no matter by whom they are given, are to be tested by recourse to the texts themselves in the presence of the church.[21] The Bereans of Acts 17 are a model for the Christian response to all preaching and writing. Second, he placed engagement with the Bible in a larger, spiritual context. Instead of appealing to the weakness of the human mind (he in fact argued that 'nothing is more fitting for understanding the words of God than such weakness'), he spoke of the malice of Satan, who 'sits enthroned in our weakness, resisting the word of God'.[22] There is more to reading and believing the Scriptures than meets the eye.

Which leads us to one of Luther's most distinctive contributions, his delineation of two kinds of clarity in Scripture.[23] There is, he insisted, an 'external clarity', which concerns the public accessibility of Scripture. God has graciously chosen to express himself in the

---

[20] 'For what still sublimer thing can remain hidden in the Scriptures now that the seals have been broken, the stone rolled from the door of the sepulchre, and the supreme mystery brought to light . . . Take Christ out of the Scriptures, and what will you find left in them?' (Luther 1525: 25–26 [*WA* XVIII, 606.24–26, 29 = *LW* 33, 25–26]).

[21] Luther 1525: 91 (*WA* XVIII, 653.28 = *LW* 33, 91).

[22] Luther 1525: 99–100 (*WA* XVIII, 659.27–31 = *LW* 33, 99–100).

[23] Thompson 2004: 228–235.

ordinary conventions of human language, with the result that 'everything there is in the Scriptures has been brought out by the Word into the most definite light, and published to all the world'.[24] This is the aspect of clarity that makes the public ministry of the word possible as well as the appeal to Scripture in all matters of doctrine and Christian living. Yet there is another aspect of Scripture's clarity: 'internal clarity'. There is a sense in which, to use his words, 'no man perceives one iota of what is in the Scriptures unless he has the Spirit of God'.[25] It is possible to know how to quote Scripture, to recite everything in it in a way that makes perfect sense and to 'apprehend and truly understand nothing of it'. Understanding, in the true Christian sense, is more than making sense of the words on the page. The clarity of Scripture, Luther argued, needs to be understood at both of these levels, external and internal, and we must remember that God involves himself in both. The clarity of Scripture is no mere once and for all accomplishment, 'a static property of the text', to use the popular caricature. Scripture remains God's word by which he addresses the human heart. God's clear word is made clear to believers by God.

The debate with Erasmus was not the first or last time Luther would discuss the clarity of Scripture.[26] It is a consistent theme in his writing and in other contexts he was happy to assert this conviction without detailed explanation and without qualification. Yet *De servo arbitrio* remains his critical contribution to the discussion of the topic, and the arguments he mounted here were repeated by others in the decades and centuries that followed. Within months Erasmus had produced a response to Luther, in which he delighted in pointing out the differences emerging between the Reformation theologians themselves as further proof that the clarity of Scripture is an illusion.[27] But Luther considered this next instalment to be facile and told his

[24] Luther 1525: 28 (*WA* XVIII, 609.13–14 = *LW* 33, 28).

[25] Luther 1525: 28 (*WA* XVIII, 609.6–7 = *LW* 33, 28).

[26] Thompson 2004: 193–205.

[27] 'Finally, why do your "brothers" disagree so much with one another? They all have the same Scripture, they all claim the same spirit. And yet Karlstadt disagrees with you violently. So do Zwingli and Oecolampadius and Capito, who approve of Karlstadt's opinion though not of his reasons for it. Then again Zwingli and Balthazar are miles apart on many points. To say nothing of images, which are rejected by others but defended by you, not to mention rebaptism rejected by your followers but preached by others, and passing over in silence the fact that secular studies are condemned by others but defended by you. Since you are all treating the subject matter of Scripture, if there is no obscurity in it, why is there so much disagreement among you?' (Erasmus 1526: 130–131).

colleagues that it added nothing new to the discussion. He did not even bother to reply. However, two decades later, when the Roman Catholic Church finally convened a General Council to deal with the theology of the Reformers (amongst other things), it made no attempt to take Luther's arguments seriously. It simply reiterated the official position.[28]

## The saint and the professor

A significant extension of the Luther–Erasmus debate took place in the wake of the Council of Trent. One of the great champions of the council and its doctrine was Roberto Bellarmino.[29] In November 1576 he began his tenure as Professor of Controversial Theology at the Roman College (later incorporated into the Gregorian University). His appointment was part of Gregory XIII's plan to 'stem the tide of heresy' and win back those who had been deceived by it. Though only 34 at the time, Bellarmino soon made a name for himself as a controversialist who could answer the teaching of the heretics and give new courage to Catholics in the 'lost lands'. Ten years later the first volume of his great *Disputationes de controversiis christianae fidei adversus hujus temporis hereticos* (Disputations on the Controversies of the Christian Faith against the Heretics of Today) appeared, with significant attention devoted to the Reformation teaching on Scripture.[30] Many of the arguments found in Erasmus are rehearsed in this work, yet with considerably more detail, extensive references both to Scripture and the church Fathers, and a great deal more passion. He built his case against the clarity or perspicuity of Scripture around five basic arguments.[31]

---

[28] 'Furthermore, in order to curb impudent clever persons, the synod decrees that no one who relies on his own judgment in matters of faith and morals, which pertain to the building up of Christian doctrine, and that no one who distorts the Sacred Scripture according to his own opinions, shall dare to interpret the said Sacred Scripture contrary to the sense which is held by holy mother Church, whose duty it is to judge regarding the true sense and interpretation of the Holy Scriptures, or even contrary to the unanimous consent of the Fathers, even though interpretations of this kind were never intended to be brought to light' (*Decretum de editione et usu sacrorum librorum*, Council of Trent, Session IV, 8 April 1546 [Denzinger 1954: 245 (no. 786)]).

[29] Roberto Bellarmino is probably best known by the anglicized version of his name, Robert Bellarmine.

[30] Bellarmino 1586.

[31] The arguments made by Bellarmino are most accessible in the response by William Whitaker (Whitaker 1588: 367–380). However, the high regard Bellarmino is reported to have had for Whitaker's scholarship suggests we can expect Whitaker to have presented his opponent's case truthfully, if not sympathetically.

1. *The authority of Scripture*. Bellarmino drew attention to David's prayer for understanding, which occurs five times in Psalm 119.[32] How is such a prayer to be reconciled with the clarity of Scripture? Also, it seems that the disciples on the Emmaus road (Luke 24:27) needed Jesus to interpret the Scriptures to them. Evidently, the Scriptures are difficult to understand without such aid. He then turned to the case of the Ethiopian eunuch (Acts 8), who once again needed an interpreter before he could understand the passage he was reading. Finally, Bellarmino cites the words of Peter about difficulties in Paul's writing (2 Pet. 3:16). Scripture itself, he concludes, testifies to its own difficulty and so the Protestant doctrine of the clarity of Scripture cannot stand.

2. *The common consent of the ancient Fathers*. Bellarmino cites eight key patristic witnesses in an attempt to demonstrate that this Protestant doctrine is a novelty that finds no place in apostolic Christianity. Irenaeus, Origen, Ruffinus, Chrysostom, Ambrose, Jerome, Augustine and Gregory are all quoted confessing the difficulties they had in their own reading of the text and the necessity of careful study. Irenaeus' simple approach ('in the Scriptures we understand some things and some things we commend to God') stands in stark contrast to the exaggerated claims of the Reformers.[33] Augustine's explanation of the usefulness of obscurity ('to tame our pride and rouse our understanding from listlessness') had been ignored by them.[34] The difficulty of Scripture has long been a part of the church's teaching.

3. *Necessary reasoning*. Under this heading Bellarmino drew attention to the connection between the profundity of Scripture's subject matter and the difficulties only to be expected in understanding the text. This connection between 'the things spoken and the way in which they are spoken' should not be lightly dismissed. Divine mysteries such as the Trinity and the incarnation of Christ cannot be

[32] Ps. 119: 34, 73, 125, 144, 169.

[33] The full quote reads, 'In regard to those things which we investigate in the Scriptures (which are throughout spiritual), we are able by the grace of God to explain some of them, while we must leave others in the hands of God' (Irenaeus 189: 399 [*Adversus haereses* II.xxviii.3 (*PG* VII, 806 = *ANF* I, 399)]).

[34] The full quote reads, 'Some of the expressions are so obscure as to shroud the meaning in thickest darkness. And I do not doubt that all this was divinely arranged for the purpose of subduing pride by toil, and of preventing a feeling of satiety in the intellect, which generally holds in small esteem what is discovered without difficulty' (Augustine 426: 537 [*De doctrina christiana* II.6 (*CCSL* XXXII, 36 = *NPNF*, 1st Series, II, 537)]).

expressed without straining our language and framework of thinking. Furthermore, we need to consider the complicated features of biblical language, including apparent contradictions, ambiguous terms, figurative language, foreign phrases and idioms, disrupted sentences, and apparent confusions of order in some narratives. Even leaving aside its sublime subject matter, the forms of expression in Scripture are enough to raise questions about unqualified assertions of Scripture's clarity.

4. *Common experience.* The fourth argument began with an observation of the phenomenon of biblical commentaries, at least as prevalent amongst the Protestants as in the church of Rome. Why were so many necessary if Scripture is so clear? Bellarmino then pointed to the variety of interpretation represented by these commentaries. If Scripture is clear, why haven't learned and godly men been able to agree on its meaning and significance? These differences, he was at pains to point out, were not just between Catholics and Protestants; they were a feature of the Reformers' own engagement with the Scriptures.

5. *The confession of the Protestants themselves.* Bellarmino's final argument was really a collection of comments by Luther, Brentius, Chemnitz and other Protestant writers, admitting difficulty with individual passages of Scripture and encouraging continued study in order to understand the biblical text. Bellarmino suggested that either the Reformers were inconsistent in their approach to Scripture on the basis of this doctrine or the claims made by this doctrine were disingenuous.

Bellarmino's brilliance as a controversialist is evident more than four hundred years later. His extraordinary contribution to a revitalized Catholicism in the early seventeenth century was recognized by his contemporaries, despite an acrimonious debate with Pope Sixtus V over continuing papal claims to temporal authority in Europe.[35] Undoubtedly, his was the most carefully argued refutation of *claritas scripturae* in the post-Reformation period. Few were able to marshall the resources of the Catholic tradition in the way he did. Many Protestant scholars attempted to respond to his work, but by his own reckoning the most significant answer came from the Regius Professor of Divinity at Cambridge, William Whitaker.

---

[35] It was most likely this continuing debate about papal authority that delayed his canonization for a little over three centuries. His cause was argued on a number of occasions in the seventeenth and eighteenth centuries but he was only finally canonized by Pope Pius XI in 1930 and declared a Doctor of the universal church a year later.

Whitaker had been at Cambridge for over twenty years when he published his response to Bellarmino and others on the doctrine of Scripture in 1588. His *Disputatio de sacra scriptura contra hujus temporis papistas* (Disputation on Holy Scripture against the Papists of Today) was the product of extended engagement with a large number of contemporary Catholic apologists, but it was tied in structure and argument to the work of Bellarmino, as Whitaker himself indicated in the preface.[36] After dealing first with the extent of the canon, the question of which version of the Bible should be used, and then the authority of the Scriptures, Whitaker turned his attention to the perspicuity or clarity of Scripture.[37]

His treatment of the topic was divided into four chapters. In the first he sought to establish the state of the question with reference to Luther and Erasmus, but also Eck, Bellarmino, Stapleton and a number of others. In this introduction to the topic, Whitaker sounded a note that would be repeated throughout his exposition. Catholic apologists have exaggerated the Protestant claim, he argued, making it absolute and leaving no room for real and continuing difficulty with particular passages. He strongly denied that this had ever been the Protestant position. Instead, he insisted,

> our fundamental principles are these: First, that the Scriptures are sufficiently clear to admit of their being read by the people and the unlearned with some fruit and utility. Secondly, that all things necessary to salvation are propounded in plain words in the Scriptures. Meanwhile, we concede that there are many obscure places, and that the Scriptures need explication; and that, on this account, God's ministers are to be listened to when they expound the word of God, and the men best skilled in Scripture are to be consulted.[38]

Whitaker explicitly argued that this was in all respects the same argument as that published by Luther sixty years earlier. The clarity of Scripture did not mean, and had never meant, that there are no difficulties at all in Scripture. The Catholic caricature of this doctrine was a simple and commonplace rhetorical device: it is always easier to knock over a straw man than the real thing. Luther and those

---

[36] Whitaker 1588: 19.
[37] Whitaker 1588: 359–401.
[38] Whitaker 1588: 364.

others who had dealt with this topic on the Protestant side, Whitaker asserted, had always recognized the reality of difficulties and had even suggested reasons why this might be so. In fact, as the next chapter in Whitaker's exposition went on to demonstrate with reference to the early church Fathers, the difficulties that still exist in clear Scripture can themselves be seen as part of God's good provision for his people. By such difficulties God calls us to prayer, excites our diligence, keeps our interest, causes us to value the Scriptures, subdues our pride, and much else besides.[39]

It is in the third chapter that Whitaker attempts a point-by-point refutation of Bellarmino's five arguments.[40] It is a masterful, if somewhat wordy, response. David's prayer in Psalm 119 is the prayer of every Christian. It is never enough just to know the words of Scripture. What is more, that understanding of the heart which shows itself in faith and obedience is a gift of God, and so prayer for it is entirely appropriate. The disciples on the Emmaus road and the eunuch on the road to Gaza were in distinctive situations. The disciples were stricken with grief and the eunuch was unskilled and unfamiliar with Scripture. In any event, the clarity of Scripture has never meant that the aid of those more familiar with the Scriptures is irrelevant, unhelpful or, particularly when the case of young Christians is considered, unnecessary. Peter's words about Paul need to be weighed carefully. Yes, some things in Paul's letters are hard to understand, but not everything in them. Furthermore, Peter does encourage the reading of Paul's letters at the same time. Bellarmino's appeal to these passages paid too little attention to the context of each.

Next, Whitaker dealt with Bellarmino's quotations from the Fathers. He acknowledged that the Fathers do in fact speak of difficulties, but again he denied that the exclusion of all talk of difficulty had ever been part of the doctrine of Scripture's clarity. Yet, alongside this concession, Whitaker argued that Bellarmino had repeatedly overstated his case. A confession of ignorance is not the same thing as an argument that understanding is not possible. What obscurities there are in the Scriptures are not such that they would prevent ordinary Christians from reading them. Indeed, such reading was encouraged by the Fathers. In addition, the Fathers demonstrated a confidence that, with further prayerful study, those difficulties which do exist could be resolved.

---

[39] Whitaker 1588: 365–366.
[40] Whitaker 1588: 367–380.

Whitaker deals similarly with the arguments from necessary reasoning and common experience. Bellarmino had failed to appreciate the difference between true knowledge and exhaustive or complete knowledge. We do not know everything there is to know about God and his purposes. There is a limit to what we can say, simply because there is a limit to what God has made known. Yet what he has made known, what he has caused to be written about the sublime subjects of the faith, is plain. Whitaker took up Bellarmino's own examples:

> For example, that God is one in substance and three in persons, that God was made man, and such like, although they be in themselves, if we regard the nature of the things themselves, so obscure that they can by no means be perceived by us; yet they are proposed plainly in Scripture, if we will be content with that knowledge of them which God hath chosen to impart to us.[41]

On the subject of the writing of commentaries, Whitaker argued, Bellarmino had again failed to make a critical distinction, this time that between writing with the goal of making Scripture understood and writing with the goal of making Scripture better and more easily understood. Scripture can be understood without the commentaries. They are not necessary in this sense. Yet gifted teachers are themselves God's gift to his people and they serve their fellows by encouraging better understanding and more wholehearted appropriation. The diversity of opinion amongst the commentators ought not to be exaggerated beyond its actual extent. There was, Whitaker argued, a remarkable unanimity amongst the Reformed commentators on most matters. The real differences that exist were more a product of 'our slowness and inconstancy' than anything in the text itself.[42]

Bellarmino's final argument, the Protestants' own confession of difficulty in Scripture, concerned Whitaker least of all. He had already shown that the Reformers, like the Fathers before them, could concede some difficulties in Scripture without abandoning their commitment to its clarity. As far as Whitaker was concerned, Bellarmino had expended all this effort on proving something he and his friends

---

[41] Whitaker 1588: 376. Though Whitaker himself makes no use of this passage, his argument here parallels that of Deut. 29:29.

[42] Whitaker 1588: 379–380.

would willingly concede and had attacked a notion of absolute transparency and simplicity that they had never defended!

The final chapter of Whitaker's exposition of this topic was devoted to his own argument for the clarity of Scripture, although at each point he also presented Bellarmino's counter-argument and sought to refute it.[43] He began with five Scriptural passages and themes: the accessibility of the commandment (Deut 30:11); the image of Scripture as a light (Pss. 19; 119; Prov. 6:22); Jesus' description of the apostolic band, those future authors of the New Testament, as 'the light of the world' (Matt. 5:14); Peter's appeal to the sure word of prophecy as 'a lamp shining in a dark place' (2 Pet. 1:19); and Paul's words to the Corinthians that 'if our gospel be hid, it is hid to them that are lost' (2 Cor. 4:3, AV). There was nothing new here. These verses had been used by others before him.[44] His argument that since 'the sum of the whole Scripture' is clear we are able to say that Scripture is clear, was likewise far from novel. However, it did require him to engage Bellarmino's argument that if the doctrines of Scripture were indeed clear, there would be no controversy about them. Whitaker's reply was straightforward: 'there is nothing in Scripture so plain that some men have not doubted it'.[45]

Whitaker did claim to go beyond earlier arguments at a number of points, most notably a development of the theological argument we identified in Luther's response to Erasmus:

> If the Scriptures be so obscure and difficult to be understood, that they cannot be read with advantage by the people, then this hath happened, either because the Holy Spirit could not write more plainly, or because he would not. No one will say that he could not: and that he would not, is repugnant to the end of writing . . . The Holy Spirit willed the Scriptures to be consigned to writing in order that we might understand them; and that this was the end which he proposed there are many things in the Scriptures themselves that testify: therefore, they are so written as to be intelligible by us, or else the Holy Spirit hath not gained his end; which cannot be thought without impiety.[46]

---

[43] Whitaker structures his argument in twelve parts, no doubt with some eye on how this would appear to dwarf his opponents' presentation (Whitaker 1588: 381–401).

[44] Whitaker readily admits that the first nine of his twelve arguments are attributable to Martin Luther and Johann Brentius of Würtemberg (Whitaker 1588: 381).

[45] Whitaker 1588: 389.

[46] Whitaker 1588: 392.

What is said about the Scriptures cannot be said in isolation from the rest of Christian theology. In the final analysis, for Whitaker, as for Luther and a considerable number of patristic writers before him, the power and benevolence of God undergirds the doctrine of Scripture's clarity.

William Whitaker was a scholar, as learned an opponent as any Bellarmino faced in his lifetime. Yet he was also driven by pastoral concerns. He was convinced that opposition to the doctrine of Scripture's clarity could be used, and was in fact being used by some, to dissuade Christian people from private reading and study of the Bible. His own defence of the doctrine was laced with references to the importance and usefulness of reading Scripture. The word of God is too valuable, in a sense too powerful, to be left in the hands of scholars or in the control of the hierarchy of the Roman Church. Instead, their undoubted contribution should equip and encourage every Christian man or woman to read the Bible for themselves. Whitaker summarized his position in just these terms: 'Our opinion is, that the Scriptures are not so difficult, but that those who read them attentively may receive from thence advantage and the greatest edification, even laymen, plebeians and the common mass of mankind.'[47]

## On appreciating the classical inheritance

When examined carefully and in context, the great classical treatments of this doctrine during the time of the Reformation are more robust and less naive than is generally acknowledged. While the doctrine always remained the clarity *of Scripture*, so that the text of Scripture is not bypassed in an appeal to some clear but disembodied meaning, it is richly theological in the sense that it speaks about God and his activity amongst us. Even if we were to move forward into the seventeenth century and the so-called Protestant Scholasticism of François Turretin in his *Institutio theologicae elencticae* (Institutes of Elenctic Theology) – much maligned by those who have read very little of it – a commitment to the relevance of God's presence, his sovereign power and his rich benevolence remains, despite a clear difference of structure, style and, to some degree, emphasis. 'The perspicuity of Scripture is further proved: (1) by their efficient cause (viz. God, the Father of men, who cannot be said either to be unwilling or unable to speak plainly without impugning his perfect goodness and wisdom) . . .'[48]

---

[47] Whitaker 1588: 381.
[48] Turretin 1679–85: 145.

It has been fashionable since the nineteenth century to suggest that in classical Reformed theologies a consciousness of God's involvement in the process of a faithful reading of Scripture was transformed into a static property of the text itself.[49] Undoubtedly, incautious statements were made by some who sought to defend the doctrine. A number of these arise in the midst of the controversies surrounding the authority of Scripture in the late nineteenth and early twentieth centuries. Building upon the Reformation notion of the priesthood of all believers, some affirmed the 'right of private judgment' as a religious correlate of the individual's civil rights in a democracy.[50] But the strongest and most enduring of the classical treatments of this doctrine cannot fairly be cast in that same light. A significant emphasis on the ongoing ministry of the Spirit is to be found in these, together with a recognition of the usefulness of reading in and with the church. To quote Turretin again:

> The question does not concern a perspicuity which excludes the means necessary for interpretation (i.e., the internal light of the Spirit, attention of mind, the voice and ministry of the church, sermons and commentaries, prayer and watchfulness). For we hold these means not only to be useful but also necessary ordinarily. We only wish to proscribe the darkness which would prevent the people from reading the Scriptures as harmful and perilous and compel them to have recourse to tradition when they might rest in the Scriptures alone.[51]

[49] '[L]ater accounts ran the risk of so talking about Scripture's clarity *in se* and *ante usum* that it became extracted from its proper dogmatic location and rendered as a natural property of the Bible *qua* text' (Webster 2005: 35). Heinrich Heppe's influential *Die Dogmatik der evangelisch-reformierten Kirche* includes such an aside in the midst of a quotation from Wendelin: 'Therefore H. Scripture has the attribute of perspicuity – [attributing to the book what is the gift of God?] – by which the things necessary to be known for salvation are so plainly and clearly unfolded in Scripture that they may be understood even by unlearned believers who read with devotion and attention' (Heppe 1861: 32–33).

[50] I have already made mention of Charles Hodge in this regard (Hodge 1871: 186).

[51] Turretin 1679–85: 144. George Giger's translation has been modified slightly at this point in order to make it more readable. The first sentence in Turretin's Latin original reads, 'Non quaeritur de Perspicuitate quae non excludat media ad Interpretationem necessaria; ut lucem Spiritus internam, attentionem animi, vocem et ministerium Ecclesiae, conciones et commentaries, preces et vigilias; agnoscimus enim talia media non modo utilia, sed etiam necessaria esse ordinarie: sed proscriptam tantum volumes eam obscuritatem, quae plebem arcet a lectione Scripturae quasi noxia sit et periculosa, et quae cogat ad Traditionem confugere, ubi subsistendum erat in sola Scriptura.'

There is an obvious awareness in the writing of Luther, Whitaker and Turretin that it is possible to claim too much in the name of this doctrine. Yet each of them refuses to withdraw from a bold statement of Scripture's clarity, particularly (but not exclusively) in those things necessary for salvation. In the final analysis, the clarity and sufficiency of Scripture were kept together in their thinking: Scripture is clear enough to provide a firm basis for doctrine and an unambiguous call to holiness.

# A doctrine for the times

The Christian theological tradition provides resources such as these that can sharpen and deepen any contemporary treatment of the clarity of Scripture. Yet these resources have frequently suffered from superficial readings and caricature. In addition, it should be frankly admitted that there has been, in some circles, a real neglect of the classical exposition, fuelled by an untenable commitment to the priority of the recent over the ancient, of the novel over the traditional, and an uncritical acceptance of the conclusions of nineteenth- and twentieth-century historical criticism. Notions of the evolution of religious ideas were a staple part of the diet of liberalism in the Harnack mode, and contemporary theology has not thrown off that yoke completely even yet. The most recent treatment of a theological topic is not always or necessarily the best. Twenty-first century theology in general needs to listen more carefully to the theological tradition on its own terms, rather than through the prism of twentieth-century concerns and nineteenth-century anthologies.

Nevertheless, an appreciation of the classic expositions of this doctrine does not mean they are, in and of themselves, sufficient for the needs of the moment. A theological reappropriation of contributions such as those of Luther, Whitaker and Turretin cannot afford to be purely reactive, refusing to do anything but restate them verbatim or in a contemporary paraphrase. There have been many very significant advances in understanding over the last four hundred years. Furthermore, the culture (in particular the intellectual culture) in which the contemporary reading of Scripture takes place, asks many of the same questions in a very different way as well as coming up with some of its own. The recovery of a robust doctrine of Scripture for the twenty-first century requires both faithfulness and confidence, a commitment to pass on the apostolic gospel combined with a serious engagement with the thought world of our contemporaries.

This ought not to be represented as a surrender to apologetic interests that will undoubtedly swamp the declaratory nature of Christian theology and necessarily distort its content. There is a pretentiousness and even an air of self-deception about the insistence that Christian dogmatics should keep itself pure from apologetic entanglements. Of course God's self-revelation must set the agenda for theological work, not the culture into which that gospel is proclaimed. Nevertheless, the act of faithfully speaking about God and his purposes does not occur in a vacuum and theology abstracted to such a level that this seems possible fails to fulfil its most basic responsibility. Christian doctrine and Christian living amidst God's people in the eyes of the world are more deeply intertwined than that. In particular, a doctrine concerned with the accessibility and intelligibility of God's self-revelation in the words of Scripture cannot avoid the questions of the moment.

As I have noted on more than one occasion, our decisions about this doctrine have a significant impact upon the approach to reading the Bible taken in the course of ordinary Christian discipleship. The biblical exhortation to read and hear and teach the Scriptures has been echoed in the Christian tradition, but the task seems much more complex in the light of contemporary questions about truth and sophisticated theories about texts and meaning. Has the modern equivalent of the ploughboy got a chance? With so many claiming that the text does not mean what it seems to mean, with others insisting that meaning consists of what each individual brings to the text, with influential church leaders openly rejecting the teaching of Scripture at the very points at which it calls our own culture to account, there is little incentive to 'take and read' as Augustine did in that garden in Milan over sixteen hundred years ago. This can only compound that widespread biblical illiteracy that has emerged in the past two generations.[52]

It is undoubtedly significant that so much classical interest in the doctrine of Scripture's clarity is driven by a concern to encourage direct engagement with the Scriptures by those who are not scholars or specialists in biblical studies. The advocates of this doctrine understood that without a confidence that Scripture is clear, few could be expected to begin or to persevere in reading the Bible. They knew too that without it the public reading of Scripture would soon be

---

[52] For current statistical information on the level of biblical literacy amongst American teenagers see Gallup 2005.

swamped by other activities that seem to generate a more direct connection with God (Luther believed this was something that could be observed both in the Roman Church and amongst the *Schwärmer* [fanatics]). Yet they argued from their own experience that a robust confidence in the clarity of Scripture stimulated interest in the word of God. It generated expectations of hearing God's address and it nurtured wholehearted faith and fulsome obedience. Although assaults upon this doctrine may not be responsible for the contemporary malaise in much Western Christian life and thought, a confident and responsible reaffirmation of the clarity of Scripture may play a significant role in its remedy.

Another important cutting edge of this doctrine at the beginning of the twenty-first century lies in the field of ethics. An argument that the meaning of Scripture is unclear, or irrelevant because of its location amidst the historical particularities and thought world of antiquity, has featured in debates over gender relationships (especially over how these are reflected in church life), human sexuality (especially over the acceptability or otherwise of homosexual behaviour) and the sanctity of yet unborn life (especially when this debate is redefined in terms of 'rights': the right to choose versus the right to life). It would be easy in passing reference to these debates to caricature them. It must be emphasized that not everyone who wishes to revise classical Christian teaching on these subjects argues that the Bible is unclear at these points and so, because it is unclear, we are free to decide the issues on other grounds. The discussion in each case is more complex than that. Nevertheless, it is a simple matter of the historical record that some participants in these debates have published contributions that advance precisely this argument.[53] They insist that there are hard questions that traditional positions, relying on traditional readings of particular biblical texts, need to answer. Yet surely the hard questions need to be asked in both directions. One of those hard questions concerns whether the suggestion that Scripture is unclear is sustainable in the light of traditional as well as contemporary biblical scholarship and the Christian understanding of God as one who speaks effectively. If not, perhaps the real problem lies in the challenge the Bible presents to today's ideological commitments.

Ethical discussion involves a decision about the clarity of Scripture. Is the biblical text sufficiently clear to give us, in Anthony

---

[53] Groothuis 1997: 215–216; Nathan 2002: 142–145; Cowdell 2004.

Thiselton's words, 'a ground on which we may confidently proceed'.[54] Of course, as I have repeatedly indicated, some individual texts will be difficult. We have no promise that we will have *all* the answers. On some issues there will be room for the legitimate exercise of Christian freedom. Yet our confidence in the goodness of God and his capacity to make his mind known to us without distortion should generate an expectation that the basic contours of a Christian response to even the most recent developments in thought and practice can be found in the Scriptures. God has given us what we need to live as his people in the last days. Such a theological perspective should also generate a concern, not to hedge in the application of any particular biblical teaching, but precisely because it is the good word of a good God, to appropriate it to the full.

However, these are not the only, or even the most important, aspects of contemporary thought and life upon which our consideration of this doctrine has an immediate and urgent bearing. In a world overshadowed by global terrorism, where the demand for security and social harmony means we can no longer avoid the diversity of religious convictions, the clarity of Scripture's testimony to Jesus Christ is itself being questioned. There is increasing pressure (political, social and ecclesiastical) for less 'exclusive' readings of texts like John 14:6 and Acts 4:12. To understand these texts as teaching the uniqueness of Jesus or that salvation and blessing are to be found only by those who belong to him is portrayed as the mere repetition of an ancient bigotry, a defensive strategy that, like most defensive strategies, operates to exclude or oppress those we fear. Genuine interfaith dialogue demands a suspension if not a repudiation of such claims and so another way of understanding these texts must be found. A reality we can no longer avoid demands we read the Bible differently.[55]

To appeal to texts such as John 14:6, Acts 4:12 and a myriad of others as clear affirmations of the uniqueness of Jesus Christ and the reality of salvation only in him is, in the current climate, considered to be scandalous. Yet an appreciation of 'the scandal of particularity' has long been part of the Christian theological tradition (1 Cor. 1:22–24). It was as unfashionable in the first century to proclaim Jesus as the Son of the living God, the only one who can save men and women, as it is in the twenty-first. People were offended then too,

---

[54] Thiselton 1992: 184–185.

[55] With different degrees of sophistication, arguments to this end can be found in Doctrine Commission 1995: 168; Dupuis 1997: 286–288; Swidler 1997: 185.

social structures were disrupted, violence was not an uncommon repercussion of making the claim. Furthermore, the unambiguous testimony of Scripture in this regard is the engine room of Christian mission, which is fuelled by love rather than fear or a desire to extinguish difference. The consequences of a denial that these are clear and unambiguous claims from Jesus himself and those commissioned to speak his words into the world are catastrophic and expose once again the spiritual context in which all our reading, and all our talk about reading, takes place. Any demand that the call to come to Jesus be silenced or modified so as not to offend those who already have other commitments can only have one ultimate origin.

There is a spiritual context in which all engagement with Scripture takes place, whether at the corporate or individual level. The doctrine of the clarity of Scripture cannot be isolated from that context as if it were a neutral and purely academic matter about textual intelligibility, hermeneutical sophistication and the shared life of readers and texts. The idea that none of us is a disinterested reader is more acceptable at the moment than it has been in the past. Gadamer and his successors have done us a service at this point. Yet the moral and spiritual propensity to avoid the meaning of a text (not least by claiming it is unclear) is still not often recognized. One of those things we bring to the reading of the biblical text is our own rebellious struggle against the sovereign right of God to determine what is true and what is right. As John Webster reminds us, it is that struggle that binds the clarity of Scripture and prayer:

> the very act of interpretation is itself an episode in the struggle between faith and repudiation of God. We can cloak our own darkness by calling it the obscurity of the text; we can evade the judgement which Scripture announces by endless hermeneutical deferral; we can treat Scripture not as the clear Word of judgement and hope but as a further opportunity for the imagination to be puzzled, stimulated and set to work . . . That is why the promise of *claritas scripturae* is inseparable from the prayer: 'Open my eyes, that I may behold wondrous things out of thy law'.[56]

There is more than one way to harden our hearts, as the writer to the Hebrews put it in the first century (Heb. 3:7 – 4:13). It is possible to

[56] Webster 2005: 67.

understand the word that has been spoken to us and yet still refuse to align ourselves with it.

# A clear and present word

A contemporary restatement of the doctrine of the clarity of Scripture needs to take both its classical exposition and its present context seriously. The objections raised by late modern and postmodern philosophy, literary theory and theology, to a much unappreciated extent, have been anticipated in the debates of the past. The limitations and imperfections of our knowledge, given our location in history rather than outside it or at the point of its fulfilment, were highlighted by Bellarmino. Questions about the adequacy of human language to convey or even depict spiritual realities were raised by Erasmus and many others before him. The patristic and medieval discussions of figurative language anticipated concerns about genre and literary form. They were also preliminary skirmishes in the battle over the extent to which the author or the author's situation determine the meaning of the text. Meanwhile, the intense struggle over the role of the church in the process of interpretation, its shaping of the reader and its adjudication between conflicting readings takes on a new dimension in the wake of the work of Gadamer and Fish.

Nevertheless, whereas there are many more similarities between current and previous discussions of these issues than is often realized, there can be little doubt that each of these questions has been intensified by the contributions of contemporary philosophy, literary theory and theological studies. In addition a number of new concerns have emerged, including an appreciation of the range of illocutionary possibilities in human discourse and a new sensitivity to the way an appeal to a clear text can be used to serve the interests of those with power. Furthermore, most of the traditional discussions took place within a theological framework, where the reality and relevance of God and his unique relation to the biblical text were accepted on all sides. Today the discussion is very often conducted within the bounds of naturalism. Jowett's suggestion that Scripture should be read like any other book has achieved axiomatic status.

As I have attempted to demonstrate, the principal response to almost all the objections raised against this doctrine, whether traditional or contemporary, is in fact located in the field of theology rather than that of historical or literary studies. This is not to ignore or minimize the positive contribution of historians or literary theorists. Nor is it to remain blind to the character of the Bible as a piece of literature anchored in an important way to certain periods of human history. Nevertheless, the effectiveness of this text as a piece of communication depends ultimately on the power and benevolence of the God who gives it to us. In other words, the clarity of Scripture is in essence a divine gift rather than a human achievement. It is a gift that cannot be isolated from this text as a text – in this sense the language of gift and textual attribute come together in a theological account of the doctrine. Yet it is God himself who ensures he will be known by those who are his. He does not leave them in the dark about his character, his purposes or his promises. In these genuinely human words, which are never less than genuinely human while at the same time remaining in the fullest possible sense the word of God to us, God presents his Son to the world. The offence caused by such a message in the world at large is itself a testimony to its clarity. There are no insurmountable obstacles to God's communicative purposes.

It is God's involvement with this text, not just at the point of composition but all the way through to the activity of reading the Bible at the beginning of the third millennium, that calls into question the assumptions made by many who oppose the clarity of Scripture. While the Bible remains a written text, a book of words open to investigation as a piece of literature or as a testimony to history, it will not fit into such categories neatly or without remainder. This text is *sui generis*; the attempt to read it 'like any other book' is, in the final analysis, to overlook its critical otherness. The origin of the Scriptures can and to some extent must be explained in terms of the activity of figures such as Moses, David, Isaiah and the apostle Paul. The human authorship of each part of the Bible is never simply incidental. Yet to explain the origin of the Bible in human terms alone is deeply inadequate in the light of the phenomena of the texts and their own explicit claims. The Bible as a whole, and each part, has its ultimate origin in the communicative activity of the living God. As I have stressed previously, this generates an extraordinary situation when it comes to reading these texts: they are never read in the absence of the God who speaks in and through them. Luther's external and internal clarity of Scripture are both God's work rather than ours. God has not abandoned his word to the vicissitudes of ordinary literary engagement. The same Spirit who moved men to write these words moves in the hearts of men and women to bring about an understanding that demonstrates itself in repentance and faith.

Embedded within such an understanding of the text and its relation to God as its ultimate author is a theological perspective on the
phenomenon of human language. It is not enough to speak of human
language as a creaturely phenomenon that is commandeered, or even
'sanctified', as a vehicle for divine self-revelation.[57] God is himself the
source of human language. He is the first speaker and invests language with a deep significance for generating and nourishing personal relationships. Far from being an unsuitable or inadequate
vehicle for God's revelation of himself and his purposes, the first use
of human language has precisely this function. God makes promises
that can be trusted. It is God's intention that his people trust those
promises. Of course the deeply textured nature of human language
must also be taken seriously. We do not always speak or write in a
literal mode: there is a rich variety of form, genre, style and literary
or rhetorical device that when ignored heightens the risk of misunderstanding. None of this subtlety in linguistic structure is insig-
nificant. It is part of the wonder of the divine gift. Precisely for this
reason, a plain reading of the Bible should never be confused with a
uniformly flat or literal reading of the Bible. There is a dynamic
quality to human language generally that is reflected at various levels
in the biblical text.

At the heart of God's involvement with this text is the centrality of
its witness to Jesus Christ – his person, work and words. In the final
analysis, all the words God has spoken testify to him. A theological
perspective that does not find the critical centre of Scripture's clarity
at this point has not taken God or this text seriously enough. The
living God is not known apart from, behind or alongside Jesus
Christ. To know him is to know the Father, and to know him is life.
This is at least part of the reason why classical treatments of this doctrine stressed the clarity of Scripture in 'those things necessary to
salvation'.[58] The clarity of Scripture radiates from this point because
this is the centre of God's purposes. God's intention is not mere intellectual enrichment but salvation from sin and judgment, and this

---

[57] The proper dogmatic location of the doctrine of Scripture is within revelation, or
better the knowledge of God, rather than sanctification; contra de Senarclens 1959:
294–297; Webster 2003a: 17–30 (though note p. 39).

[58] For instance, *The Westminster Confession of Faith* (1647), I.vii, reads, 'All things
in Scripture are not alike plain in themselves, nor alike clear unto all; yet those things
which are necessary to be known, believed, and observed for salvation, are so clearly
propounded and opened in some place of Scripture or other, that not only the learned,
but the unlearned, in a due use of the ordinary means, may attain unto a sufficient
understanding of them.'

salvation is realized only in Jesus Christ. A reading of Scripture that does not relate its parts to this centre runs the risk of being fragmentary, of stressing diversity over fundamental unity, of 'reading against the grain'. The shape of the biblical canon, the internal dynamic of promise and fulfilment, and the explicit statements of the New Testament about the testimony of the Old Testament to the person and work of Jesus all point in this direction. The Scriptures are a rich tapestry that finds its basic unity in the Father's presentation of the Son. God is active by his Spirit to this very end as the Scriptures are read.

Once again, this personal and present activity of the living God does not mean that each passage of Scripture is simple or that its meaning is transparent. God does not ensure that understanding is uniformly automatic or intuitive, nor has any serious affirmation of Scripture's clarity ever denied the continuing reality of difficulty at points. Such difficulty continues to be explained in a variety of ways. There is a depth to the purposes of God: they encompass judgment as well as salvation; God is concerned both to nourish faith and to encourage the exercise of a faithful mind. In addition, our lack of familiarity with the text, with its language and structure or its deeply coherent message (biblical theology), can complicate the picture. However, beyond all of these considerations lies another that is often neglected. A theological perspective is required, not only on the nature of human language and the production of this text, but on the conditions under which it is read in the world between the resurrection and the return.

As mentioned a moment ago, the Bible is read in the midst of a world that continues to assert its own perspective, its own right to self-determination. In other words, it is read not only in the presence of God but in the presence too of human repudiation of God, a repudiation that continues to echo, however faintly, in every individual reader and in every corporate audience. Our readerly limitations, not merely in terms of acquaintance with this text and its context, nor simply in terms of creaturely contingence and finitude, but limitations in the moral and spiritual sphere, impact upon our reception of this text and its message. Even as a reader the Christian remains *simul iustus et peccator* (at the same time righteous and a sinner). In the face of such a reality, a message does not have to be obscure or ambiguous to be misunderstood.

Another feature of a theological perspective on the context of our reading is the importance of the churches as proper interpretative communities. There should be little doubt that the Reformers' concerns about authorized ecclesiastical interpretations need to be taken seriously. Where such decisions are treated as beyond criticism, even criticism based on the words of Scripture itself, the Bible is in effect deprived of its authoritative status. I have already touched upon ways in which this possibility continues to be realized in certain contemporary debates. The decisions of the churches do not determine the meaning of Scripture. At their best creeds and confessions are recognition statements, acknowledging the antecedent meaning of Scripture and remaining open to correction by appeal to the actual words of the biblical text. Yet too often in the centuries since the Reformation this legitimate concern was expanded into a call for detachment from any ecclesiastical context. Reading was assumed to take place apart from the churches as purely a matter of personal and individual interaction between the reader and this text. In such cases the clarity *of Scripture* was transformed into the right of private judgment: 'The churches have no right to say that I am wrong.' The similarity of this result with a certain postmodern insistence on the integrity of every reading of a text is glaring in retrospect.

The fear of opening a door to ecclesiastical control should not keep us from recognizing that there is a legitimate role for the Christian churches in the reading of Scripture. One of the important contributions of contemporary hermeneutics and literary theory is the recognition that reading is rarely, if ever, independent of presuppositions, conventional decisions about method, and the influence of interpretative communities. In theological terms, faithful reading is done in the context of faith and discipleship, an essential component of which is other-centred service. The churches are by God's design the arena of such faith and service. The role of the churches consists not in *determining* the meaning of Scripture but in *facilitating* the recognition and embrace of that meaning. Their rich resources include the rule of faith, the creeds, the exegetical tradition and God's gift of pastors and teachers – all manifestations of the communion of saints. We do not read alone. We read together; not just alongside each other, but to and with each other. It is not a matter of the church clarifying the text. As Webster puts it, 'the church interprets the Word by confessing and exhibiting its [antecedent] clarity'.[59]

The Bible remains a public document. To insist that faithful reading occurs within the community of faith is not to suggest that

---

[59] Webster 2005: 57–58.

the Bible is a book of 'gnostic secrets', a mysterious book that can be decoded only by the initiated.[60] Luther's explanation of the twofold clarity of Scripture is once again helpful here. The words make sense as they stand in their context. They do have an external clarity.[61] Yet because of who we are as readers, understanding at the deepest level of acknowledgment and appropriation, a recognition that we are in fact addressed by these words and must respond in repentance and faith, is also the work of the Spirit. It is not separable in the end from the text of Scripture and so, with Luther, we might properly speak of the internal clarity *of Scripture*. Yet it is always a sovereign work of the Spirit of God. The word borne to the human heart by the Spirit generates faith in God and its corollaries, repentance and obedience.

Nevertheless, faithful reading of the Scriptures in the last days is a distinctive phenomenon. The presence of God by his Spirit, the whole Bible as an interpretative context for each part, and the resources of the communion of saints all give the faithful reading of this text a particular shape. Engagement with the Scriptures is not simply the beginning of the knowledge of God, but is an ongoing characteristic of Christian discipleship. The clear Scripture always has more to deliver. The Christian reader grows in understanding. Whether novice or scholar we are given a true knowledge of God, but not complete or exhaustive knowledge. We can expect to learn from those whose engagement with the text of Scripture has been more intense than our own, or has occurred over a longer period. Difficulty with individual passages may rightly be seen as contingent and temporary in principle. Others may help me to see what I should have seen but have not, due to my own prejudices, ignorance or lack of attention. Yet we all read the Bible as people living in the midst of the end but not there yet. There is room for study, an appropriate place for teachers and commentaries, and a right appreciation of fresh insight, all without for a moment compromising the clarity of Scripture.

So what then is the clarity of Scripture? How might we summarize our exploration of this doctrine? *The clarity of Scripture is that quality of the biblical text that, as God's communicative act, ensures its*

---

[60] Carnley 2004: 109; Cowdell 2004: 125; Weber 1955: 281.

[61] A significant debate within early Pietism arose in Danzig between 1621 and 1628 over whether anything in Scripture was intelligible without the illuminating work of the Holy Spirit in the human heart. It surrounded the teaching of Hermann Rahtmann. See Steiger 1998.

*meaning is accessible to all who come to it in faith.*[62] To confess the clarity of Scripture is to adopt the same attitude as Jesus demonstrated in his own use of the Old Testament. It is to align ourselves with the confidence of the apostolic writers, who appealed to the Old Testament as intelligible and decisive even when addressing predominantly Gentile audiences. It is to be bold, even brazen, as we follow the example of Augustine and 'take and read'. The practice of reading in the light of this confession will be serious and attentive. It will not be content with superficiality or with a uniform literalism that flattens the variety of genre and literary feature found throughout this text. It will take seriously the text we have (not pining for some ideal text beyond our reach) and expects that these very words have the power to cut deep and to heal profoundly even today. In short, a confession of the clarity of Scripture is an aspect of faith in a generous God who is willing and able to make himself and his purposes known. God has something to say and he is very good at saying it.

---

[62] In the light of the previous chapters, our definition can be somewhat more robust than that of Kevin Vanhoozer: 'clarity means that the Bible is sufficiently unambiguous in the main for any well-intentioned person with Christian faith to interpret each part with relative adequacy' (Vanhoozer 1998: 315). What is missing here is an explicit reference to the source of Scripture's clarity in God's communicative intention. Even less explicitly theological is the summary offered by James Callahan: 'Scripture's clarity is, simply put, how Christians account for the union of text, reader and reading' (Callahan 2001: 19).

# Bibliography

Abraham, W. J. (1998), *Canon and Criterion in Christian Theology*, Oxford: Clarendon.

Ahlstrom, S. (1955), 'The Scottish Philosophy and American Theology', *Church History* 24: 257–272.

Allison, G. R. (1995), 'The Protestant Doctrine of the Perspicuity of Scripture: A Reformulation on the Basis of Biblical Teaching', PhD thesis, Trinity Evangelical Divinity School, Illinois.

Alston, W. (1989), 'Can We Speak Literally of God?', in *Divine Nature and Human Language: Essays in Philosophical Theology*, Ithaca: Cornell University Press, 39–63.

Anderson, F. I. (1967), 'The Instrument at Hand: The Problem of the Language of Scripture', *Interchange* 1.2: 67–70.

Aston, W. M. (ed.) (2000), *Theology in the Service of the Church: Essays in Honor of Thomas W. Gillespie*, Grand Rapids: Eerdmans.

Augustine, A. (391), *De utilitate credendi*, trans. J. H. S. Burleigh, in *Augustine: Earlier Writings*, LCC 6, 291–323, Philadelphia: Westminster, 1953.

——(426), *De doctrina christiana*, trans. J. F. Shaw, 1886, as *On Christian Doctrine*, in P. Schaff (ed.), *A Select Library of the Nicene and Post-Nicene Fathers of the Christian Church*, vol. 2, 519–597, Grand Rapids: Eerdmans, repr. 1979.

Austin, J. L. (1962), *How to Do Things with Words*, Oxford: Clarendon.

Barrett, C. K. (1994), *A Critical and Exegetical Commentary on Acts*, ed. J. A. Emerton, C. E. B. Cranfield and G. N. Stanton, ICC, 2 vols., Edinburgh: T. & T. Clark.

Barth, K. (1917), *Die neue Welt in der Bibel*, trans. D. Horton as 'The Strange New World within the Bible', in *The Word of God and the Word of Man*, 28–50, Gloucester, MA: Smith, 1978.

——(1918), *Der Romerbrief*, 6th ed., trans. E. C. Hoskyns as *The Epistle to the Romans*, London: Oxford University Press, 1933.

——(1932), *Kirchliche Dogmatik I/1*, trans. G. W. Bromiley as *Church Dogmatics I/1 The Doctrine of the Word of God*, ed. G. W. Bromiley and T. F. Torrance, Edinburgh: T. & T. Clark, 1975.

——(1938), *Kirchliche Dogmatik I/2*, trans. G. W. Bromiley et al., as *Church Dogmatics I/2 The Doctrine of the Word of God*, ed. T. F. Torrance and G. W. Bromiley, Edinburgh: T. & T. Clark, 1956.

Barthes, R. (1968), 'La mort de l'auteur', trans. Stephen Heath, 1977, as 'The Death of the Author', in S. Burke (ed.), *Authorship from Plato to the Postmodern: A Reader*, 125–130, Edinburgh: Edinburgh University Press, 1995.

Bavinck, H. (1895), *Gereformeede Dogmatiek*, trans. J. Vriend, ed. J. Bolt, as *Reformed Dogmatics*, 4 vols., Grand Rapids: Baker, 2003–.

Bebbington, D. W. (1989), *Evangelicalism in Modern Britain: A History from the 1730s to the 1980s*, London: Unwin Hyman.

Beisser, F. (1966), *Claritas Scripturae bei Martin Luther*, Forschungen zur Kirchen- und Dogmengeschichte 18, Göttingen: Vandenhoeck & Ruprecht.

Bellarmino, R. (1586), *Disputationes de controversiis christianae fidei adversus hujus temporis haereticos*, 4 vols., Venice: Apud Societatem Minimam.

Berkouwer, G. C. (1966–7), *De Heilige Schrift*, trans. and ed. J. B. Rogers, as *Holy Scripture*, Grand Rapids: Eerdmans, 1975.

Blenkinsopp, J. (1988), *Ezra-Nehemiah*, OTL, London: SCM.

Blocher, H. (1987), 'The "Analogy of Faith" in the Study of Scripture', in N. M. de S. Cameron (ed.), *The Challenge of Evangelical Theology: Essays in Approach and Method*, 17–38, Edinburgh: Rutherford House.

Bolt, P. G. (2004), *The Cross from a Distance: Atonement in Mark's Gospel*, NSBT 18, Leicester: Apollos.

Brecht, M. (1986), *Martin Luther: Zweiter Band: Ordnung und Abgrenzung der Reformation, 1521–1532*, trans. J. L. Schaaf as *Martin Luther: Shaping and Defining the Reformation 1521–1532*, Minneapolis: Fortress, 1990.

Brown, W. P. (2002), *Seeing the Psalms: A Theology of Metaphor*, Louisville: Westminster John Knox.

Bruce, F. F. (1982), *Commentary on Galatians*, NIGTC, Exeter: Paternoster.

Brunner, E. (1941), *Offenbarung und Vernunft: Die Lehre von der christlichen Glaubenserkenntnis*, trans. O. Wyon as *Reason and Revelation: The Christian Doctrine of Faith and Knowledge*, London: SCM, 1946.

Bullinger, H. (1549), *Decades*, trans. H. I., ed. T. Harding, Cambridge: Parker Society, 1849.

Callahan, J. (2001), *The Clarity of Scripture: History, Theology and Contemporary Literary Studies*, Downers Grove: IVP.

Calvin, J. (1559), *Institutio christianae religionis*, trans. F. L. Battles as *Institutes of the Christian Religion*, ed. J. T. McNeill, LCC 20.21, Philadelphia: Westminster, 1960.

Caneday, A. B. (2004), 'Is Theological Truth Functional or Propositional? Postconservatism's Use of Language Games and Speech-Act Theory', in M. J. Erickson, P. K. Helseth and J. Taylor (eds.), *Reclaiming the Center: Confronting Evangelical Accommodation in Postmodern Times*, 137–159, Wheaton, IL: Crossway.

Carnley, P. (2004), *Reflections in Glass: Trends and Tensions in the Contemporary Anglican Church*, Pymble, NSW: HarperCollins.

Carson, D. A. (1991), 'The Role of Exegesis in Systematic Theology', in J. D. Woodbridge and T. E. McComiskey (eds.), *Doing Theology in Today's World: Essays in Honor of Kenneth S. Kantzer*, 39–76, Grand Rapids: Zondervan.

——(1996), *The Gagging of God: Christianity Confronts Pluralism*, Leicester: Apollos.

——(1997), 'Is the Doctrine of "Claritas Scripturae" Still Relevant Today?', in E. Hahn, R. Hille and H.-W. Neudorfer (eds.), *Dein Wort ist die Wahrheit: Beiträge zu einer schriftgemäßen Theologie*, FS G. Maier, 97–111, Wuppertal: Brokhaus.

——(2004), 'The Vindication of Imputation: Of Fields of Discourse and Semantic Fields', in M. Husbands and D. J. Treier (eds.), *Justification: What's at Stake in the Current Debates*, 46–78, Downers Grove: IVP; Leicester: Apollos.

——(2005), *Becoming Conversant with the Emerging Church: Understanding a Movement and Its Implications*, Grand Rapids: Zondervan.

Chalke, S. (2003), *The Lost Message of Jesus*, Grand Rapids: Zondervan.

Childs, B. S. (1979), *Introduction to the Old Testament as Scripture*, London: SCM.

——(1992), *Biblical Theology of the Old and New Testaments*, London: SCM.

Christensen, D. L. (2002), *Deuteronomy 21:10 – 34:12*, ed. J. D. Watts and J. W. Watts, WBC 6b, Nashville: Nelson.

Coleridge, S. T. (1840), *Confessions of an Inquiring Spirit*, New York: Chelsea House, repr. 1983.

Cowdell, S. (2004), 'Homsexuality and the Clarity of Scripture: Reflecting with Peter Jensen', in S. Cowdell and M. Porter (eds.), *Lost in Translation? Anglicans, Controversy and the Bible*, 114–130, Thornbury, Vic.: Desbooks.

Craigie, P. C. (1976), *The Book of Deuteronomy*, ed. R. K. Harrison, NICOT, Grand Rapids: Eerdmans.

Cranfield, C. E. B. (1975), *A Critical and Exegetical Commentary on the Epistle to the Romans*, ed. J. A. Emerton and C. E. B. Cranfield, ICC, 2 vols., Edinburgh: T. & T. Clark.

Cuneo, T. and R. van Woudenberg (2004), *The Cambridge Companion to Thomas Reid*, Cambridge Companions to Philosophy, Cambridge: Cambridge University Press.

Daube, D. (1956), *The New Testament and Rabbinic Judaism*, Jordan Lectures 1952, London: Athlone.

Davies, G. F. (1999), *Ezra and Nehemiah*, Berit Olam: Studies in Hebrew Narrative and Poetry, ed. D. W. Cotter, Collegeville: Liturgical Press.

Davies, W. D. and D. C. Allison (1988–97), *A Critical and Exegetical Commentary on The Gospel According to Saint Matthew*, ed. J. A. Emerton, C. E. B. Cranfield and G. N. Stanton, ICC, 3 vols., Edinburgh: T. & T. Clark.

Denzinger, H. (1954), *Enchiridion symbolorum*, revised K. Rahner, trans. R. J. Deferrari as *The Sources of Catholic Dogma*, 13th ed., St. Louis: Herder, 1957.

Derrida, J. (1967a), *De la grammatologie*, trans. G. C. Spivak as *Of Grammatology*, Baltimore: Johns Hopkins University Press, 1974.

——(1967b), *L'écriture et la difference*, trans. A. Bass as *Writing and Difference*, London: Routledge & Kegan Paul, 1978.

——(1988), *Limited Inc.*, trans. S. Weber, Evanston: Northwestern University Press.

Descartes, R. (1641), *Meditationes de prima philosophia*, trans. J. Cottingham as *Meditations on First Philosophy*, Cambridge: Cambridge University Press, 1986.

Doctrine Commission (1995), *The Mystery of Salvation: The Story of God's Gift. A Report of the Doctrine Commission of the General Synod of the Church of England*, London: Church House.

Driver, S. R. (1895), *A Critical and Exegetical Commentary on Deuteronomy*, ed. S. R. Driver, A. Plummer and C. A. Briggs, ICC, Edinburgh: T. & T. Clark.

Duff, J. N. (1998), 'A Reconsideration of Pseudepigraphy in Early Christianity', DPhil thesis, University of Oxford.

Duggan, M. W. (2001), *The Covenant Renewal in Ezra-Nehemiah (Neh. 7:72b – 10:40): An Exegetical, Literary and Theological Study*, ed. M. V. Fox and M. A. Powell, SBL Dissertation Series 164, Atlanta: SBL.

Dupuis, J. (1997), *Toward a Christian Theology of Religious Pluralism*, New York: Orbis.

Eco, U. (1990), *The Limits of Interpretation*, Bloomington: University of Indiana Press.

——(1992), *Interpretation and Overinterpretation*, ed. S. Collini, Tanner Lectures 1990, Cambridge: Cambridge University Press.

Ellis, E. E. (1957), *Paul's Use of the Old Testament*, Grand Rapids: Eerdmans.

——(1999), *The Making of the New Testament Documents*, Leiden: Brill.

Enns, P. (2005), *Inspiration and Incarnation: Evangelicals and the Problem of the Old Testament*, Grand Rapids: Baker.

Erasmus, D. (1524a), *De libero arbitrio diatribhl sive collatio*, trans. E. Gordon Rupp and A. N. Marlow as 'On the Freedom of the Will', in *Luther and Erasmus: Free Will and Salvation*, LCC 17, 35–97, Philadelphia: Westminster, 1969.

——(1524b), *Erasmus Roterodamus regi angliae Henrico (ep. 1493)*, trans. R. A. B. Mynors and A. Dalzell, in *The Correspondence of Erasmus: Letters 1356 to 1534 (1523 to 1524)*, Collected Works of Erasmus 10, 373–374, Toronto: University of Toronto Press, 1992.

——(1526), *Hyperaspistes liber unus*, trans. C. H. Miller as *A Warrior Shielding a Discussion of Free Will against the Enslaved Will by Martin Luther, Book One*, in C. Trinkaus (ed.), *Collected Works of Erasmus* 76, 93–297, Toronto: University of Toronto Press, 1999.

Erickson, M. J., P. K. Helseth and J. Taylor (eds.) (2004), *Reclaiming the Center: Confronting Evangelical Accommodation in Postmodern Times*, Wheaton, IL: Crossway.

Evans, G. R. (1984), *The Language and Logic of the Bible: The Earlier Middle Ages*, Cambridge: Cambridge University Press.

——(1985), *The Language and Logic of the Bible: The Road to Reformation*, Cambridge: Cambridge University Press.

Ferretter, L. (2003), 'Towards a Christian Literary Theory', in E. Jay and D. Jasper (eds.), *Cross Currents in Religion and Culture*, Basingstoke: Palgrave Macmillan.

Fish, S. (1980), *Is There a Text in This Class? The Authority of Interpretive Communities*, Cambridge, MA: Harvard University Press.

Foucault, M. (1977), 'Truth and Power', in P. Rabinow (ed.), *The Foucault Reader*, 51–75, New York: Pantheon, 1984.

——(1979), 'What Is an Author?', in P. Rabinow (ed.), *The Foucault Reader*, 101–120, New York: Pantheon, 1984.

Fowl, S. E. (1998), *Engaging Scripture: A Model for Theological Interpretation*, ed. G. Jones and L. Ayres, Challenges in Contemporary Theology, Oxford: Blackwell.

Fowler, A. (1982), *Kinds of Literature: An Introduction to the Theory of Genres and Modes*, Oxford: Clarendon.

Fowler, R. M. (1991), *Let the Reader Understand: Reader-Response Criticism and the Gospel of Mark*, Minneapolis: Fortress.

France, R. T. (1982), 'Evangelical Disagreements about the Bible', *Churchman* 96: 226–240.

Franke, J. R. (2004), 'Scripture, Tradition and Authority: Reconstructing the Evangelical Conception of Sola Scriptura', in V. Bacote, L. C. Miguélez and D. L. Okholm (eds.), *Evangelicals and Scripture: Tradition, Authority and Hermeneutics*, 192–210, Downers Grove: IVP.

Frei, H. W. (1974), *The Eclipse of Biblical Narrative: A Study in Eighteenth and Nineteenth Century Hermeneutics*, New Haven: Yale University Press.

——(1975), *The Identity of Jesus Christ: The Hermeneutical Bases of Dogmatic Theology*, Philadelphia: Fortress.

Gadamer, H.-G. (1974), 'Hermeneutik', in J. Ritter (ed.), *Historisches Wörterbuch der Philosophie*, vol. 3, cols. 1061–1073, Basel: Schwabe.

——(1984), *Wahrheit und Methode*, trans. and revised J. Weinsheimer and D. G. Marshall as *Truth and Method*, 5th ed., New York: Continuum, 1994.

Gaffin, R. (2004), 'Speech and the Image of God: Biblical Reflections on Language and its Uses', in D. VanDrunen (ed.), *The Pattern of Sound Doctrine: Systematic Theology at the Westminster Seminaries. Essays in Honor of Robert B. Strimple*, 181–193, Phillipsburg: P. & R.

Gallup (2005), 'Teenagers' Knowledge of the Bible', *The Bible Literacy Report: What Do American Teens Need to Know and What Do They Know?* New York: Bible Literacy Project.

Goldingay, J. (1994), *Models for Scripture*, Grand Rapids: Eerdmans.

Greco, J. (2000), *Putting Skeptics in their Place: The Nature of Skeptical Arguments and their Role in Philosophical Inquiry*, Cambridge: Cambridge University Press.

Green, J. B. and M. D. Baker (2000), *Recovering the Scandal of the Cross: Atonement in the New Testament and Contemporary Contexts*, Downers Grove: IVP.

Greer, R. C. (2003), *Mapping Postmodernism: A Survey of Christian Options*, Downers Grove: IVP.

Gregory (583–90), *Moralia in Iob*, trans. members of the English Church, ed. E. B. Pusey et al., in *A Library of Fathers of the Holy Catholic Church Anterior to the Division of the East and West*, 3 vols., Oxford: Parker Society, 1844–50.

Grenz, S. J. (2000), *Renewing the Center: Evangelical Theology in a Post-Theological Era*, Grand Rapids: Baker.

Grenz, S. J. and J. R. Franke (2001), *Beyond Foundationalism: Shaping Theology in a Postmodern Context*, Louisville: Westminster John Knox.

Groothuis, D. (2000), *Truth Decay: Defending Christianity Against the Challenges of Postmodernism*, Downers Grove: IVP.

Groothuis, R. M. (1997), *Good News for Women: A Biblical Picture of Gender Equality*, Grand Rapids: Baker.

Guelich, R. A. (1989), *Mark 1 – 8:26*, WBC 34a, Dallas: Word.

Gunton, C. E. (1985), *Enlightenment and Alienation: An Essay towards a Trinitarian Theology*, London: Marshall Pickering.

——(1995), *A Brief Theology of Revelation*, Edinburgh: T. & T. Clark.

——(1997), *The Promise of Trinitarian Theology*, 2nd ed., Edinburgh: T. & T. Clark.

——(1999), 'A Rose by Any Other Name? From "Christian Doctrine" to "Systematic Theology"', *IJST* 1.1: 4–23.

Guthrie, D. (1962), 'The Development of the Idea of Canonical Pseudepigrapha in New Testament Criticism', *VE* 1: 43–59.

Harrington, D. J. (1991), *The Gospel of Matthew*, SP 1, Collegeville: Liturgical Press.

Harris, H. (1998), *Fundamentalism and Evangelicals*, Oxford Theological Monographs, Oxford: Clarendon.

Harrisville, R. A. and W. Sundberg (2002), *The Bible in Modern Culture: Baruch Spinoza to Brevard Childs*, 2nd ed., Grand Rapids: Eerdmans.

Hays, R. B. (1989), *Echoes of Scripture in the Letters of Paul*, New Haven: Yale University Press.

Heidegger, M. (1927), *Sein und Zeit*, trans. J. Macquarrie and E. Robinson as *Being and Time*, Oxford: Blackwell, 1962.

Helm, P. (1982), *Divine Revelation: The Basic Issues*, Foundations for Faith, London: Marshall, Morgan & Scott.

——(2004), *John Calvin's Ideas*, Oxford: Oxford University Press.

Helseth, P. K. (2004), 'Are Postconservative Evangelicals Fundamentalists? Postconservative Evangelicalism, Old Princeton, and the Rise of Neo-Fundamentalism', in M. J. Erickson, P. K. Helseth and J. Taylor (eds.), *Reclaiming the Center: Confronting Evangelical Accommodation in Postmodern Times*, 223–250, Wheaton, IL: Crossway.

Heppe, H. (1861), *Reformierte Dogmatik: Die Dogmatik der evangelisch-reformierten Kirche*, revised and ed. E. Bizer, 1935, trans. G. T. Thomson as *Reformed Dogmatics*, London: George Allen & Unwin, repr. 1950.

Hicks, P. (1998), *Evangelicals and Truth: A Creative Proposal for a Postmodern Age*, Leicester: Apollos.

Hodge, C. (1871), *Systematic Theology*, 3 vols., London: Nelson.

Hopko, T. (1995), 'The Church, the Bible, and Dogmatic Theology', in C. E. Braaten and R. W. Jenson (eds.), *Reclaiming the Bible for the Church*, 107–118, Grand Rapids: Eerdmans; Edinburgh: T. & T. Clark.

Horton, M. S. (2002), *Covenant and Eschatology: The Divine Drama*, Louisville: Westminster John Knox.

——(2005), *Lord and Servant: A Covenant Christology*, Louisville: Westminster John Knox.

Irenaeus (189), *Adversus haereses*, trans. A. Roberts and J. Robertson, 1867, as *Irenaeus against Heresies*, revised A. C. Coxe, 1885, 315–567, Grand Rapids: Eerdmans, repr. 1985.

Jeanrond, W. G. (1986), *Text und Interpretation als Kategorien theologischen Denkens*, trans. T. J. Wilson as *Text and Interpretation as Categories of Theological Thinking*, New York: Crossroad, 1988.

——(1991), *Theological Hermeneutics: Development and Significance*, New York: Crossroad.

——(1993), 'After Hermeneutics: The Relationship between Theology and Biblical Studies', in Francis Watson (ed.), *The Open Text: New Directions for Biblical Studies?* 85–102, London: SCM.

Jensen, P. F. (1997), 'Teaching Doctrine as Part of the Pastor's Role', in R. J. Gibson (ed.), *Interpreting God's Plan: Biblical Theology and the Pastor*, Explorations 11, 75–90, Carlisle: Paternoster.

——(2002), *The Revelation of God*, ed. G. Bray, Contours of Christian Theology, Leicester: IVP.

Jenson, R. W. (1995), 'Hermeneutics and the Life of the Church', in C. E. Braaten and R. W. Jenson (eds.), *Reclaiming the Bible for the*

*Church*, 89–105, Grand Rapids: Eerdmans; Edinburgh: T. & T. Clark.

——(1997), *Systematic Theology*, vol. 1: *The Triune God*, New York: Oxford University Press.

Jowett, B. (1860), 'On the Interpretation of Scripture', in B. Jowett (ed.), *Essays and Reviews*, 8th ed., 330–433, London: Longman, Green, Longman & Roberts, 1861.

Jüngel, E. (1977), *Gott als Geheimnis der Welt*, trans. D. L. Guder as *God as the Mystery of the World: On the Foundation of the Theology of the Crucified One in the Dispute between Theism and Atheism*, Grand Rapids: Eerdmans, 1983.

Kant, I. (1781), *Kritik der reinen Vernunft*, trans. N. K. Smith as *Critique of Pure Reason*, London: Macmillan, 1933.

——(1798), *Der Streit der Fakultäten*, trans. M. J. Gregor and R. Anchor as 'The Conflict of the Faculties', in A. W. Wood and G. Di Giovanni (eds.), *Religion and Rational Theology*, 233–328, Cambridge: Cambridge University Press, 1996.

Kermode, F. (1979), *The Genesis of Secrecy: On the Interpretation of Narrative*, Cambridge, MA: Harvard University Press.

Kierkegaard, S. (1851), *Til Selvprøvelse: Samtiden Anbefalet*, trans. E. Hong and H. Hong as *For Self-Examination*, Minneapolis: Augsburg, 1940.

Klauber, M. I. and G. S. Sunshine (1990), 'Jean-Alphonse Turretini on Biblical Accommodation: Calvinist or Socinian?', *CTJ* 25: 7–27.

Knox, D. B. (1982), *The Everlasting God*, Welwyn, Herts.: Evangelical Press.

——(2000), 'The Implications of the Doctrine of the Trinity for Theology and for Ordinary Life', in *D. B. Knox, Selected Works*, vol. 1: *The Doctrine of God*, 153–170, Kingsford, NSW: Matthias Media.

Kolb, R. (2005), *Bound Choice, Election, and Wittenberg Theological Method: From Martin Luther to the Formula of Concord*, Grand Rapids: Eerdmans.

Köstenberger, A. J. and P. T. O'Brien (2001), *Salvation to the Ends of the Earth: A Biblical Theology of Mission*, ed. D. A. Carson, NSBT 11, Leicester: IVP.

Kraftchick, S. J. (2002), *Jude, 2 Peter*, ANTC, Nashville: Abingdon.

Lakeland, P. (1997), *Postmodernity: Christian Identity in a Fragmented Age*, Minneapolis: Fortress.

Liechty, D. (1990), *Theology in Postliberal Perspective*, London: SCM.

Lindbeck, G. A. (1984), *The Nature of Doctrine: Religion and Theology in a Postliberal Age*, London: SPCK.

——(2002), *The Church in a Postliberal Age*, London: SCM.

Long, J. (2004), *Emerging Hope: A Strategy for Reaching the Postmodern Generations*, Downers Grove: IVP.

Longenecker, R. N. (1975), *Biblical Exegesis in the Apostolic Period*, Grand Rapids: Eerdmans.

Luther, M. (1520a), *An den christlichen Adel deutscher Nation von des christlichen Standes Besserung*, trans. C. M. Jacobs, revised J. Atkinson as 'To the Christian Nobility of the German Nation Concerning the Reform of the Christian Estate', in H. T. Lehmann (ed.), *Luther's Works*, vol. 44, 123–217, Philadelphia: Fortress, 1966.

——(1520b), *Assertio omnium articulorum M. Lutheri per bullam Leonis X novissimam damnatorum*, repr. in *D. Martin Luthers Werke: Kristische Gesamtausgabe, Schriften*, ed. J. K. F. Knaake, G. Kawerau et al., vol. 7, 94–115, Weimar: Böhlaus Nachfolger, 1883–.

——(1522), *Eyn kleyn unterricht, was man ynn den Evangelijs suchen und gewartten soll*, trans. E. Theodore Bachmann as 'A Brief Instruction on What to Look for and Expect in the Gospels', in H. T. Lehmann (ed.), *Luther's Works*, vol. 35, 117–124, Philadelphia: Fortress, 1960.

——(1525), *De servo arbitrio*, trans. P. S. Watson and B. Drewery, 1969, as 'The Bondage of the Will', in H. T. Lehmann (ed.), *Luther's Works*, vol. 33, 15–295, Philadelphia: Fortress, repr. 1972.

——(1527), *Vorlesung über den 1. Brief des Johannes*, trans. W. A. Hansen as 'Lectures on the First Epistle of St. John', in J. Pelikan (ed.), *Luther's Works*, vol. 30, 219–327, St. Louis: Concordia, 1967.

——(1535), *In epistolam S. Pauli ad Galatas commentarius*, trans. J. Pelikan as 'Lectures on Galatians 1535', in J. Pelikan (ed.), *Luther's Works*, vols. 26–27, St. Louis: Concordia, 1963.

——(1535–45), *Vorlesungen über 1. Mose*, trans. G. V. Schick and P. D. Pahl as 'Lectures on Genesis', in J. Pelikan (ed.), *Luther's Works*, vols. 1–8, St. Louis: Concordia, 1958–66.

Lyotard, J.-F. (1979), *La condition postmoderne: rapport sur le savoir*, trans. G. Bennington and B. Massumi as *The Postmodern Condition: A Report on Knowledge*, Theory and History of Literature 10, Minneapolis: University of Minnesota Press, 1984.

Malley, B. (2004), *How the Bible Works: An Anthropological Study of Evangelical Biblicism*, Cognitive Science of Religion Series, ed. H. Whitehouse and L. H. Martin, Walnut Creek, CA: Altamira.

Manson, T. W. (1931), *The Teaching of Jesus*, Cambridge: Cambridge University Press.

Marquard, O. (1981), 'Frage nach der Frage, auf die Hermeneutik die Antwort ist', trans. R. M. Wallace as 'The Question, To What Question is Hermeneutics the Answer?', in D. E. Christensen et al. (eds.), *Contemporary German Philosophy*, vol. 4, 9–31, University Park: Pennsylvania State University Press, 1984.

Marsden, G. M. (1980), *Fundamentalism and American Culture: The Shaping of Twentieth Century Evangelicalism 1870–1925*, New York: Oxford University Press.

Marshall, I. H. (1999), *A Critical and Exegetical Commentary on the Pastoral Epistles*, ed. J. A. Emerton, C. E. B. Cranfield and G. N. Stanton, ICC, Edinburgh: T. & T. Clark.

McCormack, B. L. (2004), 'The Being of Holy Scripture is in Becoming', in V. Bacote, L. C. Miguéléz and D. L. Okholm (eds.), *Evangelicals and Scripture: Tradition, Authority and Hermeneutics*, 55–75, Downers Grove: IVP.

McFague, S. (1983), *Metaphorical Theology: Models of God in Religious Language*, London: SCM.

McGrath, A. E. (1996), *A Passion for Truth: The Intellectual Coherence of Evangelicalism*, Leicester: Apollos.

——(1999), *Reformation Thought: An Introduction*, 3rd ed., Oxford: Blackwell.

McLaren, B. D. (2004), *A Generous Orthodoxy*, El Cajon, CA: Emergent.

McQuilkin, R. and B. Mullen (1997), 'The Impact of Postmodern Thinking on Evangelical Hermeneutics', *JETS* 40.1: 69–82.

Molland, E. (1934), *Das paulinische Euangelion: Das Wort und die Sache*, Oslo: Dybwad.

Moreland, J. P. and G. De Weese (2004), 'The Premature Report of Foundationalism's Demise', in M. J. Erickson, P. K. Helseth and J. Taylor (eds.), *Reclaiming the Center: Confronting Evangelical Accommodation in Postmodern Times*, 81–107, Wheaton, IL: Crossway.

Morrison, J. D. (2004), 'Barth, Barthians, and Evangelicals: Reassessing the Question of the Relation of Holy Scripture and the Word of God', *TJ* 25 NS: 187–213.

Motyer, J. A. (1993), *The Prophecy of Isaiah*, Leicester: IVP.

Muers, R. (2004), *Keeping God's Silence: Towards a Theological Ethics of Communication*, Oxford: Blackwell.

Nathan, R. (2002), *Who Is My Enemy? Welcoming People the Church Rejects*, Grand Rapids: Zondervan.

Nichols, A. (2002), *Discovering Aquinas: An Introduction to His Life, Work, and Influence*, Grand Rapids: Eerdmans.

Noll, M. (1994), *The Scandal of the Evangelical Mind*, Grand Rapids: Eerdmans.

O'Brien, P. T. (1999), *The Letter to the Ephesians*, ed. D. A. Carson, Pillar New Testament Commentary, Grand Rapids: Eerdmans; Leicester: Apollos.

——(2004), 'Was Paul Converted?', in D. A. Carson, P. T. O'Brien and M. A. Seifrid (eds.), *Justification and Variegated Nomism*, vol. 2: *The Paradoxes of Paul*, 361–391, WUNT 2, Reihe 181, Tübingen: Mohr Siebeck.

O'Donovan, O. (1996), *The Desire of the Nations: Rediscovering the Roots of Political Theology*, Cambridge: Cambridge University Press.

——(2002), 'Response to Walter Moberly', in C. Bartholomew et al. (eds.), *A Royal Priesthood? The Use of the Bible Ethically and Politically*, Scripture and Hermeneutics Series 3, 65–68, Carlisle: Paternoster; Grand Rapids: Zondervan.

Okakura, K. (1906), *The Book of Tea: A Japanese Harmony of Art, Culture and the Simple Life*, ed. E. F. Bleiler, New York: Dover, repr. 1932.

Osborne, G. R. (1991), *The Hermeneutical Spiral: A Comprehensive Introduction to Biblical Interpretation*, Downers Grove: IVP.

Packer, J. I. (1978), *The Evangelical Anglican Identity Problem: An Analysis*, Latimer Studies 1, Oxford: Latimer House.

Pannenberg, W. (1988), *Systematische Theologie*, I, trans. G. W. Bromiley 1991 as *Systematic Theology*, vol. 1, Edinburgh: T. & T. Clark.

Parker, J. (2004), 'A Requiem for Postmodernism – Whither Now?', in M. J. Erickson, P. K. Helseth and J. Taylor (eds.), *Reclaiming the Center: Confronting Evangelical Accommodation in Postmodern Times*, 307–321, Wheaton, IL: Crossway.

Polanyi, M. (1962), *Personal Knowledge*, London: Routledge & Kegan Paul.

——(1966), *The Tacit Dimension*, New York: Doubleday.

Preus, R. (1955), *The Inspiration of Scripture: A Study of the*

*Theology of the Seventeenth Century Lutheran Dogmaticians*, Edinburgh: Oliver & Boyd.

Prior, M. (1989), *Paul the Letter-Writer and the Second Letter to Timothy*, JSNTSup 23, Sheffield: JSOT.

Raschke, C. A. (1982), 'The Deconstruction of God', in T. J. J. Altizer et al. (eds.), *Deconstruction and Theology*, 1–33, New York, Crossroad.

——(2004), *The Next Reformation: Why Evangelicals Must Embrace Postmodernity*, Grand Rapids: Baker.

Reid, T. (1785), *Essays on the Intellectual Powers of Man*, London: Griffin, repr. 1854.

Ricœur, P. (1976), *Interpretation Theory: Discourse and the Surplus of Meaning*, Fort Worth: Texas Christian University Press.

——(1977), 'Toward a Hermeneutic of the Idea of Revelation', trans. D. Pellauer, *HTR* 70.1–2: 1–37.

——(1981), *Hermeneutics and the Human Sciences: Essays on Language, Action and Interpretation*, ed. and trans. J. B. Thompson, Cambridge: Cambridge University Press; Paris: Editions de la Maison des Sciences de l'Homme.

Robinson, D. W. B. (1951), *Josiah's Reform and the Book of the Law*, Tyndale Monographs, London: Tyndale.

Rogers, J. B. and D. K. McKim (1979), *The Authority and Interpretation of the Bible: An Historical Approach*, San Francisco: Harper & Row.

Rorty, R. (1979), *Philosophy and the Mirror of Nature*, Princeton: Princeton University Press.

Rothen, B. (1990), *Die Klarheit der Schrift*. I: *Martin Luther: Die wiederentdeckten Grundlagen*. Und II: *Karl Barth: Eine Kritik*, Vandenhoeck & Ruprecht.

Ryle, J. C. (1871), *Knots Untied*, condensed and revised C. S. Carter, London: Clarke, repr. 1954.

Sandin, R. T. (1983), 'The Clarity of Scripture', in M. Inch and R. Youngblood (eds.), *The Living and Active Word of God: Studies in Honor of Samuel J. Schultz*, 237–253, Winona Lake: Eisenbrauns.

Saussure, F. de (1916), *Cours de linguistique générale*, trans. R. Harris as *Course in General Linguistics*, London: Duckworth, 1983.

Schleiermacher, F. (1809–10), 'General Hermeneutics', trans. and ed. A. Bowie, in *Hermeneutics and Criticism and Other Writings*, 227–268, Cambridge: Cambridge University Press, 1998.

——(1830), *The Christian Faith*, trans. H. R. Mackintosh and J. S. Stewart, Edinburgh: T. & T. Clark, repr. 1999.

Schneider, S. M. (1991), *The Revelatory Text: Interpreting the New Testament as Sacred Scripture*, San Francisco: Harper.

Schreiner, T. R. (1998), *Romans*, Baker Exegetical Commentary 6, Grand Rapids: Baker.

Searle, J. R. (1969), *Speech Acts: An Essay in the Philosophy of Language*, Cambridge: Cambridge University Press.

——(1996), 'What Is a Speech Act?', in H. Geirsson and M. Losonsky (eds.), *Readings in Language and Mind*, 110–121, Oxford: Blackwell.

Seifrid, M. A. (2000), *Christ, our Righteousness: Paul's Theology of Justification*, ed. D. A. Carson, NSBT 9, Leicester: Apollos.

Senarclens, J. de (1959), *Héritiers de la Réformation*, trans. and ed. G. W. Bromiley as *Heirs of the Reformation*, London: SCM, 1963.

Silva, M. (1987), *Has the Church Misread the Bible? The History of Interpretation in the Light of Current Issues*, Foundations of Contemporary Interpretation 1, Grand Rapids: Zondervan.

——(1993), 'Old Testament in Paul', in G. F. Hawthorne, R. P. Martin and D. G. Reid (eds.), *Dictionary of Paul and his Letters*, 630–642, Leicester: IVP.

Smalley, B. (1941), *The Study of the Bible in the Middle Ages*, 3rd ed., Oxford: Blackwell, 1983.

Smith, J. K. A. (2000), *The Fall of Interpretation: Philosophical Foundations for a Creational Hermeneutic*, Downers Grove: IVP.

Smith, R. S. (2004), 'Language, Theological Knowledge, and the Postmodern Paradigm', in M. J. Erickson, P. K. Helseth and J. Taylor (eds.), *Reclaiming the Center: Confronting Evangelical Accommodation in Postmodern Times*, 109–133, Wheaton, IL: Crossway.

Sosa, E. and L. Bonjour (2003), *Epistemic Justification: Internalism vs Externalism, Foundation vs Virtues*, Great Debates in Philosophy, Oxford: Blackwell.

Soskice, J. M. (1985), *Metaphor and Religious Language*, Oxford: Clarendon.

Sproul, R. C. (1977), *Knowing Scripture*, Downers Grove: IVP.

Steiger, J. A. (1998), '"Das Wort sie sollen lassen stahn . . ." Die Auseinandersetzung Johann Gerhards und der lutherischen Orthodoxie mit Hermann Rahtmann und deren abendmahlstheologische und christologische Implikate', *ZTK* 95: 338–365.

Stein, R. H. (1981), *An Introduction to the Parables of Jesus*, Philadelphia: Westminster.

Steinmetz, D. C. (1980), 'The Superiority of Pre-Critical Exegesis', *ThTo* 37.1: 27–38.

——(1984), 'Luther and Calvin on Church and Tradition', in *Luther in Context*, 85–97, Bloomington: Indiana University Press, repr. 1986.

Stott, J. R. W. (1970), *Christ the Controversialist: The Basis of Belief*, Leicester: IVP.

——(1973), *Guard the Gospel: The Message of 2 Timothy*, BST, London: IVP.

——(1977), *What Is an Evangelical?* London: Church Pastoral Aid Society.

Swidler, L. (1997), 'Epilogue', in L. Swidler and P. Mojzes (eds.), *The Uniqueness of Jesus: A Dialogue with Paul F. Knitter*, 183–189, New York: Orbis.

Taylor, M. C. (1984), *Erring: A Postmodern A/Theology*, Chicago: University of Chicago Press.

Taylor, V. (1952), *The Gospel According to St. Mark*, London: Macmillan.

Tertullian (207), *Adversus Marcionem*, trans. P. Holmes, 1868, as 'The Five Books against Marcion', in A. Roberts and J. Donaldson (eds.), *The Ante-Nicene Fathers: Translations of the Writings of the Fathers Down to A.D. 325*, vol. 3, 271–475, Grand Rapids: Eerdmans, repr. 1980.

Thielicke, H. (1948), *Die Frage der Entmythologisierung des Neuen Testaments*, trans. R. H. Fuller, 1953, as 'The Restatement of New Testament Mythology', in H.-W. Bartsch (ed.), *Kergyma and Myth: A Theological Debate*, 138–174, London: SPCK, repr. 1972.

Thiselton, A. C. (1980), *The Two Horizons: New Testament Hermeneutics and Philosophical Description with Special Reference to Heidegger, Bultmann, Gadamer, and Wittgenstein*, Exeter: Paternoster; Grand Rapids: Eerdmans.

——(1992), *New Horizons in Hermeneutics: The Theory and Practice of Transforming Biblical Reading*, Grand Rapids: Zondervan.

Thompson, M. D. (1998a), '*Claritas Scripturae* in the Eucharistic Writings of Martin Luther', *WTJ* 60.1: 23–41.

——(1998b), 'Reformation Perspectives on Scripture: The Written Word of God', *RTR* 57: 105–120.

——(2000), 'The Missionary Apostle and Modern Systematic Affirmation', in P. G. Bolt and M. D. Thompson (eds.), *The Gospel to the Nations: Perspectives on Paul's Mission*, FS P. T. O'Brien, 365–382, Leicester: Apollos.

——(2004), *A Sure Ground on which to Stand: The Relation of Authority and Interpretive Method in Luther's Approach to Scripture*, Carlisle: Paternoster.

Tigay, J. H. (1996), *Deuteronomy*, ed. N. M. Sarna, Jewish Publication Society Torah Commentary, Philadelphia: Jewish Publication Society.

Tomlinson, D. (1995), *The Post-Evangelical*, London: Triangle.

Torrance, T. F. (1965), 'Knowledge of God and Speech about him according to John Calvin', in *Theology in Reconstruction*, 76–98, London: SCM.

——(1969), *Theological Science*, London: Oxford University Press.

——(1982), *Reality and Evangelical Theology: The Realism of Christian Revelation*, Downers Grove: IVP, repr. 1999.

——(1996), *The Christian Doctrine of God, One Being Three Persons*, Edinburgh: T. & T. Clark.

Tracy, D. (1994), *On Naming the Present: God, Hermeneutics, and Church*, New York: Orbis; London: SCM.

Turretin, F. (1679–85), *Institutio theologicae elencticae*, trans. G. M. Giger, ed. J. T. Dennison, as *Institutes of Elenctic Theology*, 3 vols., Phillipsburg: P. & R., 1992.

Vander Stelt, J. C. (1978), *Philosophy and Scripture: A Study in Old Princeton and Westminster Theology*, Marlton, N.J.: Mack.

Vanhoozer, K. J. (1994a), 'From Canon to Concept: "Same" and "Other" in the Relation between Biblical and Systematic Theology', *SBET* 12: 96–124.

——(1994b), 'God's Mighty Speech-Acts: The Doctrine of Scripture Today', in P. E. Satterthwaite and D. F. Wright (eds.), *A Pathway into the Holy Scripture*, 143–181, Grand Rapids: Eerdmans.

——(1998), *Is There a Meaning in This Text? The Bible, the Reader, and the Morality of Literary Knowledge*, Grand Rapids: Zondervan.

——(2002), *First Theology: God, Scripture and Hermeneutics*, Downers Grove: IVP; Leicester: Apollos.

Vincent (434), *Commonitorium*, trans. C. A. Heurtley as 'The Commonitory of Vincent of Lérins', in P. Schaff (ed.), *A Select Library of Nicene and Post-Nicene Fathers of the Christian Church*, 2nd Series, vol. 11, 131–156, Grand Rapids: Eerdmans, repr. 1982.

Wallace, B., A. Ross and J. B. Davies (2003), 'Applied Hermeneutics and Qualitative Safety Data: The CIRAS Project', *Human Relations* 56.5: 587–607.

Ward, T. (2002), *Word and Supplement: Speech Acts, Biblical Texts, and the Sufficiency of Scripture*, Oxford: Oxford University Press.

Watson, F. (1994), *Text, Church and World: Biblical Interpretation in Theological Perspective*, Edinburgh: T. & T. Clark.

——(2002), 'An Evangelical Response', in P. Helm and Carl R. Trueman (eds.), *The Trustworthiness of God: Perspectives on the Nature of Scripture*, 285–289, Grand Rapids: Eerdmans; Leicester: Apollos.

Weber, O. (1955), *Grundlagen der Dogmatik*, trans. D. L. Guder as *Foundations of Dogmatics*, 2 vols., Grand Rapids: Eerdmans, 1981.

Webster, J. B. (1997), *Theological Theology: An Inaugural Lecture Delivered before the University of Oxford 27 October 1997*, Oxford: Clarendon.

——(1998), 'Hermeneutics in Modern Theology: Some Doctrinal Reflections', *SJT* 51.3: 307–341.

——(2003a), *Holy Scripture: A Dogmatic Sketch*, ed. I. Torrance, Current Issues in Theology, Cambridge: Cambridge University Press.

——(2003b), 'The Ethics of Reconciliation', in C. E. Gunton (ed.), *The Theology of Reconciliation*, 109–124, Edinburgh: T. & T. Clark.

——(2005), *Confessing God: Essays in Christian Dogmatics*, vol. 2, London: T. & T. Clark.

Weinandy, T. (2000), *Does God Suffer?* Edinburgh: T. & T. Clark.

Wells, D. (1991), 'The Theologian's Craft', in J. D. Woodbridge and T. E. McComiskey (eds.), *Doing Theology in Today's World*, FS K. S. Kantzer, 171–194, Grand Rapids: Zondervan.

Wellum, S. J. (2004), 'Postconservatism, Biblical Authority, and Recent Proposals for Re-doing Evangelical Theology: A Critical Analysis', in M. J. Erickson, P. K. Helseth and J. Taylor (eds.), *Reclaiming the Center: Confronting Evangelical Accommodation in Postmodern Times*, 161–197, Wheaton, IL: Crossway.

Wenham, J. W. (1993), *Christ and the Bible*, The Christian View of the Bible 1, Guildford, Surrey: Eagle.

Westermann, C. (1966), *Das Buch Jesaia, 40–66*, trans. D. M. G. Stalker as *Isaiah 40–66*, OTL, London: SCM, 1969.

Westphal, M. (2001), *Overcoming Onto-Theology: Toward a Postmodern Christian Faith*, New York: Fordham University Press.

——(2003), 'Blind Spots: Christianity and Postmodern Philosophy', *ChrCent* (14 June): 32–35.

Whitaker, W. (1588), *Disputatio de sacra scriptura contra hujus temporis papistas*, trans. and ed. W. Fitzgerald as *Disputations on Holy Scripture against the Papists, Especially Bellarmine and Stapleton*, Cambridge: Parker Society, 1849.

Williams, R. (1991), 'Theological Integrity', in *On Christian Theology*, Challenges in Contemporary Theology, 3–15, Oxford: Blackwell, repr. 2000.

——(1994a), 'Being Alone', in *Open to Judgment: Sermons and Addresses*, 143–149, London: Darton, Longman & Todd.

——(1994b), 'The Dark Night', in *Open to Judgment: Sermons and Addresses*, 95–100, London: Darton, Longman & Todd.

——(2003), 'Chris Moore talks to Dr Rowan Williams, the Archbishop of Canterbury at Lambeth Palace', *Daily Telegraph*, 12 February 2003. Online at http//:www.dailytelegraph.co.uk/news/main.jhtml?xml=/news/2003/02/12/nbish112.xml.

Williams, T. (2005), 'The Doctrine of Univocity Is True and Salutary', *Modern Theology* 21.4: 575–585.

Williamson, H. G. M. (1985), *Ezra, Nehemiah*, WBC 16, Waco: Word.

Wimsatt, W. K. and M. C. Beardsley (1946), 'The Intentional Fallacy', *Sewanee Review* 54: 468–483.

Wolterstorff, N. (1995), *Divine Discourse: Philosophical Reflections on the Claim that God Speaks*, Cambridge: Cambridge University Press.

——(2001), 'The Promise of Speech-Act Theory for Biblical Interpretation', in C. Bartholomew et al. (eds.), *After Pentecost: Language and Biblical Interpretation*, Scripture and Hermeneutics Series 2, 73–90, Carlisle: Paternoster; Grand Rapids: Zondervan.

Wood, C. M. (1981), *The Formation of Christian Understanding: An Essay in Theological Hermeneutics*, Philadelphia: Westminster.

Wright, N. T. (2005), *Scripture and the Authority of God*, London: SPCK.

Zavarzadeh, M. (1982), 'Review of Jonathan Culler's *The Pursuit of Signs: Semiotics, Literature, Deconstruction* (Cornell University Press, 1981)', *Journal of Aesthetics and Art Criticism* 40: 329–33.

Zinn, G. A. (1997), 'Hugh of St. Victor's *De scripturis et scriptoribus sacris* as an *Accessus* Treatise for the Study of the Bible', *Traditio* 52: 111–134.

# Index of authors

# Index of Scripture references

Printed and bound by CPI Group (UK) Ltd, Croydon, CR0 4YY

25/03/2025

14647344-0004